A Journey Through The Last Dance

Activities & Resources

Lynne Ann DeSpelder

Cabrillo College

Albert Lee Strickland

McGraw Hill

Boston   Burr Ridge, IL   Dubuque, IA   Madison, WI   New York   San Francisco   St. Louis
Bangkok   Bogotá   Caracas   Kuala Lumpur   Lisbon   London   Madrid   Mexico City
Milan   Montreal   New Delhi   Santiago   Seoul   Singapore   Sydney   Taipei   Toronto

Higher Education

This book is printed on acid-free paper.

1 2 3 4 5 6 7 8 9 0   BKM/BKM   0 9 8 7 6 5 4

ISBN 0-07-293047-0

Vice president and Editor-in-chief: *Thalia Dorwick*
Publisher/Sponsoring editor: *Stephen Rutter*
Development editor: *Kirsten Stoller*
Media producer: *Ginger Bunn*
Marketing manager: *Melissa Caughlin*
Project manager: *Mel Valentín*
Production supervisor: *Tandra Jorgensen*
Compositor: *Noyes Composition and Graphics*
Typeface: *11/13 Palatino*
Printer: *Bookmart Press*

Cover:
"Edvard Munch, *The Dance of Life*. 1889–1900. Oil on canvas. 49-1/4" x 74-3/4". National Gallery, Oslo. (c) 2003 The Munch Museum/The Munch-Ellingsen Group/Artists Rights Society (ARS), New York. Photo: J. Lathion. (c) Nasjonalgalleriet, Oslo 1997."

www.mhhe.com

Contents

CHAPTER 2:

CHAPTER 3:

PART III: RESOURCES FOR LEARNING AND WRITING ABOUT DEATH AND DYING

PART IV: APPENDIX

Using This Book

We have designed *A Journey Through The Last Dance* to help you achieve two important goals in learning about death and dying. First, it will make it easier for you to study, review, and comprehend the material from the seventh edition of *The Last Dance: Encountering Death and Dying.* Although it is true that each of us already has knowledge about death, dying, and bereavement, the amount of new information—as well as the number of terms and ideas presented in your class and textbook—may surprise you. *A Journey Through The Last Dance* will help you increase your success in learning, retaining, and integrating essential information.

Second, and of equal importance, this book will give you opportunities to think about death, dying, and bereavement in the context of your own life. You will find areas where theory, research, and practice apply to your experiences. Death studies is not just about death, dying, and bereavement. It is a subject that draws on your psychological, cultural, and ethical makeup. Perhaps more than any other course you will take in college, the ideas you will be learning about, the objective information that is presented, and the applications that are possible have the potential to affect your behavior and personal development. One student summed it up by saying: "We all will survive loss and one day each of us will be dead. This course tells me about how I want to live in the face of death."

To begin, Part I, the Introduction, prepares you to think about your attitudes and values, as well as the resources you will draw on to gain information about death studies. The section titled **Getting Acquainted with Your Text: A Self-Guided Tour** gives you an overview of *The Last Dance* and suggests ways to use each feature, sometimes directing you to perform a specific activity and then report on the results. The next section of the Introduction, **Death and Dying on the Web: Evaluating and Using Internet Resources**, suggests ways to understand the materials you find on the Internet, followed by an activity that applies what you have learned. The third section of the Introduction, **Examining Your Attitudes and Experiences**, gives you information and activities (marked with the symbol ➠) for examining your past experiences and attitudes, including further directions for applying the learnings from these exercises to help you write an essay. The fourth section of the Introduction, **Writing Your Deathography,** will lead you to reflect and learn more about your past experiences of loss through writing an autobiographical essay. Students say time and again that the information from this essay has provided relief, resolution, and understanding about current beliefs and past experiences. We hope these explorations will help you as well.

Part II contains materials for each of the fifteen chapters in *The Last Dance.* Each chapter in this book begins with a narrative **Chapter Summary**. Read this summary *before* you begin reading the chapter in the text. It will help you get an idea of the focus of the chapter. Following the summary are the **Objectives**. You will likely find this listing of the concepts included in the chapter beneficial before reading the text chapter. **Key Terms**

and Concepts are also listed. As you read the text, you will find the terms printed in italic the first time they are mentioned. Note the definitions. While some texts provide glossaries with terms defined, we have found that you are more likely to remember a term if you have seen the definition in context. Keep your list of key terms with you while you are reading a chapter in the text. Students find it helpful to check off each term as they discover it in the text. You can make notes in the margins of this book to remind you of any terms that seem difficult at first. The next section is titled **Questions for Guided Study and Review.** We suggest that you use these questions to reflect on the material you have read in the chapter and also as a guide for test review. Each chapter includes **Practice Test Questions,** consisting of multiple choice and true/false questions as well as a matching question. Answers to the Practice Test Questions can be found in Part IV of this book. The section **Related Readings** gives you additional resources and expands the information from Further Readings in the corresponding chapter of *The Last Dance.* In this book, readings are divided by topic and selections from *The Path Ahead: Readings in Death and Dying* are also included (indicated by the symbol 📖). The next section, **Organizations and Internet Resources,** provides a selected listing of resources that can be used to expand your knowledge and obtain more information about the topics that pertain to each chapter. As noted at the end of this section, additional resources are available online at the web site for *The Last Dance* (directions for accessing this site are provided in the Introduction under the heading "Evaluating and Using Internet Resources"). This listing of resources is followed by a list of the **Major Points in this Chapter.** Use this section to get a quick overview of the material in the chapter. You might want to look at this section both before and after reading the chapter in your text. **Observations and Reflections** gives you an opportunity to think about how this chapter's material might influence your attitudes and experiences. Finally, you will find **Activities** (marked with the symbol ➠) designed to make the class content more relevant and meaningful. Some activities ask you to observe or evaluate information others include exercises to analyze how the information in the chapter relates to your experiences, behavior, and opinions. Computer activities are indicated by the symbol 💻.

Part III is composed of additional resources for your study of death, dying, and bereavement. Here you will find information about reading a journal article and writing a research paper, as well as guidelines and suggestions for completing a research project. These tools will assist you in learning and writing about topics in death studies.

Part IV, the Appendix, contains the answers to the Practice Tests and a Glossary.

Every student in this course has a unique background and unique feelings about death, dying, and bereavement. We believe that your efforts in completing the activities in this book will give you new insights and, more importantly, encourage you to re-examine your attitudes and behaviors, as well as provide an understanding of the place of death in your life.

Over the years, many students and professors have made helpful suggestions about the activities and information most useful for understanding death, dying, and bereavement. We thank all those who have contributed to the resources included here.

L.A.D.

A.L.S.

⇒ *Getting Acquainted with Your Text: A Self-Guided Tour*

Over the next few months, you will be spending considerable time with the seventh edition of *The Last Dance: Encountering Death and Dying*. Along with lectures, discussions, and other learning activities, your textbook is an important tool. We have given a great deal of thought to how the various elements of this edition of *The Last Dance* fit together. These elements form a whole that aims to further your understanding of death, dying, and bereavement.

The following questions provide you with a self-guided tour through your textbook. Write your responses to the "tour guide's" questions in the spaces provided. Your responses should be brief; a sentence or two will help you remember your full answers. (Note that this is an activity marked with the symbol ⇒ to alert you to the exercise.)

1. Take a few minutes to browse through *The Last Dance* to get a feel for it. What is your first impression of the book?

   _____

   _____

   _____

   _____

   _____

2. Read through the Contents. These pages give you an overview of the material in the textbook. What is the title of the chapter that looks the most interesting to you?

   _____

   _____

   _____

   _____

   _____

- In which chapters do you have extensive information?

_____

_____

_____

- In which chapters would you like to have more information?

_____

_____

_____

3. Read the Preface. What purposes of the book are most interesting to you? Briefly list them.

_____

_____

_____

_____

4. Read the Prologue. What is the message about death in this story by David Gordon?

_____

_____

_____

_____

5. Each chapter begins with a photograph, and, throughout the chapter, there are additional photos, as well as boxed materials, tables, figures, and usually a cartoon. Each chapter concludes with a list of Further Readings (which are organized by topic in this Study Guide, along with readings from *The Path Ahead: Readings in Death and Dying*, edited by DeSpelder and Strickland (New York: McGraw-Hill, 1995). Skim through these elements in Chapter 1 of the textbook. List some of the most interesting elements and include the page numbers.

_____

_____

_____

_____

6. In your textbook, information that relates to the numbered endnotes has been placed at the back of the book, beginning on page 555. This style of citation allows us to provide additional information that expands on the basic source data associated with the note. For example, look in the endnotes for the full text of Note 3 on Page 88. What additional information did you find?

_____

_____

_____

_____

7. Key terms are italicized in the text and defined in the context of the material you are reading. Look on page 11 of the text and write a brief definition of the term *epidemiologic transition*:

_____

_____

_____

_____

Some students find it useful to prepare flash cards for Key Terms and Concepts to familiarize themselves with the language of death studies.

8. In your tour of the *The Last Dance*, look at the end of a chapter for the Further Readings. Which resource looks the most interesting to you?

_____

_____

_____

_____

Check the same chapter in this companion book to see if the Related Readings section contains an additional resource that looks interesting. List it here:

_____

_____

_____

_____

_____

9. In your tour of *The Last Dance,* look through the photographs for each chapter. Don't read the captions just yet. Just pay attention to the images. As you think about how your own life history may relate to the photographs, respond to the following questions:

- Which images are the most provocative?

_____

_____

_____

_____

- What thoughts and feelings are provoked?

_____

_____

_____

_____

10. We have created a detailed index to help you find the information you are looking for in *The Last Dance.* Look up two or three topics in the index. Write down the topics and the page numbers:

_____

_____

_____

Turn to those pages in the text. Is the information where it should be? How does it help you to see it in the context of a chapter?

_____

_____

_____

11. Evaluate your tour of *The Last Dance.* Did we leave anything out that you think would be good for students to know before they start reading the book?

_____

_____

_____

Death and Dying on the Web: Evaluating and Using Internet Resources

While you are using *A Journey Through The Last Dance*, there will be opportunities for learning activities using the Internet. To provide better understanding of the websites you access, here is a discussion of criteria for evaluating an Internet site as well as an activity giving you the opportunity to evaluate several sites. When working with Internet-based research, you can refer back to this information.

Each chapter in this book has a section that lists Organizations and Internet Resources. These resources have been selected to expand your study of dying, death, and bereavement. At the end of this section, you will see a notice that additional resources are available online at mhhe.com. To access the Online Learning Center (OLC) and the website for *The Last Dance: Encountering Death and Dying,* go to www.mhhe.com. On the left side of the screen, under "Website Gallery," click on "Humanities and Social Sciences." When that page loads, click on "Psychology." Websites for various books are listed alphabetically by author. Clicking on "DeSpelder/Strickland, *The Last Dance: Encountering Death and Dying,* 7e, 2004," will take you to the book's site. Explore the student section of this site to locate additional organizations and Internet resources, as well as activities, practice test questions, and further information about the book and its authors.

Evaluating Internet Information

The Internet offers students, teachers, and researchers opportunities to gather information from around the world. It is important to recognize, however, that the Internet is unregulated. Thus, many Internet sites lack the "safety net" of peer review and the critical eye of a competent editor. To compensate for the scarcity of filters between you and the information you find on the Internet, you must carefully evaluate the quality of every Internet resource you use. Thinking critically about such information is vital in the absence of the peer-review process. Since excellent resources reside alongside dubious ones, it is necessary to develop skills to evaluate what you find. There are more issues concerning evaluating quality with respect to Internet sites than with traditional print resources. Along with the need to evaluate the objectivity and accuracy of the information available on the Internet, the technology itself introduces additional criteria that must be evaluated.[1] Keep the following questions in mind.

1. Can you access the site regularly? Is it well organized and easy to navigate?
2. Do the pages load quickly?
3. Do the links work, taking you to relevant material?
4. Can you print content easily and quickly?

5. Are the graphics on the site informative without being flashy or overpowering?
6. If the site has received awards, are they for design or for content? Can you confirm claims of award-winning quality?

Resources devoted to gathering information and developing skills for thinking critically about information are available both in print and online.[2] One of the best online sites, developed by librarians Jan Alexander and Marsha Tate, includes criteria for evaluation, along with examples of information posted on the Internet designed to demonstrate principles of critical thinking.[3]

What follows is a brief discussion of some of the major criteria by which you can and should evaluate information presented on the Internet.[4]

AUTHORSHIP

Who is the author of the document or site? Is the author well known in the field? Is there a biography of the author stating his or her credentials? Is he or she even identified? Are there other Internet publications by this author that you trust? Does the author support his or her statements with other published work? Can you contact the author to request further information? Is the author's e-mail link "live" (that is, active), and does he or she respond to your questions?

PUBLISHING BODY

Can you tell if this is a personal home page established and maintained by the author? Is the name of any organization given on the page or in the document, or is a link to a sponsoring organization provided? Is this a recognized and respected organization in the field? Is it an appropriate organization for your topic? Are you able to determine what the relationship is between the author and the publishing body—assuming, of course, that it is not self-published?

POINT OF VIEW OR BIAS

Does the organization under which the author is publishing have a specific bias or stake in the issue? You might find clues in a web site's mission statement or purpose. Is this a business web site intended to market or sell products? Is the information from the website of an organization that has a political or philosophical agenda? Keep in mind the definition of bias and how such thinking might influence the form and content of the web-page documents and links.

REFERRAL TO AND KNOWLEDGE OF THE LITERATURE

Does the document include a bibliography? Does the author appropriately reference the work of others, including citations and documentation? Does the author demonstrate knowledge of the field that is generally consistent with the theories, schools, and viewpoints prevalent within the field? Does the author discuss the limitations of his or her perspective, approach, and technique? If the subject is controversial, does the author acknowledge this fact?

ACCURACY OR VERIFIABILITY OF DETAILS

In the case of a research report, are the research *methods* described as well as the *findings?* Are the methods appropriate to the topic? Are traditional print resources cited in a bibliography? Are links provided to other Internet-based documents? Can all these be checked for accuracy?

CURRENCY

Are dates provided for material on the page? Is the page itself dated? Does it include information on the most recent update? If the page is updated on a regular basis, is there any indication of when this occurs? Is a copyright date included?

Understanding and Decoding URLs

Uniform Resource Locators (URLs) are the Internet addresses that you see on the location bars at the top or bottom of your web browser. URLs provide a standard format for the transmission and reception of a wide variety of information types. This is how they are constructed:

transfer protocol://servername.domain/directory/subdirectory/filename.filetype

Every URL must have at least the first two elements shown above (the information directly before and after the //). Here is an example:

http://www.growthhouse.org/books/despeld.htm

In this example, "http" is the transfer protocol, "www.growthhouse" is the server name, and "org" is the domain. The directory is "books," the subdirectory is "despeld," and the file type is "htm." (Note that in URLs with "www," it is no longer necessary to type "http://"—The transfer protocol is automatically used.)

Understanding the different elements that make up a URL will help you know what to expect before you click on a link. You will also be able to see what kind of organization or institution is providing the information. The following categories of Internet domains are important to recognize:

.edu: An educational institution (for example, msu.edu [Michigan State University, East Lansing, Michigan]).

.org: An organization that is typically part of the nonprofit sector (for example, adec.org [Association for Death Education and Counseling]).

.com: A commercial enterprise, including commercial online services (for example, aol.com [America Online]).

.net: Usually an Internet Service Provider (ISP); that is, an individual or group that provides access to the Internet (for example, earthlink.net).

.gov: A governmental body (for example, loc.gov [Library of Congress, Washington, D.C.]).

Citing Electronic References

The range of materials on the Internet, and the way it is structured, generates challenges for identifying useful references. The American Psychological Association suggests the following guidelines:[5]

1. Direct readers as closely as possible to the information being cited. Whenever possible, reference specific documents rather than "home" or menu pages.
2. Provide addresses that work. Broken links are the bane of academic research. Keep in mind the reasons that URLs do not work: first, they are typed incorrectly and, second, the document has been moved or deleted. Test the addresses in your references regularly. Remove any links that no longer point to your sources.

Notes

1. David R. Campbell and Mary V. Campbell, *The Student's Guide to Doing Research on the Internet* (Reading, Mass.: Addison-Wesley, 1995); John M. Grohol, *Insider's Guide to Mental Health Resources Online* (New York: Guilford, 1997); and Bernard Robin, Elissa Keeler and Robert Miller, *Educator's Guide to the Web* (New York: MIS Press, 1997), pp. 217–231.
2. Jan Alexander and Marsha Tate, *Web Wisdom: How to Evaluate and Create Information Quality on the Web* (Mahwah, N.J.: Lawrence Erlbaum Associates, 1999); and Internet Detective, "An Interactive Tutorial on Evaluating the Quality of Internet Resources," www.sosig.ac.uk/desire/internet-detective.html (accessed December 15, 2003).
3. Jan Alexander and Marsha Tate, "Evaluating Web Pages: Links to Examples of Various Concepts," www2.widener.edu/Wolfgram-Memorial-Library/webevaluation/examples/htm (accessed December 15, 2003).
4. Joe Barker, "Evaluating Web Pages: Experience Why It's Important," www.lib.berkeley.edu/TeachingLib/Guides/Internet/Evaluate.html (accessed December 15, 2003).
5. American Psychological Association, "Electronic References," www.apastyle.org/elecmedia.html (accessed December 15, 2003).

🖥 ⇒ *Evaluating Internet Resources*

Directions: *Read the section entitled "Evaluating and Using Internet Resources." For each of the websites listed below, answer the questions about information and quality. Include any additional notes about the usefulness of each site.*

Bereavement Care Centre: < www.bereavementcare.com.au>

1. What is the URL?_____

2. What is the country of origin?_____

3. Can you access the site regularly? _____

4. Is it well organized and easy to navigate? _____

   _____

5. Do the links work? _____

6. Do they help you access relevant material? _____

   _____

   _____

7. Can you print content easily and quickly? _____

8. Are graphics informative without being flashy or overpowering? _____

9. Are advertisements embedded in the site?_____

10. Has the site received awards for design or content?_____

    _____

    _____

11. Can you authenticate these claims? _____

12. Who is (are) the author(s)?_____

    _____

    _____

13. Who is the publishing body?_____

    _____

    _____

14. Is a point of view or bias implied or specifically stated? If so, what is it?_____

_____

15. Do the documents posted include authorship, bibliographies, and information that are generally consistent with theories, schools and viewpoints within the field? Give examples. _____

_____

_____

_____

16. What are the recent dates on information posted to the website?_____

17. Describe the most interesting feature of this site.

_____

_____

_____

_____

_____

_____

_____

_____

The Centre for Grief Education: < www.grief.org.au>

1. What is the URL?_____

2. What is the country of origin?_____

3. Can you access the site regularly? _____

4. Is it well organized and easy to navigate?_____

_____

5. Do the links work? _____

6. Do they help you access relevant material? _____

_____

7. Can you print content easily and quickly? _____

8. Are graphics informative without being flashy or overpowering? _____

9. Are advertisements embedded in the site? _____

10. Has the site received awards for design or content? _____

_____

11. Can you authenticate these claims? _____

12. Who is (are) the author(s)? _____

_____

13. Who is the publishing body? _____

_____

14. Is a point of view or bias implied or specifically stated? If so, what is it? _____

_____

15. Do the documents posted include authorship, bibliographies, and information that

    are generally consistent with theories, schools, and viewpoints within the field?

    Give examples. _____

_____

_____

_____

16. What are the recent dates on information posted to the website? _____

17. Describe the most interesting feature of this site.

_____

_____

_____

_____

_____

_____

Site of your choice: Select a death, dying, or bereavement site that interests you and answer the following questions.

1. What is the URL?_____

2. What is the country of origin?_____

3. Can you access the site regularly? _____

4. Is it well organized and easy to navigate?_____

   _____

5. Do the links work? _____

6. Do they help you access relevant material? _____

   _____

7. Can you print content easily and quickly? _____

8. Are graphics informative without being flashy or overpowering?_____

9. Are advertisements embedded in the site? _____

10. Has the site received awards for design or content? _____

    _____

11. Can you authenticate these claims?_____

12. Who is(are) the author(s)? _____

    _____

13. Who is the publishing body?_____

    _____

14. Is a point of view or bias implied or specifically stated? If so, what is it? _____

    _____

15. Do the documents posted include authorship, bibliographies, and information that

    are generally consistent with theories, schools and viewpoints within the field?

    Give examples. _____

    _____

    _____

16. What are the recent dates on information posted to the website?_____

    _____

17. Describe the most interesting feature of this site.

_____

_____

_____

_____

_____

_____

Use the space provided below and on the following page to explain what you have learned about Internet research as a result of visiting and evaluating these three sites. Include notes about your ability to evaluate information found on the Internet. Review your readings about evaluating a website and make specific suggestions for enhancing each of these sites.

_____

_____

_____

_____

_____

_____

_____

_____

_____

_____

_____

_____

_____

_____

Examining Your Attitudes and Experiences

Though the goals and objectives of each death, dying, and bereavement course differ, one theme uniting them is the application of the information and concepts presented in class to your attitudes, beliefs, values, and behavior.

A variety of challenges may arise when you begin to examine your attitudes and experiences. For instance, you may have only incomplete memories of previous loss experiences. We suggest that you contact those adults who might be willing and able to fill in the gaps in your knowledge. Uncomfortable and sometimes painful feelings may result from reading, writing, and talking about certain experiences, perhaps for the first time. Students have reported that being in an environment where they are "not the only ones" exploring past experiences is helpful. Permission to "pass" in class discussions is an important safety valve. Give yourself that freedom. You can say something like, "I'd prefer not to get into that right now." Decisions about what you choose to address publicly during the course and in the following activities are yours. We suggest that you both prepare yourself to take some risks and protect yourself when you are feeling vulnerable.

Over the years of teaching about death, dying, and bereavement, we have observed many students discover that exploring their attitudes and subsequently writing a "Deathography" is a valuable experience. This essay will lead you to reflect on past experiences of loss.

The three activities that follow provide you with basic information about yourself. Begin with a survey of your attitudes. Continue by examining childhood losses. And finish with an overview of losses in your life to the present time. Completing these three activities will also give you the information needed for your "Deathography" essay, which is discussed more fully in the next section of this Introduction.

Time and again, students have been thankful for the opportunity to look closely at their attitudes and experiences and find, on paper, the various influences on their behavior. Insights about current beliefs and information about possible changes for the future are greatly valued.

⟫➡ *Questionnaire: You and Death*

Directions: *Begin by completing the* ⟫➡ ***Questionnaire: You and Death*** *located on the next several pages. Note that a question may have several different answers, possibly even conflicting ones. Check all that apply. If your response is not listed, write it in. Use this activity to explore your attitudes and experiences. After you have completed the questionnaire, go back through it and code the questions using the following categories:*

PE = Answer based on personal experience

S = Answer about which you feel strongly

D = Question is difficult to answer

A = Answer about which you feel ambiguous

SB = Answer based on spiritual or religious beliefs

You may find that some questions seem to have no codes that you can apply to them. Other questions may have all five. This analysis will give you information about your experiences with particular areas of death studies. Finish this exercise by making notes about your learnings in the space below.

_____

_____

_____

_____

_____

_____

_____

_____

_____

_____

_____

_____

_____

))⇒ *Questionnaire: You and Death*

Answer the following questions by checking all the responses that apply. You may have more than one answer, or your answers may conflict. If you have a response that is not listed, write it in.

1. **Who died in your first personal involvement with death?**
   a. Grandparent or great-grandparent
   b. Parent
   c. Brother or sister
   d. Other family member
   e. Friend or acquaintance
   f. Stranger
   g. Public figure
   h. Animal

2. **To the best of your memory, at what age were you first aware of death?**
   a. Under three
   b. Three to five
   c. Five to ten
   d. Ten or older

3. **When you were a child, how was death talked about in your family?**
   a. Openly
   b. With some sense of discomfort
   c. Only when necessary and then with an attempt to exclude the children
   d. As though it were a taboo subject
   e. Never recall any discussion

4. **Which of the following best describes your childhood conceptions of death?**
   a. Heaven and hell concept
   b. After-life
   c. Death as sleep
   d. Cessation of all physical and mental activity
   e. Mysterious and unknowable
   f. Something other than the above
   g. No conception
   h. Can't remember

5. **Which of the following most influenced your present attitudes toward death?**
   a. Death of someone close
   b. Specific reading
   c. Religious upbringing
   d. Introspection and meditation
   e. Ritual (e.g., funerals)
   f. TV, radio or motion pictures
   g. Longevity of my family
   h. My health or physical condition
   i. Other (specify):_____
   _____

6. **How much of a role has religion played in the development of your attitude toward death?**
   a. A very significant role
   b. A rather significant role
   c. Somewhat influential, but not a major role
   d. A relatively minor role
   e. No role at all

7. **To what extent do you believe in a life after death?**
   a. Strongly believe in it
   b. Tend to believe in it
   c. Uncertain
   d. Tend to doubt it
   e. Convinced it does not exist

8. **Regardless of your belief about life after death, what is your wish about it?**
   a. I strongly wish there were a life after death.
   b. I am indifferent as to whether there is a life after death.
   c. I definitely prefer that there not be a life after death.

9. **To what extent do you believe in reincarnation?**
   a. Strongly believe it
   b. Tend to believe it
   c. Uncertain
   d. Tend to doubt it
   e. Convinced it cannot occur

10. **How often do you think about your own death?**
    a. Very frequently (at least once a day)
    b. Frequently
    c. Occasionally
    d. Rarely (no more than once a year)
    e. Very rarely or never

11. **If you could choose, when would you die?**
    a. In youth
    b. In the middle prime of life
    c. Just after the prime of life
    d. In old age

12. **When do you believe that, in fact, you will die?**
    a. In youth
    b. In the middle prime of life
    c. Just after the prime of life
    d. In old age

13. **Has there been a time in your life when you wanted to die?**
    a. Yes, mainly because of great physical pain
    b. Yes, mainly because of great emotional pain
    c. Yes, mainly to escape an intolerable social or interpersonal situation
    d. Yes, mainly because of great embarrassment
    e. Yes, for a reason other than above
    f. No

14. **What does death mean to you?**
    a. The end; the final process of life
    b. The beginning of a life after death; a transition, a new beginning
    c. A joining of the spirit with a universal cosmic consciousness

d. A kind of endless sleep; rest and peace
e. Termination of this life but with survival of the spirit
f. Don't know
g. Other (specify): _____

_____

15. **What aspect of your own death is the most distasteful to you?**
    a. I could no longer have any experience.
    b. I am afraid of what might happen to my body after death.
    c. I am uncertain as to what might happen to me if there is a life after death.
    d. I could no longer provide for my family.
    e. It would cause grief to my relatives and friends.
    f. All my plans and projects would come to an end.
    g. The process of dying might be painful.
    h. Other (specify): _____

    _____

16. **Based on your present feelings, what is the probability of your taking your own life in the near future?**
    a. Extremely high (I feel very much like killing myself)
    b. Moderately high
    c. Between high and low
    d. Moderately low
    e. Extremely low (very improbable that I would kill myself)

17. **In your opinion, at what age are people most afraid of death?**
    a. Up to 12 years
    b. Thirteen to 19 years
    c. Twenty to 29 years
    d. Thirty to 39 years
    e. Forty to 49 years
    f. Fifty to 59 years
    g. Sixty to 69 years
    h. Seventy years and over

18. **What is your belief about the causes of most deaths?**
    a. Most deaths result directly from the con-

scious efforts of the person who dies.
    b. Most deaths have strong components of conscious or unconscious participation by the persons who die (in their habits and use, misuse, nonuse, or abuse of drugs, alcohol, medicine, etc.).
    c. Most deaths just happen; they are caused by events over which individuals have no control.
    d. Other (specify): _____

    _____

19. **To what extent do you believe that psychological factors can influence (or even cause) death?**
    a. I firmly believe that they can.
    b. I tend to believe that they can.
    c. I am undecided or don't know.
    d. I doubt that they can.

20. **When you think of your own death (or when circumstances make you realize your own mortality), how do you feel?**
    a. Fearful
    b. Discouraged
    c. Depressed
    d. Purposeless
    e. Resolved, in relation to life
    f. Pleasure, in being alive
    g. Other (specify): _____

    _____

21. **What is your present orientation to your own death?**
    a. Death-seeker
    b. Death-hastener
    c. Death-accepter
    d. Death-welcomer
    e. Death-postponer
    f. Death-fearer

22. **How often have you been in a situation in which you seriously thought you might die?**
    a. Many times
    b. Several times
    c. Once or twice
    d. Never

23. **To what extent are you interested in having your image survive after your own death through your children, books, good works, etc.?**
    a. Very interested
    b. Moderately interested
    c. Somewhat interested
    d. Not very interested
    e. Totally uninterested

24. **For whom or what might you be willing to sacrifice your life?**
    a. For a loved one
    b. For an idea or a moral principle
    c. In combat or a grave emergency where a life could be saved
    d. Not for any reason

25. **If you had a choice, what kind of death would you prefer?**
    a. Tragic, violent death
    b. Sudden but not violent death
    c. Quiet, dignified death
    d. Death in line of duty
    e. Death after a great achievement
    f. Suicide
    g. Homicidal victim
    h. There is no "appropriate" kind
    i. Other (specify): _____

    _____

26. **If it were possible, would you want to know the exact date on which you are going to die?**
    a. Yes
    b. No

27. **If your physician knew that you had a terminal disease and a limited time to live, would you want him/her to tell you?**
    a. Yes
    b. No
    c. It would depend on the circumstances

28. **If you were told that you had a terminal disease and a limited time to live, how would you want to spend your time until you died?**
    a. I would make a marked change in my life style;

satisfy hedonistic needs (travel, sex, drugs, other experiences).

b. I would become more withdrawn; reading contemplating or praying.

c. I would shift from my own needs to a concern for others (family, friends).

d. I would attempt to complete projects; tie up loose ends.

e. I would make little or no change in my life style.

f. I would try to do one very important thing.

g. I might consider dying by suicide.

h. I would do none of these.

29. **How do you feel about having an autopsy done on your body?**

a. Approve

b. Don't care one way or the other

c. Disapprove

d. Strongly disapprove

30. **To what extent has the possibility of massive human destruction by nuclear war influenced your present attitudes toward death or life?**

a. Enormously

b. To a fairly large extent

c. Moderately

d. Somewhat

e. Very little

f. Not at all

31. **Which of the following has influenced your present attitudes toward your own death the most?**

a. Pollution of the environment

b. Domestic violence

c. Television

d. Wars

e. The possibility of nuclear war

f. Poverty

g. Existential philosophy

h. Changes in health conditions and mortality statistics

i. Other (specify): _____

32. **How often have you seriously contemplated suicide?**

a. Very often

b. Only once in a while

c. Very rarely

d. Never

33. **Have you ever attempted suicide?**

a. Yes, with an actual very high probability of death

b. Yes, with an actual moderate probability of death

c. Yes, with an actual low probability of death

d. No

34. **Whom have you known who has died by suicide?**

a. Member of immediate family

b. Other family member

c. Close friend

d. Acquaintance

e. No one

f. Other (specify): _____

35. **How do you estimate your lifetime probability of suicide?**

a. I plan to do it some day.

b. I hope that I do not, but I am afraid that I might.

c. In certain circumstances, I might very well do it.

d. I doubt that I would do it in any circumstances.

e. I am sure that I would never do it.

36. **Suppose that you were to die by suicide, what reason would most motivate you to do it?**

a. To get even or hurt someone

b. Fear of insanity

c. Physical illness or pain

d. Failure or disgrace

e. Loneliness or abandonment

f. Death or loss of a loved one

g. Family strife

h. Atomic war

i. Other (specify): _____

37. **Suppose you were to die by suicide, what method would you be most likely to use?**

a. Barbiturates or pills

b. Gunshot

c. Hanging

d. Drowning

e. Jumping

f. Cutting or stabbing

g. Carbon monoxide

h. Other (specify): _____
_____

38. **Suppose you were ever to die by suicide, would you leave a suicide note?**

a. Yes

b. No

39. **To what extent do you believe that suicide should be prevented?**

a. In every case

b. In all but a few cases

c. In some cases, yes; in others, no

d. In no case; if a person wants to die by suicide, society has no right to stop him

40. **What efforts do you believe ought to be made to keep a seriously ill person alive?**

a. All possible effort; transplantations, kidney dialysis, etc.

b. Efforts that are reasonable for that person's age, physical condition, mental condition, and pain

c. After reasonable care has been given, a person ought to be permitted to die a natural death

d. A senile person should not be kept alive by elaborate artificial means

41. **If or when you are married would you prefer to outlive your spouse?**

a. Yes; I would prefer to die second and outlive my spouse.

b. No; I would rather die first and have my spouse outlive me.

c. Undecided or don't know

42. **What is your primary reason for the answer which you gave for the question above?**
   a. To spare my spouse loneliness
   b. To avoid loneliness for myself
   c. To spare my spouse grief
   d. To avoid grief for myself
   e. Because the surviving spouse could cope better with grief or loneliness
   f. To live as long as possible
   g. None of the above
   h. Other (specify): _____
   _____

43. **How important do you believe mourning and grief ritual (such as wakes and funerals) are for the survivors?**
   a. Extremely important
   b. Somewhat important
   c. Undecided or don't know
   d. Not very important
   e. Not important at all

44. **If it were entirely up to you, how would you like to have your body disposed of after your death?**
   a. Burial
   b. Cremation
   c. Donation to medical school or science
   d. I am indifferent

45. **Would you be willing to donate your heart for transplantation (after you die)?**
   a. Yes, to anyone
   b. Yes, but only to a relative or friend
   c. I have a strong feeling against it
   d. No

46. **What kind of a funeral would you prefer?**
   a. Formal, as large as possible
   b. Small, relatives and close friends only
   c. Whatever my survivors want
   d. None

47. **How do you feel about "lying in state" in an open casket at your funeral?**
   a. Approve
   b. Don't care one way or the other
   c. Disapprove
   d. Strongly disapprove

48. **What is your opinion about the costs of funerals today?**
   a. Very much overpriced
   b. No one has to pay for what he doesn't want
   c. In terms of costs and services rendered, prices are not unreasonable

49. **In your opinion, what would be a reasonable price for a funeral?**
   a. Under $500
   b. From $500 to $2500
   c. From $2500 to $4500
   d. From $3500 to $5500
   e. From $5500 to $7500
   f. From $7500 to $9500
   e. More than $9500

50. **What are your thoughts about leaving a will?**
   a. I have already made one.
   b. I have not made a will, but intend to do so some day.
   c. I am uncertain or undecided.
   d. I probably will not make one.
   e. I definitely won't leave a will.

51. **To what extent do you believe in life insurance to benefit your survivors?**
   a. Strongly believe in it; have insurance
   b. Tend to believe in it; have or plan to get insurance
   c. Undecided
   d. Tend not to believe in it
   e. Definitely do not believe in it; do not have and do not plan to get insurance

52. **Who do you feel should be the one to tell you that you are dying?**
   a. Doctor
   b. Nurse

   c. Family member
   d. Close friend

53. **Which aspect of yourself would you want to take time with if you knew you would die soon? (Rate 1-10 for urgency with 1 being most urgent.)**
   a. Physical
   b. Emotional
   c. Activities and plans
   d. Spiritual
   e. Relationships
   f. Playful
   g. Financial and practical
   h. Other (specify): _____
   _____

54. **List four things you would most like to learn, change, or do, before you die. (Number 1 through 4 in order of greatest to least priority.)**
   _____
   _____
   _____
   _____

55. **If your parent, child, or close friend had a terminal illness, who would you want to tell them?**
   a. Doctor
   b. Nurse
   c. Myself
   d. Minister
   e. Other (specify): _____
   _____

56. **Which rituals, or activities—(a) thru (q)—do you feel may be helpful for survivors, and their grief process?**
   Mark V=Very helpful, M= Moderately helpful, Q=Questionable, N=Not helpful, D=Detrimental
   a. Embalming, open casket
   b. Viewing body, not embalmed
   c. Memorial service
   d. Getting rid of photos and belongings
   e. Taking trip later
   f. Remembering dead on anniversary, holidays
   g. Talking about deceased a lot

h. New social activities, dating
i. Wearing black
j. Taking a trip right away
k. Restricting social activities
l. Keeping belongings
m. Moving, selling house (when not necessary)
n. Join widows group
o. Grieving alone
p. Sharing grief with children
q. Suggested activities not mentioned: _____

_____

57. **Most often, how do you feel you probably will die?**
a. Long illness
b. Stroke or heart attack
c. Auto accident
d. War
e. Violent encounter
f. Other (specify): _____

_____

58. **The present generation of adults has been called "hibakusha" or "explosion affected" like the survivors of Hiroshima and Nagasaki due to growing up with the cold war, air-raid sirens, the nuclear threat, Vietnam, and terrorism. How much does this awareness affect you?**

a. Daily life
b. Decisions for future
c. Never think about it
d. No respect

59. **What is your most vivid experience with death?**
Age: _____
a. Dream
b. Experience with close person
c. Animal
d. Experience with stranger
e. Story
f. News story
If your answer was (a), (c), or (f), briefly describe: ____

_____

60. **How is death talked about in your family at this time?**
a. Openly
b. Some discomfort
c. Only when necessary

d. Excludes children
e. Taboo
f. Never recall talking
g. Excludes dying person or survivor

61. **Question #10 asked how often you think about death. What was your answer? (a), (b), (c), (d), (e). Why do you think/not think about death with this frequency?**
a. If I don't think about it, it won't happen
b. Figure I'll die suddenly
c. Preoccupied with death
d. Too much fear
e. Seems very real to me
f. Very unreal to me
g. Other (specify): _____

_____

62. **At what age have you experienced the most fear of death?**

_____

Do you know what was on your mind then?

_____
_____
_____

63. **If you knew you had only a limited time to live, would you want to know the exact date of your death?**
a. Yes
b. No

64. **If death was sudden, would you be willing to donate your or a close relative's . . .**
a. Needed organ
b. Heart
c. Retinas
d. Body for research

Do you have a donor card for this?
a. Yes
b. No

65. **Presuming a home death, how do you feel about friends and family viewing your body at home right after the death?**
a. Good idea
b. Don't care
c. Up to family
d. Don't like the idea

66. **If you had a terminal illness, who would you want to talk with about your "difficult" feelings? (Number in preferential order, with 1 being the most preferred.)**
a. Spouse
b. Close family member
c. Doctor
d. Another patient
e. Friend
f. Nurse
g. Therapist
h. Clergy or spiritual friend
i. Understanding third party

67. **If a doctor told you that an immediate family member was going to die, would you want them told?**
a. Yes
b. No
c. Depends

68. **If your close friend was dying, felt depressed, and wanted to talk, how would you feel?**
a. Comfortable
b. Embarrassed
c. Distressed
d. Willing
e. Not sure
f. Would visit less

69. **When thinking of dying, I mostly fear . . . (Rate H=High fear, M=Moderate fear, L=Low fear.)**
a. Being alone
b. Mentally disoriented
c. Pain
d. Disfigurement
e. Dependence on others
f. Loss of control over physical functions
g. What happens at/after death
h. Hospitalization & treatment
i. Other (specify): _____

_____

70. **When notified of a funeral—not immediate family—I usually . . .**
a. Decline
b. Hate to go
c. Happy to go
d. Attend if at all possible
e. Dread going

71. The cause of death I'm most afraid of is . . .
    a. Accident
    b. Cancer
    c. Bomb
    d. Infection
    e. Nerve disease
    f. Heart failure
    g. Kidney failure
    h. Stroke
    i. Violence
    j. Other (specify): _____
    _____

72. As of this date I _____ made out a will.
    a. Have
    b. Have not

73. When I die the thing(s) I would like to happen to my body is/are (check one or more of the following) . . .
    a. Funeral (body present)
    b. Memorial service
    c. Cremation
    d. Embalming
    e. Organ donation
    f. Body donation
    g. Cemetery burial
    h. Above ground entombment
    i. Burial at sea
    j. Cryonics (freezing of body)
    k. Other:
    l. I don't care what happens to my body after I die.

74. My attitude toward the use of capital punishment for first degree murder is . . .
    a. Strongly agree
    b. Agree
    c. Neutral
    d. Disagree
    e. Strongly disagree

75. My attitude toward the use of abortion to terminate a pregnancy is . . .
    a. Strongly agree
    b. Agree
    c. Neutral
    d. Disagree
    e. Strongly disagree

76. My attitude toward the use of euthanasia to terminate the life of a dying person in a vegetative state is . . .
    a. Strongly agree
    b. Agree
    c. Neutral
    d. Disagree
    e. Strongly disagree

77. If I had a choice as to where I would die it would be . . .
    a. In a hospital
    b. While fighting for a good cause
    c. At home
    d. In an accident
    e. Other

78. Research findings of people who supposedly "died" on the operating table indicate that some of them reported the following experiences: floating out of body, observing resuscitation efforts, moving through a dark tunnel to a "being" of light, reviewing life, etc. What is your opinion of this?
    a. Definitely do not believe
    b. Probably do not believe
    c. Not sure
    d. Probably do believe
    e. Definitely do believe

* * * * *

Adapted from "You and Death: A Questionnaire" by Edwin S. Shneidman et al., published in *Psychology Today* (August 1970). Reprinted by permission of Edwin S. Shneidman.

This questionnaire was originally designed by Edwin Shneidman of the Center for Advanced Study in Behavioral Sciences in consultation with Edwin Parker and G. Ray Funkhouser of Stanford University. It is a modification of a questionnaire Shneidman developed at Harvard with the help of graduate assistants Chris Dowell, Ross Goldstein, Dan Goleman, and Bruce Smith.

Use the space below to write additional questions of interest to you.

Writing Your Deathography

A Deathography is an essay that details the death and loss events in your life, along with your present understanding of how each experience has influenced your attitudes and beliefs. Begin by recalling your past experiences with death and dying. Note who in your life has influenced your attitudes toward death. Review your answers to the ⬛➡ **Questionnaire: You and Death**, noting especially those questions that were difficult to answer.

Use the first activity in this section, ⬛➡ **Childhood Loss Memories**, to focus on some of your earliest memories of loss and death.

After you have completed this exercise, turn to the next activity, ⬛➡ **Questionnaire: Loss Inventory**, to brainstorm and record other death and loss events in your life. Think about your past experiences with loss. Remember that loss events include other losses in life, as well as those related to death. Some of the topics students have written about include the experience of the loss of health through a serious illness, the loss of a relationship through divorce, the loss of country through emigration, and the loss of the childbearing experience through infertility. Later, as you sit down to write your paper, you can select the important loss events in your life and make connections to your beliefs and behavior today.

The typewritten "Deathography" paper should be five to seven pages in length, although some students' essays may be longer. (For computer printouts, please use an easily readable serif typeface of 10 to 12 points.)

As an example of the "Deathography," read the following two excerpts about prior loss events and how these students connected them to their present beliefs and behaviors:

> "In examining my somewhat wishy-washy feelings about ground burial, I began to get an idea of where the conflicting notions came from in my experience. Pictures of my mother's response to digging up a long-buried goldfish join with the childhood rhyme, 'The worms crawl in, the worms crawl out, the worms play pinochle on his snout.' No wonder I am not centered about ground burial."

> "When my little sister died at birth, I was four. During the previous months I had been prepped to be a 'big brother.' My parents came home from the hospital and picked me up at my grandparents. I asked, 'Where is my baby?' My parents responded, "She didn't live long enough to come home.' I never asked another question. For years I was sure that she didn't come home because I couldn't be a good enough big brother for her and really didn't want the job anyway. While I was writing my paper, I called my mom and dad to ask them about my baby sister's death. They told me the details. When I asked them how I reacted, they said that I never talked about her. They thought that 'no questions meant no prob-

lems.' I can see now that my reluctance to ask questions of other survivors might have come from that childhood experience."

On your "Deathography," include your name, section number, and the date, along with your age. Consider creating a title that reflects your death experiences.

Use the space below to make notes about your "Deathography."

_____

_____

_____

_____

_____

_____

_____

_____

_____

_____

_____

_____

_____

_____

_____

_____

_____

_____

_____

_____

_____

⇛ *Childhood Loss Memories*

Directions: *Reflect on your earliest memories of loss and death. Describe the "story" of your experience and respond to the following questions:*

What were your reactions?

_____

_____

_____

_____

_____

_____

_____

_____

What were the reactions of those around you?

_____

_____

_____

_____

_____

_____

_____

_____

_____

_____

In what ways do you feel that you were supported or not supported at that time?

_____

_____

_____

_____

_____

_____

_____

_____

_____

In what ways did this loss experience influence your reaction to subsequent losses in your life?

_____

_____

_____

_____

_____

_____

_____

_____

_____

⟫➡ *Questionnaire: Loss Inventory*

Directions: *Use this form to record the losses in your life. Place your age at the time of each loss in the space to the left and then briefly describe the event, including your beliefs about the impact of the loss.*

_____ 1. _____

_____

_____ 2. _____

_____

_____ 3. _____

_____

_____ 4. _____

_____

_____ 5. _____

_____

_____ 6. _____

_____

_____ 7. _____

_____

_____ 8. _____

_____

_____ 9. _____

_____

_____ 10. _____

_____

_____ 11. _____

_____

_____

____ 12. _____

_____

_____

____ 13. _____

_____

_____

____ 14. _____

_____

_____

____ 15. _____

_____

_____

____ 16. _____

_____

_____

____ 17. _____

_____

_____

____ 18. _____

_____

_____

____ 19. _____

_____

_____

____ 20. _____

_____

_____

⟫➡ *Deathography Reading Assignment*

Directions*: In course sections where your instructor's preference and class size make it possible for you to read the "Deathographies" of other students, this assignment will guide those readings. At the reserve reading desk in the library, request the binder of "Deathographies" for your section. Each binder is marked with the section number and day of the week that your class meets. Read the "Deathographies" written by your classmates. As you are reading, make notes in the following areas by answering these questions, indicating the name(s) of the student(s).*

1. Which deaths seem like ones that might be particularly difficult for you to survive?

    _____

    _____

    _____

    _____

    _____

2. What kinds of similarities do you notice between the death experiences you have written about in your "Deathography" and those of your classmates?

    _____

    _____

    _____

    _____

    _____

3. Select at least two examples from the writings of your classmates that describe ways of thinking about a death or loss that seem especially useful to you.

    _____

    _____

    _____

    _____

    _____

4. Note descriptions of understandings about loss that are helpful to you as a survivor.

_____

_____

_____

_____

_____

_____

_____

5. Identify what you believe to be a high-grief death from the experiences of your classmates.

_____

_____

_____

_____

_____

_____

_____

_____

_____

Come to class prepared with the answers to these questions, along with any other comments you have on the "Deathographies." Write down the student's name along with your answers. Use additional sheets of paper if necessary. Plan your reserve reading time carefully. You will be able to read the "Deathographies" on reserve in the library on a time-limited checkout.

You will need to begin this assignment well before it is due because there is only one source for all the students in your section.

If you see a fellow student reading, it might be possible to share the "Deathographies." Make sure you return them to the same sequence in which they appeared. Some students divide their time and read from front to back of the binder.

Attitudes Toward Death: A Climate of Change

Chapter Summary

Chapter 1 introduces the study of death and dying by focusing on individual and social attitudes toward death. The perception that death is taboo, a subject not to be discussed, is contrasted with the goal of learning about dying and death as a means to enhance personal and social choices about these significant human experiences.

The tendency to avoid talking about dying and death is not necessarily a matter of individual choice as much as it is a result of social attitudes and shared practices that have changed over time. Our forebears experienced death more frequently, and more often firsthand, than most of us do today. Typical funeral practices of the nineteenth and early twentieth centuries involved extensive participation by members of the deceased's family; today, care of the dead is usually turned over to hired professionals.

The reasons for this change in the way we deal with dying and death involve a number of social and technological factors that have tended to lessen our familiarity with death. These factors include increased life expectancy, lower mortality rates (especially among the young), geographical mobility, the displacement of death from the home to institutional settings, and significant advances in life-extending medical technologies.

Building on the awareness that attitudes and practices relative to death are not static but rather are subject to change, the chapter also introduces the wealth of cultural expressions by which we can discern both individual and social attitudes toward death. Examples are given of how euphemistic language may blur the reality of death and diminish its emotional impact and of how humor is employed to defuse anxiety toward death or provide relief from painful situations. The role of the mass media in both reflecting and shaping attitudes toward death is examined, with examples cited from news reports about death as well as entertainment programs featuring death-related themes. Attention is paid to the issue of whether images of death portrayed by the media accurately reflect the reality of death in human experience. Similarly, literature, the visual arts, and music are examined with respect to what they tell us about our own and other people's attitudes toward death.

Formal education about death and dying is traced to its foundation in contributions made by pioneers in the field, such as Herman Feifel, Elisabeth Kübler-Ross, Barney Glaser, Anselm Strauss, Cicely Saunders, Robert Fulton, Geoffrey Gorer, Jeanne Quint Benoliel, among others. The growth of professional and scholarly literature about death has been accompanied in recent years by the proliferation of courses dealing with death.

The interdisciplinary nature of death education is highlighted, as is its conjoining of both cognitive and affective content, the blending of objective facts and subjective concerns. For professionals who encounter dying and death in the course of their work—including nurses, firefighters, police officers, and emergency medical personnel—death education is an important element of training that imparts specific job-related skills.

We are now in an era when people are rethinking their assumptions about death. In a pluralistic society, there are many options for dealing with death. Unlike some other types of coursework, education about dying and death is not simply academic or theoretical. It engages not only our intellect but also our emotions. The experience of a loved one's death, or an encounter with our own mortality, makes our quest for a more meaningful understanding of death both practical and intimately relevant.

Objectives

- To identify historical antecedents of current attitudes toward death.
- To list and analyze factors that have contributed to a lessened familiarity with death.
- To describe how attitudes toward death are expressed through language, humor, mass media, music, literature, and the visual arts.
- To evaluate the usefulness of increasing an awareness of death through both formal and informal death education.
- To examine assumptions about death.

Key Terms and Concepts

causes of death
cultural lag
danger-of-death narratives
death education
death notices
"death talk"
demographics
Dies Irae
dirges
elegies
epidemiologic transition
euphemisms
geographical mobility
hibakusha
institutional denial

kanikau
laments
life expectancy
life-extending technologies
managed death
"mean world" syndrome
mortality rates
obituaries
postmodernism
public vs. private loss
revictimization
sites of memory
thanatology
"vigilante" stories

32   ∽   Chapter 1

Journey Through The Last Dance, 7th ed.
Activities and Resources

Questions for Guided Study and Review

1. Compare current customs and patterns of death and dying with those of the past.
2. Briefly describe the various factors that have had an impact on individuals' familiarity with death.
3. Distinguish between life expectancy and death rates.
4. How have death rates and causes of death changed over the past century?
5. Define the term *epidemiologic transition*.
6. What message is conveyed in the poem "Grandmother, When Your Child Died"?
7. How do language, humor, the mass media, music, literature, and the visual arts function as expressions of attitudes toward death?
8. What are some reasons for using euphemisms when speaking about death?
9. Explain how language and humor may be used to provide distance from the reality of death.
10. How do sympathy cards reflect attitudes toward death?
11. What purposes does humor serve in situations related to death and dying?
12. How is death portrayed in the news and entertainment media?
13. Explain how the news media tend to promote what is characterized as the "pornography of death" in view of the phrase "if it bleeds, it leads."
14. What is the difference between a death notice and an obituary?
15. How do the visual arts and music reflect issues and concerns related to death and dying?
16. What is a *dirge*?
17. Give examples of death themes in popular music, rock, heavy metal, and blues?
18. How is death portrayed in cartoons?
19. Describe the relationship between nineteenth-century mourning customs and the Names Project AIDS Memorial Quilt.
20. How do memorials like the Vietnam Veterans Memorial and AIDS Memorial Quilt work to counter the social taboo against public mourning?
21. What is the definition of *thanatology*?
22. What were some of the achievements of significant pioneers in death studies?
23. What factors contributed to the rise of death education?
24. Why should individuals study death and dying?
25. Is there a social taboo against mentioning or talking openly about death?
26. Define the term *institutional denial*.
27. Assess the idea that "avoidance of death" has been replaced by "obsession with death" in American society.
28. What are some benefits of death education?

Practice Test Questions

MULTIPLE CHOICE

1. Which of the following best describes attitudes toward death in modern societies?
   1. institutional denial
   2. vaguely acknowledged
   3. at the forefront of our lives
   4. both accepted and denied

   a. 1 and 2
   b. 1, 2, and 4
   c. 1, 2, and 3
   d. 1, 3, and 4

2. In applying the use of language during tragedies, the work at Ground Zero after September 11, 2001 is best described as
   a. rescue work.
   b. recovery work.
   c. rescue work becoming recovery work.
   d. search and rescue work.

3. Robert Kastenbaum defines *thanatology* as
   a. the study of life, with death left in.
   b. the study of death.
   c. a topic for reflection, study, and research.
   d. an existential problem that touches on every aspect of human existence and every field of knowledge.

4. Which of the following works written by Herman Feifel is considered to be at the forefront of the modern study of death and dying?
   a. *Death and Identity*
   b. *The Meaning of Death*
   c. *The High Cost of Dying*
   d. *The Dead*

5. Survivors of the atomic bombing of Hiroshima have been described as *hibakusha* because they
   a. have anxiety about the threat of annihilation.
   b. want to show the evil of nuclear war.
   c. do not advocate nuclear energy.
   d. are concerned about the world's reliance on oil as an energy source.

TRUE/FALSE

_____ 1. Ordinary deaths are usually emphasized in the media.

_____ 2. The image of death in the media is that it comes from outside.

_____ 3. Modern literature attempts to explore the meaning of death in situations that are seemingly incomprehensible.

_____ 4. Glaser and Strauss's studies reveal that caregivers were open to discussing death and telling patients that they were dying.

_____ 5. The first formal course in death education at an American university was initiated by Robert Fulton at the University of Minnesota in 1963.

MATCHING

Match the description on the right with the corresponding author on the left.

_____ 1. Jacques Choron's *Death and Modern Man*	a. shed light on the dying process by combining research skills and clinical experience with dying patients
_____ 2. Avery Weisman's *On Death and Dying: A Psychiatric Study of Terminality*	b. reviewed contemporary attitudes toward death
_____ 3. Cicely Saunder's *Care of the Dying*	c. discussed the fear of death and changing attitudes toward immortality
_____ 4. John Hinton's *Dying*	d. helped create demand for a new approach to caring for dying patients

❧ Answers to practice questions can be found in Part IV ☙

Related Readings

📖 Indicates selection from *The Path Ahead: Readings in Death and Dying,* ed. Lynne Ann DeSpelder and Albert Lee Strickland (Mountain View, Calif.: Mayfield, 1995).

CHANGING DEMOGRAPHICS OF DEATH

James K. Crissman. *Death and Dying in Central Appalachia: Changing Attitudes and Practices.* Urbana: University of Illinois Press, 1994.

James J. Farrell. *Inventing the American Way of Death, 1830–1920.* Philadelphia: Temple University Press, 1980.

📖 Charles E. Rosenberg, "What Is an Epidemic? AIDS in Historical Perspective," pp. 29–32.

📖 Margaret Stroebe, Mary M. Gergen, Kenneth J. Gergen, and Wolfgang Stroebe, "Broken Hearts or Broken Bonds: Love and Death in Historical Perspective," pp. 231–241.

EXPRESSIONS OF DEATH ATTITUDES

📖 Allan B. Chinen, "The Mortal King," pp. 335–336.

Martha Cooper and Joseph Sciorra. *R.I.P.: Memorial Wall Art.* New York: Henry Holt, 1994.

📖 Mary N. Hall and Paula T. Rappe, "Humor and Critical Incident Stress," pp. 289–294.

Maxine Borowsky Junge. "Mourning, Memory and Life Itself: The AIDS Quilt and the Vietnam Veterans' Memorial Wall," *Arts in Psychotherapy* 26, no. 3 (1999): 195–203.

James Kinsella. *Covering the Plague: AIDS and the American Media.* New Brunswick, N.J.: Rutgers University Press, 1990.

Lawrence L. Langer, ed. *Art from the Ashes: A Holocaust Anthology.* New York: Oxford University Press, 1995.

📖 Jack Lule, "News Strategies and the Death of Huey Newton," pp. 33–40.

Philip A. Mellor and Chris Shilling. "Modernity, Self-Identity and the Sequestration of Death," *Sociology: The Journal of the British Sociological Association* 27, no. 3 (1993): 411–431.

Albert Lee Strickland. "The Healing Power of Music in Bereavement," *The Forum: Association for Death Education and Counseling* 29, no. 2 (2003): 4–5.

DEATH EDUCATION

📖 Patrick Vernon Dean, "Is Death Education a Nasty Little Secret? A Call to Break the Alleged Silence," pp. 323–326.

📖 Herman Feifel, "Psychology and Death: Meaningful Rediscovery," pp. 19–28.

📖 Robert Kastenbaum, "Reconstructing Death in Postmodern Society," pp. 7–18.

📖 Hannelore Wass, "Visions in Death Education," pp. 327–334.

Tony Walter. *The Revival of Death.* New York: Routledge, 1994.

Organizations and Internet Resources

Association for Death Education and Counseling (ADEC): <www.adec.org>. 342 North Main Street, West Hartford, CT 06117-2507. (860) 586-7503. Fax: (860) 586-7550. ADEC is one of the oldest interdisciplinary organizations in the field of dying, death, and bereavement. Members include mental and medical health personnel, educators, clergy, funeral directors, and volunteers.

Center for Thanatology Research and Education: <www.thanatology.org/>. 391 Atlantic Avenue, Brooklyn, NY 11217. (718) 858-3026. Fax: (718) 852-1846. A nonprofit mail-order bookseller, small-press, library, museum, and referral center for thanatologic research.

Growth House: <www.growthhouse.org>. With the goal of improving the quality of care for the dying, this site offers an extensive directory of internet resources relating to life-threatening illness and end-of-life care; also offers a monthly e-mail newsletter.

International Work Group on Death, Dying, and Bereavement (IWG): c/o Robert Bendiksen, Department of Sociology/Archaeology, University of Wisconsin, La Crosse, WI 54601. (608) 785-6781. E-mail: <iwg@uwlax.edu>. Composed of clinicians, researchers, and educators, IWG is dedicated to the development of knowledge, research, and practice dealing with death, dying, and bereavement, and with education about death, dying, and bereavement.

Library of Congress: <http://lcweb.loc.gov>. Provides access to the catalogs of the Library of Congress, other libraries, databases on special topics, and other Library of Congress internet resources, including government resources, internet search tools, and resources for learning more about the internet and the World Wide Web.

Names Project Foundation AIDS Memorial Quilt: <www.aidsquilt.org>. 101 Krog Street, Atlanta, GA 30307 (404)688-5500. Fax: (404)688-5552 or (800) USA-NAMES.

E-mail: <info@aidsquilt.org>. Provides information, bookings, and resources related to the AIDS Quilt, including panel construction information and mail-order services for Quilt-related items.

National Public Radio: The End of Life—Exploring Death in America: <www.npr.org/programs/death>. Beginning in November 1998, National Public Radio broadcast regular programs in a series, "The End of Life: Exploring Death in America." At this site you can access transcripts of the original broadcasts, as well as resources, readings, and a bibliography. There is also a place to tell your own story and give feedback to the programmers. Among the topics covered in this series are palliative medicine at life's end, grief and bereavement, doctors and death, reincarnation and Tibetan Buddhism, and the biology of suicide.

The Robert Wood Johnson Foundation—Last Acts: <www.lastacts.org>. The purposes of this foundation (<www.rwjf.org>) include funding projects to improve services for people with chronic health conditions and to develop better ways of caring for the dying; it seeks to bring end-of-life issues into the public arena and help individuals and organizations do health-services research and public education.

❧ Additional resources are available online at mhhe.com ❧

Major Points in This Chapter

- Death and dying sometimes seem to be taboo topics in modern societies, a situation that may reflect both a wish to relegate these aspects of human experience to the periphery of our lives and a desire to control and master them.
- Our ancestors experienced death firsthand more often than we do today. The reasons for this include changes in life expectancy, mortality rates, causes of death, geographic mobility, the setting where death occurs, and advances in life-sustaining medical technologies.
- Attitudes toward death are expressed through language, humor, mass media, music, literature, and the visual arts.
- Death education includes both formal instruction and informal discussion.
- In examining our assumptions about death and dying, consider both our individual preferences and cultural perspectives.

Observations and Reflections

As you read through *The Last Dance*, you are likely to become aware of thoughts and feelings that relate to your own attitudes and experiences concerning death. We encourage you to notice your reactions to all of the elements that are included in the text. You may experience strong reactions in response to particular photographs or boxed materials. Your strongest responses will probably occur in the context of *perceived similarity* (that is, a sense of identification with another person's characteristics or situation). When this happens, it offers an excellent opportunity to become aware of your own life history and experience with death. Use these insights to better understand yourself and others. You may be surprised—and comforted—to find that you share many essential similarities with classmates regarding your attitudes and behaviors.

Use the blank space on the following page to record your own observations and reactions about the material in this chapter.

⟫➡ *Humor and Death: Cartoons*

Directions: *Search your comic sources for death-related cartoons. You may choose single panels (like the one on page 271 of the text) or cartoon strips (such as the "Bloom County" on page 189). Paste-up your choice(s) here and on additional sheets of paper. Be sure to identify the source, title, artist, and other information listed below for each cartoon selected.*

Source

Title: _____

Artist: _____

Date: _____

Cartoon Syndicate: _____

▪➡ *Humor and Death: Jokes*

Directions: *Gather "death jokes" by questioning your friends, family members, coworkers, and acquaintances. Take note of the person's reaction to your request, "Heard any good death jokes lately?" Use this page and the next to record the text of each joke collected along with the verbal and nonverbal reactions to your request for "good death jokes." Place source data with each joke collected.*

Humor and Death: Jokes (continued)

➤ *Music and Death*

Directions: *Review your music collection. Pay particular attention to your favorite musicians. Whatever the musical form (hip hop, grunge, rock, oldies, classical, country, gospel, etc.), choose the lyrics from one of your favorite groups or individual artists wherein the theme of the song has something to do with death. (See page 25 of the text for examples of songs.) Along with the lyrics and song title, identify the performing artist and composer.*

Lyrics:

Performer _____

Song _____

Theme _____

Music and Death (continued)

➠ *Corporate Response to Death, Dying, and Bereavement: The Airlines*

Directions: *Airlines may provide discounted tickets for travel on family emergencies related to death, dying, and bereavement. For example, United Airlines offers a fare that allows for travel on short notice at a discount from the regular fare. The discounted fare allows for flexible travel (no minimum or maximum stays required) for family emergencies as well as bereavement. In this activity, you are required to call at least five airlines that operate from your local or regional airport. Initially speak to reservations and then to a supervisor to gather information about fare discounts for family emergencies and death. In the spaces below, indicate the airline, phone number, policy, and sample price differences for a selected route of your choice, as well as the situations that airlines cover under family emergency. Note the cost of a full fare ticket and the discounted one available in family emergencies along with any other information required by the airline. Divide your research between the major carriers and the regional carriers in your area.*

1. _____
   _____
   _____
   _____
   _____
   _____
   _____
   _____
   _____

2. _____
   _____
   _____
   _____
   _____
   _____
   _____
   _____
   _____
   _____

3. _____

_____

_____

_____

_____

_____

_____

4. _____

_____

_____

_____

_____

_____

_____

5. _____

_____

_____

_____

_____

_____

_____

Learning About Death: The Influence of Sociocultural Forces

Chapter Summary

Chapter 2 deals with how individuals in a given society learn about and understand death. Such learning involves a process of adjustment and refinement as new experiences lead to a reexamination of an individual's values and responses. As children develop during their formative years, they gradually acquire what is known as a mature concept of death—that is, an understanding of death shared by most adults in the child's culture. A mature concept of death is generally described as including four basic components:

1. Death is universal. All living things eventually die, and death is inevitable and unavoidable.
2. Death is irreversible. Organisms that die cannot be made alive again.
3. Death involves nonfunctionality; that is, it is the cessation of all physiological functioning, or signs of life.
4. Death involves causality. In other words, there are biological reasons for the occurrence of death.

It is important to note, however, that individuals may also hold *nonempirical* ideas about death—that is, ideas that are not susceptible to scientific proof. Such ideas mainly have to do with notions or beliefs concerning the survival of the soul or self in some form after the death of the physical body.

A child's understanding of death is influenced by his or her level of psychosocial and cognitive development, as well as by attitudes and experiences he or she encounters in the environment. These developmental factors are explored by focusing on the models of child development devised by Erik Erikson and Jean Piaget. These models help in understanding how children usually understand death at different stages of development, beginning with infancy and toddlerhood, through the early and middle years of childhood, to adolescence—by which time children have generally acquired a mature concept of death. Although very young children may recognize the basic elements of a mature concept of death, abstract or symbolic thoughts about death usually require a longer period of development. A child's personal experiences of death are likely to have a significant impact on his or her understanding. For example, the death of a close family member may cause a child to demonstrate an understanding of death that is usually associated with children at a later stage of development.

As an aid to appreciating how different sociocultural influences help shape our understanding of death, the chapter draws upon three theoretical perspectives: structural-functionalism, symbolic interactionism, and social learning theory. The particular manner in which we relate to and understand death is influenced greatly by various "agents of socialization," including family, school and peers, the mass media, and religion. Parental messages, general cultural influences, and particular life experiences all have a part in influencing how a person understands death and his or her attitude toward it. These agents of socialization may be communicated subtly or unconsciously, as when a busy parent suggests that a dead pet be replaced without taking time to acknowledge grief resulting from the loss. Cultural ideas and attitudes about death are also communicated through the books children read and television programs they watch. Life experiences—especially those involving an encounter with a significant loss or death—can powerfully affect our beliefs and attitudes.

In contemporary multicultural societies, where there are a number of social groups with distinctive customs and life styles, we typically find a variety of attitudes and practices related to death. In the text, Hawaii is cited as an example of such cultural diversity. It illustrates such sociological concepts as "local identity," as well as the dynamics of assimilation and accommodation among groups. Enlarging our cultural perspectives provides an antidote to ethnocentrism—the fallacy of making judgments about others solely in terms of one's own assumptions and biases.

Our understanding of death evolves throughout life. The process of socialization is complex and ongoing. Even though we may be primarily identified with a particular culture or social group, we are also individuals who sometimes do things our own way. When we experience loss in our lives, previously held beliefs may be modified or exchanged for new ones that better fit our developing understanding of death and its meaning in our lives.

Objectives

- To identify the components of a mature concept of death.
- To describe the psychosocial and cognitive models of development and to demonstrate their value in comprehending a child's understanding of death.
- To identify the factors that influence a child's understanding of and attitude toward death.
- To explain how various agents of socialization influence the understanding of death.
- To describe how early experiences with death can influence later conceptions of death.
- To appraise the impact of life experiences and environment on a child's understanding of death.
- To analyze teachable moments as an aspect of socialization about death.
- To describe the way a society responds to death by using three theoretical perspectives: structural-functionalism, symbolic interactionism, and social learning.

- To assess the contributions of a variety of subcultures in understanding contemporary death customs and attitudes with particular attention to the cultural diversity found in Hawaii.

Key Terms and Concepts

accommodation
assimilation
causality
cognitive transformations
cultural competency
culture
emerging adulthood
ethnocentrism
existential dread
fantasy reasoning
irreversibility
local identity
magical thinking
mature concept of death
noncorporeal continuity
nonempirical ideas about death
nonfunctionality
parental messages

personal mortality
psychosocial development
recuerdo
religiosity
replaceability
resocialization
social construction of reality
social learning theory
social norms
social structure
socialization
society
structural-functionalism
subcultures
symbolic interactionism
tactical socialization
teachable moments
universality

Questions for Guided Study and Review

1. What are the four major characteristics of a mature concept of death?
2. What are *nonempirical* ideas about death?
3. How does Erik Erikson's model of psychosocial development help us understand children's concerns about death?
4. How does Jean Piaget's model of cognitive development help us understand children's concerns about death?
5. Briefly describe the sequence of psychosocial and cognitive stages during childhood and how they relate to a child's understanding of death.
6. How does the adolescent sense of invulnerability relate to the concept of personal death?
7. Contrast the definitions of *society* and *culture*.
8. Identify and define three theoretical perspectives on socialization, and discuss how they apply to learning about death.
9. How do cultural norms influence the expression of grief?
10. Identify at least four of the major agents of socialization, and describe their impact on learning about death.
11. Distinguish between *socialization* and *resocialization*.
12. What is the role of early childhood experiences with death in relation to processes of socialization?
13. What different meanings are found in the Western version of Little Red Riding Hood and the Chinese tale of Lon Po Po (Granny Wolf)?
14. What are some of the messages or themes communicated in lullabies?

15. What is the function of religion in societies?
16. How does religiosity differ from religious affiliation?
17. What are teachable moments?
18. What is the meaning of "cultural diversity"?
19. What are some characteristics of subcultures in relation to the larger society?
20. Why is sensitivity to other cultural groups important?
21. How might cultural diversity tend to increase anxiety about death-related attitudes and behaviors?
22. How do the concepts of *assimilation* and *accommodation* apply to the various cultural groups living in Hawaii?
23. What is "local identity"?
24. How are "fuzzy" concepts related to a mature understanding of death?

Practice Test Questions

MULTIPLE CHOICE

1. Observable facts about death include:
   a. Death is avoidable.
   b. Death is unidimensional.
   c. Death is reversible.
   d. Death is universal.

2. In Erik Erikson's model, psychosocial development depends on
   1. the environment.
   2. senses and motor abilities.
   3. relationships with others.
   4. logical abilities.

   a. 1 only
   b. 3 only
   c. 1 and 3
   d. 2 and 4

3. Which of the following is an example of nonmaterial culture?
   a. a religious belief about the soul's survival beyond physical death
   b. a funeral home in a large metropolitan city
   c. a cemetery in a small community
   d. a casket or coffin

4. Which of the following is true about teachable moments?
   1. can take place between adults
   2. can take place only between adults and children
   3. unplanned or unexpected occurrences
   4. intentionally created situations

   a. 1 and 2
   b. 1 and 3
   c. 1 and 4
   d. 1, 3, and 4

5. The most common way that the Japanese dispose of their dead is
   a. burial at sea.
   b. cremation and ashes placed into an urn.
   c. cremation and ashes scattered.
   d. entombment of the body in a mausoleum.

TRUE/FALSE

_____ 1. Finding personally satisfying answers to questions such as "What happens to an individual's personality after he or she dies?" is part of the process of acquiring a mature understanding of death.

_____ 2. People tend to acquire their learning about dying and death in an organized manner

_____ 3. Religiosity and religion are terms that mean the same thing.

_____ 4. People who see themselves as active and interesting tend to be less fearful about death.

_____ 5. Some mortuaries have kitchens and dining facilities where food can be prepared and served.

MATCHING

Match the agent of socialization on the left with the appropriate phrase on the right.

_____ 1. Family

a. in nineteenth century, portrayed violence as graphic and gory to make the desired moral impression

_____ 2. Children's stories

b. conveys lessons about death by actions as well as words

_____ 3. Mass media

c. offers solace and suggests some meaning in dying

_____ 4. Religion

d. communicates attitudes toward death to children even when messages are not purposely directed to them

❧ Answers to practice questions can be found in Part IV ❧

Related Readings

📖 Indicates selection from *The Path Ahead: Readings in Death and Dying*, ed. Lynne Ann DeSpelder and Albert Lee Strickland (Mountain View, Calif.: Mayfield, 1995).

DEVELOPMENTAL ISSUES

Jeffrey Jensen Arnett. "Emerging Adulthood: A Theory of Development from the Late Teens through the Twenties," *American Psychologist* 55, no. 5 (2000): 469–480.

Lynne Ann DeSpelder and Albert Lee Strickland. "Using Life Experiences as a Way of Helping Children Understand Death." In *Beyond the Innocence of Childhood: Factors*

Influencing Children and Adolescents' Perceptions and Attitudes Toward Death, edited by David W. Adams and Eleanor J. Deveau, 45–54. Amityville, N.Y.: Baywood, 1995.

Brenda L. Kenyon. "Current Research in Children's Conceptions of Death: A Critical Review," *Omega: Journal of Death and Dying* 43, no. 1 (2001): 63–91.

GENERAL CULTURAL STUDIES

Robert Fulton and Robert Bendiksen, eds. *Death and Identity,* 3rd ed. Philadelphia: Charles Press, 1994.

📖 James Garbarino, "Challenges We Face in Understanding Children and War: A Personal Essay," pp. 169–174.

James Garbarino, Nancy Dubrow, Kathleen Kostelny, and Carole Pardo. *Children in Danger: Coping with the Consequences of Community Violence.* San Francisco: Jossey-Bass, 1992.

STUDIES OF SPECIFIC CULTURES

📖 Ronald K. Barrett, "Contemporary African-American Funeral Rites and Traditions," pp. 80–92.

📖 Kevin E. Early and Ronald L. Akers, "It's a White Thing: An Exploration of Beliefs About Suicide in the African-American Community," pp. 198–210.

📖 Zlata Filipovic, "Zlata's Diary: A Child's Life in Sarajevo," pp. 175–178.

📖 Christopher L. Hayes and Richard A. Kalish, "Death-Related Experiences and Funerary Practices of the Hmong Refugee in the United States," pp. 75–79.

📖 Ice T, "The Killing Fields," pp. 178–181.

📖 Joseph M. Kaufert and John D. O'Neil, "Cultural Mediation of Dying and Grieving Among Native Canadian Patients in Urban Hospitals," pp. 59–74.

📖 Nancy Scheper-Hughes, "Death Without Weeping: The Violence of Everyday Life in Brazil," pp. 41–58.

Unni Wikan. "Bereavement and Loss in Two Muslim Communities: Egypt and Bali Compared." *Social Science and Medicine* 17, no. 5 (1988): 451–460.

Organizations and Internet Resources

Child Development and Death and Dying: <http://bill.psyc.anderson.edu/farmen. htm>. An article highlighting Robert Kastenbaum's dimensions of development of the concept of death.

Erikson Tutorial: <http://facultyweb.cortland.edu/~ANDERSMD/ERIK/welcome. html>. Erik Erikson's psychosocial theory of social development is explained and examined on this site.

The Jean Piaget Society: <www.piaget.org>. Department Of Human Development, Graduate School of Education, Larsen Hall, Harvard University, Cambridge, MA 02138. An international, interdisciplinary organization of scholars, teachers, and researchers interested in exploring the nature of the developmental construction of human knowledge.

Multicultural Family Institute: <www.multiculturalfamily.org/text/news.shtml>. 328 Denison Street, Highland Park, NJ 08904. (732) 565-9010. Fax: (732) 565-0703. A resource for multicultural information; includes an article by Monica McGlodrick on "Culture: A Challenge to Concepts of Normality."

Teaching Children about Death and Dying: <www.uscj.org/Explaining_Death_to_200. html>. The Rapaport House, International Headquarters of the USCJ, 155 Fifth Avenue, New York, NY 10010-6802. (212) 533-7800. Fax: (212) 353-9439. This site of the United Synagogue of Conservative Judaism focuses on creating books, films, seminars, and adult and teen study programs with application to Jewish practices relating to dying, death, and bereavement.

❧ Additional resources are available online at mhhe.com ❧

Major Points in This Chapter

- As children get older they gradually develop a mature understanding of death. This means that the child understands that death is universal, is irreversible, renders the person nonfunctional, and is caused by biological reasons.
- Theoretical frameworks such as Erikson's "psychosocial development" and Piaget's "cognitive transformations" are useful for comprehending the developmental sequence relative to the acquisition of a mature concept of death.
- Agents of socialization regarding death include family, school and peers, mass media, religion, and early experiences with death.
- Life experiences—particularly those that involve an encounter with significant loss or death—are powerful in shaping attitudes and beliefs.
- Teachable moments in death education involve adults using a spontaneous or planned event as an opportunity for teaching about death.
- Theoretical perspectives—such as structural-functionalism, symbolic interactionism, and social learning theory—are useful in helping us understand how social and cultural factors influence our attitudes and behaviors relative to death.
- By recognizing the richness of cultural diversity in a society, we can also appreciate the vast array of subcultural death rituals, beliefs, and attitudes.
- Hawaii is a unique example of cultural diversity in death customs and practices.

Observations and Reflections

In reading through this chapter, you may recall experiences of loss from your own childhood. What early childhood memories do you have concerning death and dying? Are you able to apply the examples in this chapter to your own attitudes toward death? Can you identify and appreciate contributions from your cultural heritage? In studying the developmental models and differences between them relative to a child's understanding of death, how do they apply to your own experiences? Have you ever experienced "magical thinking" even as an adult?

As you explore your childhood experiences, notice the messages about death that have come from your family, peers, school, and community, as well as from books you've read and movies you've seen. Especially reflect on the ideas and understandings that you have about death that come from your experiences. What about children raised in other cultures? Do you understand more about cultural diversity?

After reading this chapter, many students are eager to explore children's thoughts and experiences. However, before you interview a child (other than your own) about death-related subjects, be sure to obtain permission from the child's parents. You can ask if the parent(s) would like to be informed about the topics that will be discussed. If so, you can provide a list of applicable topics before interviewing the child. For young children, books about death can be used to begin a dialogue. (A list of books appropriate for children and teens is included in Chapter 10.) One way to make the interaction non-threatening is to engage the child's interest in "teaching" a grown-up.

Use the blank space below to record some of your own childhood experiences.

⇛ *Thoughts about Death*

Directions: Your answers to the following questions will provide a review of some of the issues related to death and dying.

1. How openly is death spoken about in your family, your circle of friends, and your work environment? What do you believe accounts for the ease (or lack of ease) about discussing death in each of these environments?

    _____

    _____

    _____

    _____

    _____

    _____

2. Are you afraid of death? What particular aspects of death elicit fear or anxiety in you?

    _____

    _____

    _____

    _____

    _____

    _____

3. Do you have written plans for carrying out your wishes at and after death? What are they?

    _____

    _____

    _____

    _____

    _____

4. Are there legal or consumer matters that you need to complete before your death? What are they?

_____

_____

_____

_____

_____

_____

5. What important interpersonal unfinished business would you like to complete before your death?

_____

_____

_____

_____

_____

_____

6. Do you believe that you would make changes in your life style (relationships, home, work, travel, education, etc.) if you discovered that you had a terminal illness? What would those changes include?

_____

_____

_____

_____

_____

_____

_____

➤ *A Mature Concept of Death*

Directions: *Interview two children, one between the ages of four and seven and another between the ages of eight and eleven. (Make sure parental permission is obtained.) Ask the two children the following questions related to the mature concept of death:*

Child 1: Age_____

Child 2: Age_____

1. Will all the people in the world die someday, or do some people never die?

   Child 1: _____

   _____

   _____

   _____

   _____

   _____

   Child 2: _____

   _____

   _____

   _____

   _____

   _____

2. When a person dies, can they eat? Can they breathe? Can they move?

   Child 1: _____

   _____

   _____

   _____

   _____

   _____

Child 2: _____

_____

_____

_____

_____

_____

_____

3. When a person dies, can they ever come back to life again?

Child 1: _____

_____

_____

_____

_____

_____

_____

_____

Child 2: _____

_____

_____

_____

_____

_____

_____

_____

➠ *Television as Teacher*

Directions: *Watch two or three television programs directed toward children or adolescents in which death is likely to be depicted. Provide a summary of the plot and provide answers to the following questions for each program viewed. Use additional paper as necessary to answer the questions for additional programs.*

1. What was the title of the program?

   _____

2. What was the plot or story?

   _____

   _____

   _____

   _____

   _____

3. Which character(s) died?

   _____

   _____

   _____

   _____

   _____

4. How did the character(s) die?

   _____

   _____

   _____

   _____

   _____

5. How was death determined?

_____

_____

_____

_____

_____

_____

6. What were the survivors' reactions (grief or otherwise) to death?

_____

_____

_____

_____

_____

7. Was there a funeral ritual or commemoration of the death?

_____

_____

_____

_____

_____

8. If children were depicted in the story, how were they told about the death, and what were their reactions?

_____

_____

_____

_____

_____

9. What portion of the program content included issues of cultural diversity in dying, death, or grief?

_____

_____

_____

_____

_____

10. Were the characters who died mentioned again? In what manner or context?

_____

_____

_____

_____

_____

11. What did this program teach children about death?

_____

_____

_____

_____

_____

12. How could the presentation of death-related actions or topics have been improved?

_____

_____

_____

_____

_____

Use this page to record your observations and reflections about television portrayals of dying, death, and bereavement.

_____

_____

_____

_____

_____

_____

_____

_____

_____

_____

_____

_____

_____

_____

_____

_____

_____

_____

_____

_____

_____

_____

_____

Perspectives on Death: Cross-Cultural and Historical

Chapter Summary

Chapter 3 broadens our perspective by examining how people have dealt with death in cultural and historical settings other than our own. We begin this examination by looking at traditional myths or beliefs about death. In many traditional societies, for example, the relationship between beliefs and practices is apparent in behaviors that are followed on the basis of concepts about the "power of the dead." Attitudes toward the dead are often evident in a culture's naming practices, which may involve either avoiding or memorializing the name of the deceased. The way that traditional societies explain the cause of death and its ultimate origin provide yet another avenue toward understanding central themes that still have currency in our efforts to understand death.

Attention is given to the death-related beliefs and practices that have prevailed at different times in the history of Western culture. Changes over the centuries in the manner of dying are discussed in the context of the dying person's anticipation of death and the scene around the deathbed. The attitude of survivors toward the dead is traced by examining changing fashions in burial customs, such as the contrast between anonymous burial in charnel houses and subsequent development of individual graves and memorialization of the dead. Changing attitudes about death are also revealed in the evolution of the *danse macabre*, or Dance of Death.

Our survey of historical perspectives on death and dying concludes with a discussion of "invisible death," a term that characterizes the way that death and dying have generally been dealt with by people living in modern, technological societies. It refers to the practice of delegating care of the dying and the dead to professionals and to the emphasis on delaying death by all means available, as well as to the comparative lack of social or cultural supports for placing death and dying within a meaningful context as an intrinsic part of human experience. Tracing the historical changes in death-related attitudes and customs heightens awareness of the possibility of further changes in our manner of dealing with death.

To expand our awareness of such possibilities, the chapter includes descriptions of five cultural case studies that provide enlightening comparisons with European American culture. This discussion focuses on death-related attitudes and practices associated with

Native American, African, Mexican, Asian, and Celtic traditions. The text encourages us to look for commonalties as well as differences in the ways human beings in different cultures relate to death.

The chapter concludes by noting that ultimate fulfillment, the sense of having lived one's life well, may be possible only within a community that acknowledges the significance of death. The examples of other cultures—more or less distant from our own in time or space—can offer us insights and inspiration for creating such a community.

Objectives

- To become acquainted with the diversity of death-related rituals and beliefs found in various cultures.
- To assess the correspondences among various cultures relative to death-related rituals and beliefs.
- To describe the historical changes in death-related beliefs and practices in the Western world.
- To analyze the impact of various beliefs and practices and to assess their value for survivors.

Key Terms and Concepts

ancestor worship
Black Death
butsudan
charnel house
ch'ing ming
collective destiny
danse macabre
death knells
death songs
deathbed scene
el Día de los Muertos
effigies
filial piety
fêng-shui
haka
"invisible death"
"living dead"

medicalization of dying
memento mori
memorialization
mourning restraints
name avoidance
necromancy
o-bon
origin-of-death myths
Otherworld
rites of passage
rituals of dying
Samhain
shaman
"tamed death"
Valhalla
valkyries

Questions for Guided Study and Review

1. How long have humans shown concern for the dead?
2. What are some characteristics of how death is viewed in traditional cultures?
3. What is the common theme in various myths of the origin of death?
4. How are illness and various causes of death viewed in traditional cultures?
5. What is meant by the phrase, "the power of the dead"?
6. What is name avoidance, and why is it practiced?

7. Identify the major changes that have taken place in Western attitudes toward death since the early Middle Ages (roughly C.E. 500). In framing your answer, consider the following historical periods: 500–1100, 1100–1500, 1500–1700, 1700–1900, and 1900–present.

8. What traditions illustrate these changing attitudes in Western culture? Consider, for example, deathbed scenes, burial customs, and memorialization.

9. Briefly describe the categories, "tamed death," "untamed death," and "invisible death," as used by Philippe Ariès.

10. What is the general viewpoint of Native American societies toward death?

11. What are some differences that can be noted about contrasting attitudes toward death among various Native American tribes?

12. Discuss differences in attitudes and funeral practices between the Cocopa and the Hopi.

13. Identify some practices among the Ohlone that illustrate beliefs related to the power of the dead.

14. What is a death song?

15. What is meant by the term *ancestor worship*?

16. How are treatment of the dead and the notion of the "living dead" related?

17. What are the four stages of LoDagaa mourning customs?

18. What are the two purposes served by the LoDagaa mourning rituals?

19. What meaning is given to the mourning restraints used by the LoDagaa?

20. What is the Day of the Dead?

21. What distinction is made between children and adults in customs relating to the Day of the Dead?

22. What awareness of death is reflected in Mexican death customs?

23. Using cross-cultural examples, support the theme that life and death may be perceived as a continuous process.

24. What is the role of ancestors in Asian cultures?

25. In the traditional Japanese view, what is special about the first forty-nine days after a death?

26. What is the purpose of the so-called "bone house" in Chinese mortuary practices?

27. Discuss the Celtic attitude toward death in battle?

28. What was the Celtic view of the Otherworld?

Practice Test Questions

MULTIPLE CHOICE

1. A common theme in origin-of-death myths is that death
   a. comes as a teacher.
   b. comes from outside oneself.
   c. is the result of a transgression.
   d. is a punishment.

2. A practice concerning the dead found among many traditional peoples around the world is
    a. keeping a death vigil.
    b. vision quests.
    c. name avoidance.
    d. loud wailing at funeral rituals.

3. Philippe Ariès describes the predominant attitude toward death during the period 1750–1900 as
    a. "thy death."
    b. "tamed death."
    c. "invisible death."
    d. "death denied."

4. Which culture is noteworthy for displaying a humorous or satirical attitude toward death?
    a. Hopi
    b. Mexican
    c. LoDagaa
    d. Celts

5. Elements of Celtic traditions related to death include
    1. Valhalla
    2. Ulysses
    3. Odin
    4. Valkyries

    a. 1 and 3
    b. 2 and 4
    c. 1, 2, and 4
    d. 1, 3, and 4

TRUE/FALSE

_____ 1. The attitudes prevalent in a particular culture shape the response to death.

_____ 2. The shift to a focus on death of the self in Western culture contributed to significant changes in attitudes toward death.

_____ 3. The mourning customs of the nineteenth century did little to make death seem less final or severe.

_____ 4. The size of a death notice in southwestern Nigeria can sometimes occupy a full page.

_____ 5. *Día de los Muertos* and *Samhain* occur at the same time of year.

MATCHING

Match each of the following cited examples with the appropriate topic.

_____ 1. Winnebago myth: a. causes of death
      When Hare Heard of Death

_____ 2. Senufo view of a child's death   b. memorializing the dead

_____ 3. Cemetery of Père Lachaise   c. dance of death

_____ 4. Images of skeletons on   d. origin of death
      Halloween costumes

❧ Answers to practice questions can be found in Part IV ❦

Related Readings

📖 Indicates selection from *The Path Ahead: Readings in Death and Dying,* ed. Lynne Ann DeSpelder and Albert Lee Strickland (Mountain View, Calif.: Mayfield, 1995).

HISTORICAL STUDIES

Philippe Ariès. *The Hour of Our Death.* New York: Alfred A. Knopf, 1981.

Paul Binsky. *Medieval Death: Ritual and Representation.* London: British Museum Press, 1996.

Patrick J. Geary. *Living with the Dead in the Middle Ages.* Ithaca, N.Y.: Cornell University Press, 1994.

Patricia Jalland. *Death in the Victorian Family.* New York: Oxford University Press, 1996.

Frederick S. Paxton. *Christianizing Death: The Creation of a Ritual Process in Early Medieval Europe.* New York: Cornell University Press, 1990.

Colin Platt. *King Death: The Black Death and Its Aftermath in Late-Medieval England.* London: University College of London Press, 1996.

📖 Charles E. Rosenberg, "What Is an Epidemic? AIDS in Historical Perspective," pp. 29–32.

📖 Margaret Stroebe, Mary M. Gergen, Kenneth J. Gergen, and Wolfgang Stroebe, "Broken Hearts or Broken Bonds: Love and Death in Historical Perspective," pp. 231–241.

CROSS-CULTURAL PERSPECTIVES

📖 Ronald K. Barrett, "Contemporary African-American Funeral Rites and Traditions," pp. 80–92.

John Greenleigh and Rosalind Rosoff Beimler. *The Days of the Dead: Mexico's Festival of Communion with the Departed.* San Francisco: HarperCollins, 1991.

Yoel Hoffman. *Japanese Death Poems.* Rutland, Vt.: Charles E. Tuttle, 1986.

Åke Hultkrantz. *Shamanic Healing and Ritual Drama: Health and Medicine in Native North American Religious Tradition.* New York: Crossroad, 1992.

Thomas A. Kselman. *Death and the Afterlife in Modern France.* Princeton, N.J.: Princeton University Press, 1993.

John S. Mbiti. *Introduction to African Religion,* 2nd ed. Oxford: Heinemann, 1991.

James L. Watson and Evelyn S. Rawski, eds. *Death Ritual in Late Imperial and Modern China.* Berkeley: University of California Press, 1988.

Organizations and Internet Resources

African and Egyptian Religious Beliefs: <www.geocities.com/Tokyo/Temple/9845/budge.htm>. Comparison of African and Egyptian death customs.

Artistic Expression of Life and Death in Western Cemeteries: <www.hospicecare.org.hk/education/ presentation/bbh_cemetery.PDF>. Essay by Chan-Fai Cheung from the Chinese University of Hong Kong, which draws upon the work of Phillipe Ariès.

Celtic Death Rituals: <http://ipc.paganearth.com/diaryarticles/bonus/druid/druid5.html>. Information about *Samhain* and the Otherworld.

Cross-Cultural Funeral Rites: <www.biomed.lib.umn.edu/hw/ccf.html>. Article by LaVone Hazell in the *Director* describing rituals from different cultures and religions.

Day of the Dead: <www.azcentral.com/ent/dead>. Educational site devoted to information about *El Día de los Muertos*, including history, events, food, photographs, and altars.

Medieval Art Bibliography—Death and Tombs: <www.otago.ac.nz/arthistory/medieval/deathTombs.html>. Useful references compiled by the University of Otago in New Zealand.

Simplicity or Passion? The Politics of Mourning: <www.africanews.com/article504.html>. Article by Charles Onyango-Obbo about Ugandan funeral rituals.

Tamanawit Unlimited: Suite 575, 1122 East Pike Street, Seattle, WA 98122. (206) 632-8124. Fax: (509) 463-4983. Dr. Terry Tafoya's office for consulting and education about Native American perspectives on death, dying, and bereavement.

❧ Additional resources are available online at mhhe.com ❧

Major Points in This Chapter

- Studying death in early and traditional cultures provides information about origin-of-death myths, ways of assessing the causes of death, and practices associated with the use of a deceased person's name.
- The history of attitudes toward death in Western European culture includes such phenomena as the Dance of Death (*danse macabre*) and the charnel house, as well as changes in the deathbed scene, burial customs, and practices for memorializing the dead.
- Tracing the historical changes in death-related attitudes and customs increases awareness of the possibility of further changes in our own lifetimes.
- Native American attitudes and customs relative to death vary widely among the different tribal groups, although they share a belief in the cyclic nature of life and death.

- African attitudes and customs relative to death are based on a cyclical view of birth and death whereby deceased ancestors remain part of their survivors' lives.
- LoDagaa mourning customs exemplify complex rituals that include specific ceremonies and practices to be enacted by mourners.
- The Mexican tradition of *el Día de Los Muertos* blends indigenous death rituals with the Catholic Church's commemoration of All Souls' Day to produce a unique fiesta; death is confronted by Mexican artists and writers with an attitude of humorous sarcasm.
- Respect for ancestors occupies a central place in Asian cultures. As honored members of a household, ancestors continue to be important to the lives of family members.
- During the Chinese celebration known as *ch'ing ming*, families visit graves and burn paper replicas of money, clothes, jewelry, and even modern necessities such as video cameras as a way of showing regard and care for deceased relatives.
- During the midsummer *o-bon* festival, the Japanese celebrate the return of ancestral spirits to their families. Japanese death rituals are distinctive not only because of their duration but also because of the strong association between the ancestor's spirit and ongoing benefits to the family.
- As a significant element in the lineage of European and European American culture, Celtic traditions are found in literature, music, and secular observances of Halloween, as well as in an attitude of reverence for nature and belief in personal immortality.

Observations and Reflections

A primary goal of this chapter is to help you recognize the validity of diverse cultural responses to the basic human experience of death and dying. Understanding that each culture has its own way of responding to death, you can learn to suspend judgment and recognize the value of various practices in terms of how they benefit survivors. For example, although name avoidance might at first seem to be a rather exotic practice, you may have seen the correlation between this practice as it exists in other cultures and the reluctance to mention the deceased's name to recently bereaved people in your own culture. Note, however, that the beliefs behind these two practices may differ.

You can learn to recognize that your own beliefs and practices may seem no less bizarre than the beliefs and practices of other people. This understanding allows you to evaluate the degree to which your own beliefs and practices benefit you. Reflect on the practices and beliefs that come from your own "culture."

Use the blank space below and on the following page to record some of your own beliefs and practices regarding death.

⟫➔ *Death Customs*

Directions: *Use the space below to develop a list of death customs that you have participated in or heard about. Compare and contrast these customs with those of the cultures described in* The Last Dance. *Discuss the functions served by the customs you list and the beliefs associated with each of them.*

1. Death customs I have participated in or heard about:

_____

_____

_____

_____

_____

_____

_____

_____

_____

_____

_____

_____

2. Similarities and differences between what I know about death customs and those mentioned in the text:

_____

_____

_____

_____

_____

_____

_____

_____

_____

_____

_____

_____

_____

_____

3. Functions served by the customs and the beliefs associated with each. (For example, the chapter opening photograph shows a cultural belief that manifests in a burial custom: A belief in a return of the body's elements to the "natural world" is accomplished by platform burial.)

_____

_____

_____

_____

_____

_____

_____

_____

_____

_____

_____

_____

_____

_____

⇛ 🖳 *Cultural Diversity: Internet Exercise*

Directions: *Visit at least three websites that have information about cultural diversity. Apply the criteria for evaluating a website explained in the Introduction of this book. Rate each website 1–5 (with 1 being the best and 5 the poorest). Here are several from which you may choose, or you can find others.*

http://dying.about.com/health/dying/mbody.htm
http://www.trinity.edu/~mkearl/death-1.html
http://www.health.qld.gov.au/hssb/cultdiv/guidel/death_and_dying.htm
http://www.geocities.com/Athens/1044/

1. List the websites you visited. Rate each one.

   _____

   _____

   _____

   _____

   _____

   _____

   _____

   _____

2. What kinds of cultural information did you find?

   _____

   _____

   _____

   _____

   _____

   _____

   _____

   _____

3. Pick one aspect of each website and describe its value.

_____

_____

_____

_____

_____

_____

_____

_____

_____

_____

_____

4. What did you learn from visiting the websites?

_____

_____

_____

_____

_____

_____

_____

_____

_____

_____

_____

_____

74 ∼ Chapter 3

Journey Through The Last Dance, 7th ed.
Activities and Resources

Health Care Systems:
Patients, Staff, and Institutions

Chapter Summary

Chapter 4 examines the health care system as it relates to care of individuals with life-threatening and terminal illnesses. The chapter begins with an introduction to modern health care, including issues concerning health care financing and the allocation of scarce resources. These issues raise questions about the limits of medical progress and how to achieve a balance between extension of life and quality of life.

Modern health care embodies a tripartite relationship among patient, institution, and staff. Each of the parties to this relationship contributes to the overall shape and quality of health care. Excessive bureaucratization may create situations wherein care of the dying becomes impersonal, thereby undermining the "subjecthood" of the patient. In such cases, biological death may be preceded by social death. Alternatives to such depersonalization and abstraction require that caregivers and patients alike break the illusion of immortality and recognize that all human lives have an end.

Helping professionals who work in environments where death occurs frequently are subject to high levels of stress. Decisions involving life or death may have to be made under extreme time pressures. Caregivers may have the task of delivering bad news to relatives and handling their reactions. Medical and nursing professionals need to work within a supportive environment that allows death to be discussed openly among those involved in patients' care. They must also be confident that the care they provide is appropriate, beneficial, and in patients' best interests.

Although hospitals remain an important setting for care of terminally ill patients, other options are available. Hospice and palliative care, for example, are oriented specifically toward the needs of the dying patient and his or her family. Home care is also increasingly recognized as an appropriate alternative for some patients and their families. Even within hospital settings, there is a growing emphasis on providing appropriate care for dying patients—that is, care intended to alleviate pain and other symptoms as opposed to measures intended to extend life. Most terminally ill patients use some combination of all these forms of care, depending on the stage of illness and their particular situation. Organized support groups focusing on specific interests and needs of patients are also important in the total health care system.

Emergency care for life-threatening injury and trauma is another area related to the study of death and dying. Most deaths from trauma occur immediately after injury. For those who survive with injuries, time is the enemy. Many of the advances in emergency and trauma medicine have come about from a focus on the critical "golden hour" following injury. The use of the helicopter air ambulance and the triage system for evacuating casualties have increased the chances of surviving many types of injury, as has the development of specialized trauma centers, where surgery and other medical interventions can be provided expeditiously.

Being with a person who is dying or seriously ill can elicit a confrontation with one's own mortality. People may feel uncomfortable in the presence of a person who has been diagnosed with a life-threatening illness or who is dying. An antidote to discomfort and uncertainty in such situations is to remember that the essence of caregiving and companionship involves leaving one's own agenda at the door and attending to the needs of the other person. Such situations teach us that we cannot expect ourselves to have all the answers. Being with someone who is dying can help us recognize just how precious life is, and how uncertain.

Objectives

- To list the three components of a health care system and explain how their interrelationship influences patient care.
- To describe the relationship between health care costs and the options available for treatment.
- To explain the factors influencing the onset of stress among caregivers and to identify ways of alleviating such stress.
- To summarize the various types of health care for terminally ill and dying patients and to differentiate between their functions, purposes, and methods of care.
- To assess the role of home care in the overall health care system.
- To identify psychosocial factors influencing one's relationship with a loved one who is dying.

Key Terms and Concepts

acute care
burnout
caregiver stress
chronic illness
depersonalization
diagnosis-related groups (DRGs)
elder care
gerontology
home care
hospice care
hospital
institutional neurosis
interventional cascade
life review
life-threatening illness
managed care

Medicare Hospice Benefit
nursing home
palliative care
"peaceful" death
primary caregiver
quality-adjusted life years (QALYs)
rationing
respite care
skilled nursing facility
social support
technological imperative
terminal illness
total care
trauma/emergency care
triage

Questions for Guided Study and Review

1. What are the differences between hospitals, nursing homes, and hospices?
2. What are the components of the "health care triangle"?
3. How do written and unwritten rules affect patient care?
4. How do depersonalization and abstraction affect human medical care and quality of life?
5. How is the cost of health care related to financial and technological innovations?
6. What is the definition of rationing, and when does it occur?
7. How might bureaucratic attitudes and organizational structure affect interactions among patients, family members, and health care professionals?
8. Discuss the contrast between "cure" and "care" orientations of medical care.
9. What are the main goals of palliative care?
10. Describe the settings in which palliative care is provided to patients.
11. What is the historical background of hospice care?
12. What are the goals of hospice care?
13. In what ways does St. Christopher's embody the goals and characteristics of hospice care?
14. What challenges face hospices and hospice care?
15. Summarize the Medicare guidelines for hospice care.
16. What is a primary caregiver?
17. What are the potential advantages and disadvantages to home care?
18. What is the Zen Hospice Project, and how does it work?
19. What are the central aims of social support programs for dying patients and their families?
20. What is the historical background of modern-day trauma care?
21. What is the "golden hour"?
22. Of the total number of Americans who die each year from injuries received in accidents, what is the percentage involving motor vehicles?
23. What is the definition of *trauma*?
24. How are priorities for patient care assigned in the "triage" systsem?
25. What is the survival rate for patients who receive appropriate care during the critical period following accidental injury?
26. What sources of stress may be present in caring for the dying?
27. How might caregivers deal constructively with stress related to caring for patients?
28. How is *life review* a useful counseling tool with dying people?
29. How might an individual counteract feelings of discomfort and uncertainty when in the presence of someone who is seriously ill or dying?

Practice Test Questions

MULTIPLE CHOICE

1. According to the text, what is the most commonly held fear about dying?
   a. dying in pain and loneliness
   b. causing a burden to one's families and friends
   c. the inefficient care at hospitals
   d. the high cost of health care

2. The amount of reimbursement for DRGs is based on which of the following?
    1. the patient's disease
    2. the patient's ability to pay
    3. the patient's medical history
    4. the complexity of services provided to the patient

   a. 2, 3, and 4
   b. 1, 3, and 4
   c. 1, 2, and 3
   d. 1 and 4

3. The World Health Organization defines *palliative care* as
   a. to cloak or conceal an incurable illness.
   b. to reduce the severity of an event or situation.
   c. the active total care of patients whose disease is NOT responsive to curative treatment.
   d. the active total care of patients whose disease IS responsive to curative treatments.

4. An individual with a life-threatening illness who suffers from feelings of helplessness and low self-esteem can benefit from
    1. social support organizations.
    2. respite care.
    3. home care.
    4. online patient groups.

   a. 1 and 4
   b. 2 and 3
   c. 1, 3, and 4
   d. 2 and 4

5. What does the phrase "the golden hour" refer to?
   a. the first hour after a traumatic injury
   b. the first hour of an operation
   c. the last hour of an operation
   d. the last hour before death

TRUE/FALSE

_____ 1. Hospitals are oriented toward meeting the needs of dying patients.

_____ 2. The goal of palliative care is to achieve the best possible quality of life for patients and their families.

_____ 3. One requirement in qualifying for hospice care is a doctor's certification that a patient's life expectancy is six months or less if the illness runs its normal course.

_____ 4. Home care is unsupervised medical care that is provided in the patient's home.

_____ 5. Health care professionals may experience stress because of inability to produce a cure for a patient.

MATCHING

Match each of type of elder care with the appropriate description.

_____ 1. Personal home care

_____ 2. Skilled nursing facility

_____ 3. Home health care

_____ 4. Congregate housing

a. has an organizational structure that provides the particular level of care needed by each resident.

b. provides care for residents who need minimal assistance.

c. comprehensive care, providing medical and nursing services, as well as dietary supervision.

d. ranges from medical and nursing visits to help with preparing meals and monitoring exercise.

❦ Answers to practice questions can be found in Part IV ❧

Related Readings

📖 Indicates selection from *The Path Ahead: Readings in Death and Dying*, ed. Lynne Ann DeSpelder and Albert Lee Strickland (Mountain View, Calif.: Mayfield, 1995).

HEALTH CARE SYSTEMS

📖 Daniel Callahan, "The Limits of Medical Progress: A Principle of Symmetry," pp. 103–105.

Mickey Eisenberg. *Life in the Balance: Emergency Medicine and the Quest to Reverse Sudden Death*. New York: Oxford University Press, 1997.

John D. Lantos. *Do We Still Need Doctors?* New York: Routledge, 1997.

CARE OF THE DYING

📖 William G. Bartholome, "Care of the Dying Child: The Demands of Ethics," pp. 133–143.

Ira Byock. *Dying Well: The Prospect for Growth at the End of Life*. New York: Riverhead Books, 1997.

📖 Joseph M. Kaufert and John D. O'Neil, "Cultural Mediation of Dying and Grieving Among Native Canadian Patients in Urban Hospitals," pp. 59–74.

📖 William M. Lamers, Jr., "Hospice: Enhancing the Quality of Life," pp. 116–124.

Rodger McFarlane and Philip Bashe. *The Complete Bedside Companion: No-Nonsense Advice on Caring for the Seriously Ill*. New York: Simon & Schuster, 1998.

📖 Balfour M. Mount, "Keeping the Mission," pp. 125–132.

📖 Richard S. Sandor, "On Death and Coding," pp. 144–147.

Cicely Saunders. "The Evolution of Palliative Care," *Patient Education and Counseling* 41, no. 1 (2000): 7–13.

Virginia F. Sendor and Patrice M. O'Connor. *Hospice & Palliative Care: Questions and Answers*. Lanham, Md.: Scarecrow Press, 1997.

📖 Janmarie Silvera, "Crossing the Border," pp. 301–302.

Organizations and Internet Resources

Alliance for Cannabis Therapeutics: <www.marijuana-as-medicine.org>. P.O. Box 21210, Kalorama Station, Washington, DC 20009. Information about medical uses of marijuana, including clinical studies, political action, and legal cases.

Americans for Better Care of the Dying: <www.abcd-caring.org>. 4200 Wisconsin Avenue, N.W., Fourth Floor, Washington, DC 20016. (202) 895-2660. Fax: (202) 966-5410. Organization dedicated to improving care at the end of life.

American Hospital Association: <www.aha.org>. Suite 2700, One North Franklin, Chicago, IL 60606. (312) 422-3000 or (800) 424-4301. Fax: (312) 422-4796. Represents and provides services for all types of hospitals and health care networks and for their patients in the U.S.

Caregiver Network: <www.caregiver.on.ca>. Canadian organization that offers resources to make life as a caregiver easier.

Caregiver Survival Resources: <www.caregiver911.com>. Resources to help people cope with the demands of caregiving.

Center to Improve Care of the Dying: <www.gwu.edu/~cicd/>. Suite 820, 2175 K Street NW, Washington, DC 20037. (202) 467-2222. Interdisciplinary organization focusing on research, education, and advocacy to improve care of dying patients.

Children's Hospice International: <www.chionline.org>. Suite 3C, 2202 Mount Vernon Avenue, Alexandria, VA 22301. (703) 684-0330 or (800) 242-4453. Fax: (703) 684-0226. Supports hospice care for children.

Dying Well: <www.dyingwell.com>. The website of hospice physician Ira Byock's "Missoula Demonstration Project," which promotes a definition of wellness through the end of life and includes resources for patients and families facing life-limiting illness.

Hospice Foundation of America: <www.hospicefoundation.org>. Suite 300, 2001 S Street NW, Washington, DC 20009. (202) 638-5419 or (800) 854-3402. Fax: (202) 638-5312. E-mail: <hfa@hospicefoundation.org>. Nonprofit organization promoting hospice concept of care through education and leadership.

National Association for Home Care: <www.nahc.org>. 228 7th Street SE, Washington, DC 20003. (202) 547-7424. Fax: (202) 547-3540. Information about patient home care.

National Hospice and Palliative Care Organization (NHPCO): <www.nhpco.org>. Suite 300, 1700 Diagonal Road, Alexandria, VA 22314. (703) 243-5900 or (800) 658-8898. Formerly the National Hospice Organization (NHO), NHPCO provides information about hospice care and supplies an online national directory of hospices listed by state and city.

On Our Own Terms—Public Broadcasting System: <www.pbs.org/wnet/onourownterms>. Reporting on initiatives to improve care at the end of life, this web site is a companion to the television series hosted by Bill Moyers and broadcast on PBS in September 2000. It includes information about the series, video clips, articles on the major themes of the series, descriptions of local initiatives, personal stories, and an extensive resources section.

Soros Foundation—Project on Death in America: <www.soros.org/death.htm>. Through this project, the Soros Foundation provides funding for programs and individuals who are doing research and creating models of care that address societal and technological obstacles to achieving a good death. This site is multidisciplinary, focusing on different approaches to the subject of dying, from the pragmatic to the spiritual.

Zen Hospice Project: <www.zenhospice.org>. 273 Page Street, San Francisco, CA 94102. (415) 863-2910. Fax: (415) 863-1768. This organization provides volunteer services, residential care, and educational resources.

❧ Additional resources are available online at mhhe.com ❧

Major Points in This Chapter

- The quality of health care depends on the relationships among the patient, the medical/nursing staff, and the institution.
- Individual and social choices about financing health care exert an influence on the options available for care of the seriously ill and dying.
- Emergency personnel and other caregivers are exposed to stress related to the helping role.
- Palliative care involves active total care of patients whose disease is not responsive to curative treatment.
- Hospice care is specialized palliative care of patients with terminal illness.
- Being with someone who is dying involves a confrontation with one's own mortality.

Observations and Reflections

It is important to recognize that there is nothing inherently bad or good about any particular health care system. What makes a setting good or bad are the values, beliefs, and practices of the people involved. Consequently, through education, any health care system can become more responsive to the needs of dying patients.

Use the blank space below and on the following page to brainstorm some ways that health care systems can become more responsive to the needs of dying patients and their families.

⟫➡ *Health Care Dramas: Television and the Terminally Ill*

Directions: *Watch three different medical programs on television, paying attention to how terminally ill patients, their doctors, nurses, other caregivers, family, and friends are portrayed. Then answer the following questions and bring the responses to class.*

What was the patient's age, sex, and socioeconomic level?

Program 1 _____

Program 2 _____

Program 3 _____

Describe his or her personality.

Program 1 _____

Program 2 _____

Program 3 _____

How was he or she treated by family members and medical personnel?

Program 1 _____

Program 2 _____

Program 3 _____

Was the death presented in a realistic context?

Program 1 _____

Program 2 _____

Program 3 _____

What was the cause of death?

Program 1 _____

Program 2 _____

Program 3 _____

In what ways was the death similar to or different from your own experience with death?

Program 1 _____

Program 2 _____

Program 3 _____

Was the death portrayed realistically?

Program 1 _____

Program 2 _____

Program 3 _____

What life values were expressed in the death?

Program 1 _____

Program 2 _____

Program 3 _____

What suggestions would you offer to the program writers?

Program 1 _____

Program 2 _____

Program 3 _____

Use the space below to describe what you learned while completing this activity.

_____

_____

_____

_____

_____

_____

_____

_____

➠ *Home Care*

Directions: *Imagine that your closest relative has become terminally ill and is a candidate for home care. Answer the following questions about your ability to be a caregiver.*

Given your present schedule, how much time per day (or week) would you be able to devote to caring for your relative?

_____

_____

_____

_____

What training or preparation have you had to be a caregiver?

_____

_____

_____

_____

If your relative's nurse needed assistance in carrying out the following duties, which of them would you be willing to do?

- ❑ Provide a listening ear
- ❑ Push wheelchair on outings for shopping or medical visits
- ❑ Spend the night
- ❑ Evaluate hospice care in your area
- ❑ Coordinate home health care
- ❑ Administer medication orally
- ❑ Administer medication rectally
- ❑ Administer an injection
- ❑ Clean and maintain a catheter
- ❑ Turn your relative in bed every hour to prevent bedsores
- ❑ Clean up a bowel movement
- ❑ Clean up vomit
- ❑ Be with your relative as he or she dies

Use this page to describe what you have learned by doing this exercise in combination with your readings about caregivers from *The Last Dance*.

_____

_____

_____

_____

_____

_____

_____

_____

_____

_____

_____

_____

_____

_____

_____

_____

_____

_____

_____

_____

_____

_____

_____

_____

⟫➡ *Creating a Hospice*

Directions: *Imagine you are on the advisory board for the creation of a new free-standing hospice in the community. The National Hospice and Palliative Care Organization (NHPCO) [www.nhpco.org] has descriptions of hospice care along with qualities to consider in selecting a hospice. Read about hospice care and answer the following questions:*

What characteristics would you require of the staff (medical and non-medical) hired to care for dying patients?

_____

_____

_____

_____

What would your facility look like?

_____

_____

_____

_____

What visiting hours would you permit?

_____

_____

_____

_____

Would you permit animals? If so, how would you accommodate patients who prefer not to be around animals?

_____

_____

_____

_____

What would you do to reduce staff burnout?

_____

_____

_____

_____

_____

What other ideas would you want to implement?

_____

_____

_____

_____

_____

_____

_____

_____

_____

Summarize what you have learned from this activity.

_____

_____

_____

_____

_____

_____

_____

_____

_____

Death Systems:
Matters of Public Policy

Chapter Summary

Chapter 5 surveys a number of legal, administrative, and public policy matters pertaining to death and dying. All these are aspects of a society's "death system." The topics discussed include methods of defining death, procedures involved in organ donation and transplantation, rules governing death certification, the duties of coroners and medical examiners, and autopsies.

Sophisticated medical technologies can dramatically alter the course of dying, thereby challenging conventional methods of defining and making a determination of death. Recent decades have seen the enactment of legislation recognizing the fact that, when an individual's vital processes are maintained artificially, the conventional definition of death—that is, irreversible cessation of heartbeat and breathing—sometimes proves inadequate. Organs destined for transplantation are often harvested from the bodies of donors who are "brain dead" while heartbeat and respiration are maintained artificially. Thus, when a patient is placed on a device that artificially sustains his or her vital functions, it leads to questions about how to define death.

Most efforts to expand the criteria for determining death beyond the conventional signs focus on loss of the capacity for bodily integration. This approach is based on the fact that the human body is an integrated organism with the capacity for internal regulation through complex feedback mechanisms. The loss of this capacity is popularly known as "brain death" and is usually confirmed by a flat electroencephalogram (EEG) and unresponsiveness to all external stimuli. For example, a person whose vital processes are temporarily sustained artificially during surgery is not dead. But a person who has lost the capacity for bodily integration is dead, even if the body's vital processes are maintained artificially.

The conventional definition of death suffices for determining death in most cases. However, for respirator-maintained bodies, death is now defined as the irreversible cessation of all functions of the entire brain, including the brain stem. Some experts suggest that this "whole-brain" formulation be replaced with a "higher-brain" criterion—that is, one that focuses on an individual's capacity for consciousness, social interaction, or personhood. At present, there isn't sufficient consensus or enthusiasm for making such a change in defining death.

Organ donation and transplantation, another area of interest to the student of death and dying, involves both ethical issues and the impact of governmental regulation and standardized procedures. The Uniform Anatomical Gift Act, which has been adopted in some form in all fifty states, provides for the donation of the body or specific body parts upon the donor's death. The Act was revised in 1987 to simplify organ donation by removing requirements that the document be witnessed and that next of kin give consent. Organ donation can be easily accomplished by completing a brief donor card (available from the motor vehicle department of most states). It should be noted, however, that, even though consent by next of kin is not *legally* required to effect organ donation, it is nonetheless wise to discuss plans for donation with relatives to ensure that one's wishes are carried out. A central office—known as the United Network for Organ Sharing (UNOS)—to help match donated organs with potential recipients was established as part of the National Organ Transplant Act (1984).

The official registration of death by means of the death certificate is considered to be the most important legal procedure following a death. Though often taken for granted, the death certificate can have far-reaching effects with respect to such diverse matters as distributing property and benefits to heirs, aiding in the detection of crime, tracing family genealogy, and promoting efforts to understand and prevent disease. The modes of death usually recognized by law include natural, accidental, suicidal, and homicidal. The cause of death is not always the same as the mode of death. A death caused by asphyxiation due to drowning, for example, might be classified as an accident, a suicide, or a homicide, depending on the circumstances.

Coroners and medical examiners play an important role in determining the cause and mode of death in doubtful circumstances. The cause of death is determined by various scientific procedures, possibly including an autopsy as well as other tests, analyses, and studies. Autopsy—the medical examination of a body after death to determine the cause of death or to investigate the extent and nature of changes caused by disease—is also an important tool for medical research and training.

As the variety of topics covered in this chapter makes clear, issues of public policy related to a society's death system have a significant influence on our experiences of death and dying. In some cases, these policies increase our options; in other cases, they restrict them. Either way, a basic knowledge of a society's death system and its public policies leads to more informed choices and potentially more satisfying outcomes.

Objectives

- To name four approaches to the definition of death and to evaluate the usefulness of each.
- To give an example of a practical definition of death and its application to making a determination of death.
- To describe the history of legislation defining death and the major points of view involved in its evolution.
- To describe the emotional, physical, and ethical components of organ transplantation.

- To describe the stipulations contained in the Uniform Anatomical Gift Act and to assess its pertinence for oneself.
- To describe the functions of the coroner and the medical examiner.
- To explain the functions of the death certificate.
- To explain the purposes of an autopsy.

Key Terms and Concepts

autopsy
brain death
cellular death
certification of death
clinical death
coma
coroner
death certificate
death system
definition of death
determination of death
donor card
forensic pathology
Harvard criteria for brain death

higher-brain theory
medical examiner
mode of death
National Organ Transplant Act
organ transplantation
persistent vegetative state (PVS)
postmortem
rigor mortis
Uniform Anatomical Gift Act
Uniform Determination of Death Act
United Network for Organ Sharing (UNOS)
vital signs
whole-brain theory
xenotransplantation

Questions for Guided Study and Review

1. What are the major components of what Robert Kastenbaum terms the "death system," and how do they function in society?
2. What are the traditional "signs of death"?
3. What is the distinction between *clinical death* and *cellular death*?
4. In what way does the "coffin bell-pull device" demonstrate concern about defining death?
5. What five steps are involved in the process of making decisions about the death of a human being?
6. What are the four approaches to defining and determining death outlined by Robert Veatch?
7. What is "brain death"?
8. What are the criteria for determining brain death developed by the Harvard Medical School Ad Hoc Committee?
9. What three causes generally result in irreversible loss of functions of the whole brain?
10. What is the distinction between the "higher-brain theory" and the "whole-brain" theory?
11. What is a *persistent vegetative state*?
12. What is the recent history of legislation defining death?
13. What is the purpose of the Uniform Determination of Death Act?
14. What are the major provisions of the Uniform Anatomical Gift Act?
15. How was the Uniform Anatomical Gift Act revised in 1987?
16. What does *required request* mean in terms of organ donation?

17. What are some areas of current controversy about organ donations?
18. What is the purpose of the National Organ Transplant Act?
19. What is the function of the United Network for Organ Sharing?
20. How do physicians and other medical personnel function as "gatekeepers" in cases of organ transplantation?
21. What are the main functions of a death certificate?
22. What are the four modes of death listed on the typical death certificate?
23. How does the *cause* of death differ from the *mode* of death?
24. What role do coroners and medical examiners have when a death occurs?
25. How do coroners and medical examiners differ?
26. What is *forensic pathology*?
27. What is the responsibility of the Army Central Identification Laboratory (CILHI), and how does it carry out its mission?
28. What is an autopsy?
29. Why are autopsies performed?

Practice Test Questions

MULTIPLE CHOICE

1. What medical technology renders the conventional signs of death inadequate?
   a. organ transplantation
   b. open heart surgery
   c. artificial respiration
   d. artificial nutrition

2. Which of the following questions are addressed in Robert Veatch's four levels concerning the definition and determination of death?
   1. What is the conceptual definition of death?
   2. What is the cause of death?
   3. What is the significant difference between life and death?
   4. Where does one look to determine whether death has occurred?

   a. 1, 2, and 4
   b. 2, 3, and 4
   c. 1, 3, and 4
   d. 1, 2, and 3

3. What medical procedure created the need for new methods of defining and determining death?
   a. open heart surgery
   b. artificial resuscitation
   c. brain surgery
   d. organ transplantation

4. Certification in forensic pathology refers to
   a. medical training specifically geared toward autopsy.
   b. a branch of law enforcement involved in suicide investigation.
   c. knowledge of mysterious deaths such as crib death.
   d. application of medical knowledge to questions of law.

5. A *psychological autopsy* may be employed in which of the following circumstances?
   a. an elderly woman dies after a lengthy terminal illness
   b. an intoxicated person jumps into a swimming pool with no one else around and drowns
   c. a teenager is killed in a drive-by-shooting
   d. a soldier is killed in battle

TRUE/FALSE

_____ 1. The legal definition of death warranted revision to reflect medical realities.

_____ 2. It is currently illegal to buy or sell any part of the human body.

_____ 3. Research into *xenotransplantation* has evolved because of the scarcity of human organs for transplantation.

_____ 4. Cause of death and mode of death are the same thing.

_____ 5. Studies show that autopsy results contradict the presumed cause of death in about one-quarter to one-third of the cases.

MATCHING

Match each of the definitions on the left with the appropriate term on the right.

_____ 1. cessation of vital signs   a. brain death

_____ 2. brain stem functions remain   b. cellular death

_____ 3. cessation of spontaneous breathing   c. persistent vegetative state

_____ 4. a gradual process   d. clinical death

❧ Answers to practice questions can be found in Part IV ❧

Related Readings

📖 Indicates selection from *The Path Ahead: Readings in Death and Dying,* ed. Lynne Ann DeSpelder and Albert Lee Strickland (Mountain View, Calif.: Mayfield, 1995).

THE DEATH SYSTEM

Kenneth J. Doka. "Death System," in *Macmillan Encyclopedia of Death and Dying,* ed. Robert Kastenbaum, 222–223. New York: Macmillan, 2003.

Robert Kastenbaum. "Death System," in *Encyclopedia of Death,* ed. Robert Kastenbaum and Beatrice Kastenbaum, 90–93. Phoenix, Ariz.: Oryx Press, 1989.

THE DEFINITION OF DEATH

Ronald E. Cranford. "The Persistent Vegetative State: The Medical Reality," in *Medical Ethics: Applying Theories and Principles to the Patient Encounter,* ed. Matt Weinberg, 111–120. Buffalo, N.Y.: Prometheus, 2001.

Karen G. Gervais. *Redefining Death*. New Haven, Conn.: Yale University Press, 1986.

Douglas N. Walton. *On Defining Death: An Analytic Study of the Concept of Death in Philosophy and Medical Ethics*. Montreal: McGill-Queen's University Press, 1979.

Stuart J. Youngner and Robert M. Arnold. "Philosophical Debates about the Definition of Death: Who Cares?" *Kennedy Institute of Ethics Journal* 11, no. 4 (2001): 337-358.

ORGAN TRANSPLANTATION AND ORGAN DONATION

George J. Annas. *The Rights of Patients: The Basic ACLU Guide to Patient Rights*, 2nd ed. Clifton, N.J.: Humana Press, 1991.

Albert R. Jonsen. "Ethical Issues in Organ Transplantation," in *Medical Ethics*, 2nd ed., ed. Robert M. Veatch, 239-274. Boston: Jones and Bartlett, 1997.

Stuart J. Youngner, Renée C. Fox, and Laurence J. O'Connell, eds. *Organ Transplantation: Meanings and Realities*. Madison: University of Wisconsin Press, 1996.

DEATH CERTIFICATION

📖 Jack Lule, "News Strategies and the Death of Huey Newton," pp. 33–40.

Frank Smith. *Cause of Death: The Story of Forensic Science*. New York: Van Nostrand Reinhold, 1980.

Cyril Wecht. *Cause of Death*. New York: Dutton, 1993.

CORONERS AND MEDICAL EXAMINERS

Tony Blanche and Brad Schreiber. *Death in Paradise: An Illustrated History of the Los Angeles County Department of Coroner*. Los Angeles: General Publishing Group, 1998.

Organizations and Internet Resources

Department of Health and Human Services (U.S.): <www.organdonor.gov>. Information and resources about organ donation, including donor cards.

Forensic Science Society: <www.forensic-science-society.org.uk/forcareer.html>. Forensic Science Service HQ, Sixth Floor, Priory House, Gooch Street North, Birmingham B5 6QQ, England. (0121) 607-6800. Explains the requirements for a forensic science career in England along with the functions of the society.

Hobson's College View: <www.collegeview.com/college/ask_experts/choosing_mj/pathology.html>. Suite 301, 12000 Alliance Road, Cincinnati, OH 45242. (800) 927-8439. Fax: (800)891-8531. Describes the education and training required to be a forensic pathologist. Extensive listing of links to additional information about forensic science.

Los Angeles County Department of Coroner: <http://coroner.co.la.ca.us/htm/Coroner_Home.htm>. 1104 North Mission Road, Los Angeles, CA 90033. (323) 343-7014. Information about the coroner's office and services provided.

National Kidney Foundation: <www.kidney.org>. 30 East 33rd Street, New York, NY 10016. (212) 889-2210 or (800) 662-9010. Fax: (212) 689-9261. Sponsors Gift of Life organ donation program.

New York State, Department of Health, Office of Science and Public Health: <www.health.state.ny.us/nysdoh/bsd/main.htm>. Corning Tower, Empire State Plaza, Albany, N.Y. 12237. (518) 486-1455. Fax: (518) 486.1455. New York State clinical guidelines for the determination of death, including the statute titled "Determination of Death."

President's Council on Bioethics: <www.bioethics.gov/>. Suite 700, 1801 Pennsylvania Avenue NW, Washington, DC 20006. (202) 296-4669. Provides information on ethical issues related to advances in biomedical science and technology.

Transplant Living: <www.transplantliving.org> A project of the United Network for Organ Sharing (UNOS), this site offers extensive information about organ transplantation, including facts about various organs along with advice for patients before, during, and after a transplant.

United Network for Organ Sharing (UNOS): <www.unos.org>. Suite 500, 1100 Boulders Parkway, Richmond, VA 23225. (804) 330-8500 or (800) 243-6667. Coordinates allocation and distribution of organs for transplantation.

❧ Additional resources are available online at mhhe.com ❧

Major Points in This Chapter

- As medical technology has advanced to the point that machines can sustain bodily functions, the definition of death has become more complex and new methods of determining death have been instituted.
- Legislation defining death has evolved with the expansion of sophisticated medical technologies.
- Organ transplantation involves issues of rationing that require medical personnel to act as gatekeepers in determining prospective recipients.
- Organ donation is voluntary; however, because there is a shortage of transplantable organs, most states have enacted "required request" laws that obligate hospitals to institute policies encouraging organ and tissue donations.
- Death certification, along with autopsies conducted at the direction of coroners and medical examiners, involves a legal process for reporting the cause and mode of death.

Observations and Reflections

You might have noticed some aversion to exploring some of the topics in this chapter, such as brain death, organ transplantation, the duties of coroners and medical examiners, and autopsies. Keep in mind that emotional responses are sometimes triggered by a past experience. Often, however, aversion results from a lack of information rather than too much information. It is important to be sensitive to your emotional response, but also be aware that information in itself is not harmful. Indeed, it may provide relief from discomforting thoughts or feelings about a personal experience of death.

Use the space on the following page to make notes about this chapter.

⫸ *Death Certificate*

Directions: *Obtain a copy of a death certificate for your state. Below is an example from the state of California. Review the categories of required information. Give close attention to the information provided by the coroner or medical examiner in boxes #107– #125. You might find it interesting to fill out this certificate as if it were being used to record your death.*

CERTIFICATE OF DEATH
STATE OF CALIFORNIA
USE BLACK INK ONLY / NO ERASURES, WHITEOUTS OR ALTERATIONS
VS-11 (REV 1/03)

STATE FILE NUMBER		LOCAL REGISTRATION NUMBER

DECEDENT'S PERSONAL DATA

1. NAME OF DECEDENT --- FIRST (Given)	2. MIDDLE	3. LAST (Family)

AKA. ALSO KNOWN AS --- Include full AKA (FIRST, MIDDLE, LAST)	4. DATE OF BIRTH mm/dd/ccyy	5. AGE Yrs.	IF UNDER ONE YEAR Months / Days	IF UNDER 24 HOURS Hours / Minutes	6. SEX

9. BIRTH STATE/FOREIGN COUNTRY	10. SOCIAL SECURITY NUMBER	11. EVER IN U.S. ARMED FORCES? ☐ YES ☐ NO ☐ UNK	12. MARITAL STATUS (at Time of Death)	7. DATE OF DEATH mm/dd/ccyy	8. HOUR (24 Hours)

13. EDUCATION -- Highest Level/Degree (see worksheet on back)	14/15. WAS DECEDENT SPANISH/HISPANIC/LATINO? (If yes, see worksheet on back.) ☐ YES ☐ NO	16. DECEDENT'S RACE --- Up to 3 races may be listed (see worksheet on back)

17. USUAL OCCUPATION ---- Type of work for most of life. DO NOT USE RETIRED	18. KIND OF BUSINESS OR INDUSTRY (e.g., grocery store, road construction, employment agency, etc.)	19. YEARS IN OCCUPATION

USUAL RESIDENCE

20. DECEDENT'S RESIDENCE (Street and number or location)				
21. CITY	22. COUNTY/PROVINCE	23. ZIP CODE	24. YEARS IN COUNTY	25. STATE/FOREIGN COUNTRY

INFORMANT

26. INFORMANT'S NAME, RELATIONSHIP	27. INFORMANT'S MAILING ADDRESS (Street and number or rural route number, city or town, state, ZIP)

SPOUSE AND PARENT INFORMATION

28. NAME OF SURVIVING SPOUSE --- FIRST	29. MIDDLE	30. LAST (Maiden Name)	
31. NAME OF FATHER --- FIRST	32. MIDDLE	33. LAST	34. BIRTH STATE
35. NAME OF MOTHER --- FIRST	36. MIDDLE	37. LAST (Maiden)	38. BIRTH STATE

FUNERAL DIRECTOR/ LOCAL REGISTRAR

39. DISPOSITION DATE mm/dd/ccyy	40. PLACE OF FINAL DISPOSITION	
41. TYPE OF DISPOSITION(S)	42. SIGNATURE OF EMBALMER ▶	43. LICENSE NUMBER
44. NAME OF FUNERAL ESTABLISHMENT	45. LICENSE NUMBER	46. SIGNATURE OF LOCAL REGISTRAR ▶	47. DATE mm/dd/ccyy

PLACE OF DEATH

101. PLACE OF DEATH	102. IF HOSPITAL, SPECIFY ONE ☐ IP ☐ ER/OP ☐ DOA	103. IF OTHER THAN HOSPITAL, SPECIFY ONE ☐ Hospice ☐ Nursing Home/LTC ☐ Decedent's Home ☐ Other
104. COUNTY	105. FACILITY ADDRESS OR LOCATION WHERE FOUND (Street and number or location)	106. CITY

CAUSE OF DEATH

107. CAUSE OF DEATH	Enter the chain of events --- diseases, injuries, or complications --- that directly caused death. DO NOT enter terminal events such as cardiac arrest, respiratory arrest, or ventricular fibrillation without showing the etiology. DO NOT ABBREVIATE.	Time Interval Between Onset and Death	108. DEATH REPORTED TO CORONER? ☐ YES ☐ NO REFERRAL NUMBER
IMMEDIATE CAUSE (Final disease or condition resulting in death) → (A)		(AT)	
	(B)	(BT)	109. BIOPSY PERFORMED? ☐ YES ☐ NO
Sequentially, list conditions, if any, leading to cause on Line A. Enter UNDERLYING CAUSE (disease or injury that initiated the events resulting in death) LAST	(C)	(CT)	110. AUTOPSY PERFORMED? ☐ YES ☐ NO
	(D)	(DT)	111. USED IN DETERMINING CAUSE? ☐ YES ☐ NO

112. OTHER SIGNIFICANT CONDITIONS CONTRIBUTING TO DEATH BUT NOT RESULTING IN THE UNDERLYING CAUSE GIVEN IN 107

113. WAS OPERATION PERFORMED FOR ANY CONDITION IN ITEM 107 OR 112? (If yes, list type of operation and date.)	113A. IF FEMALE, PREGNANT IN LAST YEAR? ☐ YES ☐ NO ☐ UNK

PHYSICIAN'S CERTIFICATION

114. I CERTIFY THAT TO THE BEST OF MY KNOWLEDGE DEATH OCCURRED AT THE HOUR, DATE, AND PLACE STATED FROM THE CAUSES STATED. Decedent Attended Since / Decedent Last Seen Alive (A) mm/dd/ccyy (B) mm/dd/ccyy	115. SIGNATURE AND TITLE OF CERTIFIER ▶	116. LICENSE NUMBER	117. DATE mm/dd/ccyy
	118. TYPE ATTENDING PHYSICIAN'S NAME, MAILING ADDRESS, ZIP CODE		

CORONER'S USE ONLY

119. I CERTIFY THAT IN MY OPINION DEATH OCCURRED AT THE HOUR, DATE, AND PLACE STATED FROM THE CAUSES STATED. MANNER OF DEATH ☐ Natural ☐ Accident ☐ Homicide ☐ Suicide ☐ Pending Investigation ☐ Could not be determined	120. INJURED AT WORK? ☐ YES ☐ NO ☐ UNK	121. INJURY DATE mm/dd/ccyy	122. HOUR (24 Hours)

123. PLACE OF INJURY (e.g., home, construction site, wooded area, etc.)
124. DESCRIBE HOW INJURY OCCURRED (Events which resulted in injury)
125. LOCATION OF INJURY (Street and number, or location, and city, and ZIP)

126. SIGNATURE OF CORONER / DEPUTY CORONER ▶	127. DATE mm/dd/ccyy	128. TYPE NAME, TITLE OF CORONER / DEPUTY CORONER

STATE REGISTRAR

A	B	C	D	E		FAX AUTH. #	CENSUS TRACT

Use this page to record your notes and responses to the Death Certificate activity.

_____

_____

_____

_____

_____

_____

_____

_____

_____

_____

_____

_____

_____

_____

_____

_____

_____

_____

_____

_____

_____

_____

⟫➡ *The Death System*

Directions: *Review the seven functions of a death system. Choose one function and complete a listing of additional examples of that function in your community.*

1. _____

   _____

2. _____

   _____

3. _____

   _____

4. _____

   _____

5. _____

   _____

   _____

6. _____

   _____

7. _____

   _____

   _____

8. _____

   _____

   _____

9. _____

   _____

   _____

After completing your list, write several paragraphs explaining the reason for your choice of this function of the death system. Describe your interest in the area chosen.

_____

_____

_____

_____

_____

_____

_____

_____

_____

_____

_____

_____

_____

_____

_____

_____

_____

_____

_____

_____

_____

_____

_____

_____

⟫➡ *Organ Donation*

Directions: *Prepare two arguments, one in favor of organ donation and the other against it. Then complete the third part of this activity based on your personal preferences.*

1. Organ donation is a good idea because _____

    _____

    _____

    _____

    _____

    _____

    _____

    _____

    _____

    _____

2. Organ donation is a bad idea because _____

    _____

    _____

    _____

    _____

    _____

    _____

    _____

    _____

    _____

3. Describe your own preference regarding organ donation and explain your reasons for this decision. Is your personal choice the same as the one you would make for a loved one if the need to make a decision arose and you did not know his or her own preference? Why or why not? _____

_____

_____

_____

_____

_____

_____

_____

_____

_____

_____

_____

_____

_____

_____

_____

_____

_____

_____

_____

_____

Facing Death:
Living with Life-Threatening Illness

Chapter Summary

Chapter 6 focuses on the experience of living with life-threatening illness, including its personal and social meanings. Potentially fatal diseases are often accompanied by an unjustified social stigma. Life-threatening illness may be perceived as somehow taboo. The patient may assume responsibility for the illness through the medium of magical thinking or similar self-questioning. The reality is that life-threatening illnesses affect people in all walks of life.

The personal and social costs of life-threatening illness include not only direct financial costs attributable to the disease but also the burden of disrupted lives, distorted self-concept, and anxiety about the future. Positive approaches to dealing with life-threatening illness include education, counseling, and social support. These techniques help promote an understanding that places the crisis in a more affirmative context, thus restoring a sense of personal control over a confusing situation.

The adaptive response to losses associated with life-threatening illness change as circumstances change. The ways in which individuals cope with such illness can be described in terms of the stages developed by Elisabeth Kübler-Ross in her pioneering work with dying patients, as well as in terms of more recent task-based and pattern-oriented approaches. Considered as a whole, these descriptive and theoretical approaches help provide a solid foundation for understanding how people cope with serious and life-threatening illness.

Awareness of a serious or life-threatening illness is likely to be reflected in one of four patterns of communication and interaction: closed, suspected, mutual pretense, or open. The context of awareness may change as the severity of an illness or problems related to care and treatment change. Even though certain general patterns can be distinguished, it is important to recognize that different individuals cope with life-threatening illness differently. Also, the way we might imagine the course of events leading to eventual death is not necessarily an accurate reflection of how those events will be experienced by a particular person. Idealized descriptions of how people die tend to leave out the pain, nausea, constipation, bedsores, and insomnia, as well as the loneliness, anxiety, and fear—all of which typically accompany the dying trajectory.

The options available for treating serious illness vary not only according to the particular disease and the medical techniques available but also because of decisions made by society as a whole. It is obviously not possible for all diseases and interventions to occupy the place of highest priority. Because cancer is usually viewed as the prototypic life-threatening illness, the discussion in the text focuses on the main therapies employed against this disease—surgery, radiation therapy, and chemotherapy, as well as the role of alternative, or complementary, and adjunctive therapies. "Symbolic healing," for example, may be an adjunct to conventional therapies because of its value in helping to mobilize a patient's inner resources and will to live.

Pain is the most common symptom of terminally ill patients, and managing it effectively is a chief goal of palliative care. Regardless of the therapeutic modality used to treat life-threatening illness, pain management becomes increasingly important as disease continues to progress and as patients near death. Of course, the perception of pain differs among individuals as well as cultures. The treatment of is increasingly being addressed by interdisciplinary approaches that relate to a patient's "total pain"—physical, psychological, social, and spiritual.

Until about the middle of the twentieth century, a social role for the dying person was more or less fixed by custom and circumstance. Since then, however, social and technological changes have tended to eliminate the traditional role of the dying without offering a new role to replace it. It may be that, as people become more willing to face the issues of dying and death squarely, and as hospice and palliative care become more widely available, we will see the creation of a new social role for the dying that is appropriate for our own time. Such a role would not require a terminally ill or dying patient to maintain false hope or an appearance of expecting to live forever. On the contrary, it would acknowledge the prospect of death while emphasizing an appropriate sense of empowerment whereby farewells are communicated and attention is given to the special physical, psychological, social, and spiritual needs of the end of life. The perception of a dying person's "fading away" might be accompanied by a task of redefinition, during which family members and friends begin to deal with the burden of letting go before picking up the new.

Objectives

- To list the personal and social costs of life-threatening illness.
- To design a personal strategy for health care (both physical and psychological) should one be faced with a life-threatening illness.
- To describe and assess patterns of coping with life-threatening illness.
- To identify and assess treatment strategies for individuals with life-threatening illness.
- To assess the benefits and risks of alternative therapies.
- To summarize the essential strategies for pain management.
- To distinguish among the various dying trajectories.
- To explain the factors influencing the social role of the dying patient and to create an ideal model.

Key Terms and Concepts

active dying
acute pain
adjunctive therapy
ars moriendi
biopsy
cancer
chemotherapy
chronic pain
closed awareness
complementary therapy
coping potency
coping strategies
defense mechanisms
dying trajectory
ethnomedicine
five stages
life-threatening illness

magical thinking
metastasis
middle knowledge
mutual pretense
object of hope
open awareness
pain management
prognosis
remission
social death
suffering
suspected awareness
symbolic healing
terminality
total pain
unorthodox treatment
visualization

Questions for Guided Study and Review

1. How might a person's concerns and fears change during the course of a life-threatening illness?
2. In what way is the diagnosis of life-threatening illness at times treated as something "taboo"?
3. What is "social death" and how might it be manifested?
4. What is "magical thinking" as it applies to coping with life-threatening illness?
5. How does the phrase, "adapting to living/dying" relate to life-threatening illness?
6. What are the five stages of coping with life-threatening illness as described by Elisabeth Kübler-Ross?
7. How do "task-based" models differ from "stage-based" models of coping with serious illness and dying?
8. In reviewing the models of coping behavior put forward by Charles Corr, Avery Weisman, Therese Rando, and Ken Doka, what common elements or patterns do you notice?
9. According to Barney Glaser and Anselm Strauss, what are the four awareness contexts that may be observed in communicational interactions with the dying?
10. What does it mean to "maintain coping potency"?
11. How did Presidents John Adams and Thomas Jefferson illustrate the "will to live" that may be observed in dying persons?
12. What is the definition of *metastasis*?
13. What are the advantages and disadvantages of the three main conventional cancer therapies?
14. Why are alternative and complementary therapies becoming increasingly important in health care?
15. What is *ethnomedicine*?
16. Are *adjunctive* therapies different from *alternative* or *complementary* therapies?
17. What are "unorthodox treatments"?
18. What is the most common symptom of terminally ill patients?

19. What are the two main types of pain?
20. How is pain generally managed?
21. What drug is most commonly used to relieve severe cancer pain?
22. What factors hamper adequate pain management?
23. Is "pain" a single, well-defined entity?
24. What is a "dying trajectory"?
25. How does a "lingering" trajectory differ from an "expected quick" trajectory?
26. In the last phase of a fatal illness, what are the signs of "active dying"?
27. How does the "sick role" differ from the social role of the dying patient?
28. What are three important spiritual needs of the dying?

Practice Test Questions

MULTIPLE CHOICE

1. A patient faced with life-threatening illness may have feelings of self-deprecation because he or she
   a. knows that healing will be the outcome.
   b. feels responsible for the disease.
   c. encounters people who fear they will catch the disease.
   d. knows a cure will not be discovered in his or her lifetime.

2. Which of the following behaviors are indicative of the *mutual pretense* context?
   1. family and friends pretend things are normal
   2. there is an illusion that the patient is getting well
   3. the dying person tests the medical staff to elicit information
   4. the patient recognizes the fact that death will be the outcome

   a. 1, 2, and 4
   b. 1, 2, and 3
   c. 2, 3, and 4
   d. 1, 3, and 4

3. *Defense mechanisms* differ from *coping strategies* in that they
   a. involve a conscious, purposeful effort.
   b. are employed with the intention of solving a problem.
   c. occur unintentionally and without conscious effort.
   d. function to change a person's external reality.

4. Which of the following coping strategies is used to maintain a person's sense of positive well-being?
   a. meaning-based coping
   b. problem-focused coping
   c. emotion-focused coping
   d. well-being focused coping

5. Many people fear surgery as a treatment for cancer because of the
   a. high fatality rates associated with cancer operations.
   b. possibility of disfigurement or disability.
   c. success rate of less than 10 percent.
   d. high costs involved with cancer surgery.

TRUE/FALSE

_____ 1. People with life-threatening illness can sometimes experience a kind of "social death."

_____ 2. Open awareness is a favorable interpersonal relationship pattern because it makes the situation easier.

_____ 3. The capacity to maintain a sense of self-worth reflects a "coping potency."

_____ 4. Acute pain is "an essential biological signal of the potential for or the extent of injury."

_____ 5. According to Eric Cassell, the passing of the person is a physical phenomenon whereas the death of the body is a nonphysical one.

MATCHING

Match the person on the left with his or her corresponding model.

_____ 1. Elisabeth Kübler-Ross   a. four primary dimensions

_____ 2. Avery Weisman   b. multiple tasks in three phases

_____ 3. Charles Corr   c. five stages

_____ 4. Kenneth Doka   d. three tasks and three phases

❧ Answers to practice questions can be found in Part IV ❧

Related Readings

📖 Indicates selection from *The Path Ahead: Readings in Death and Dying,* ed. Lynne Ann DeSpelder and Albert Lee Strickland (Mountain View, Calif.: Mayfield, 1995).

COPING WITH LIFE-THREATENING ILLNESS

Mitch Albom. *Tuesdays with Morrie: An Old Man, A Young Man, and Life's Greatest Lesson.* New York: Doubleday, 1997.

📖 Thomas Attig, "Coping with Mortality: An Essay on Self-Mourning," pp. 337–341.

📖 Sandra L. Bertman, "Bearing the Unbearable: From Loss, the Gain," pp. 348–354.

📖 Harold Brodkey, "To My Readers," pp. 295–300.

📖 Allan B. Chinen, "The Mortal King," pp. 335–336.

📖 Charles A. Corr, "A Task-Based Approach to Coping with Dying," pp. 303–311.

Betty Davies, Joanne Cherkryn Reimer, Pamela Brown, and Nola Martens. *Fading Away: The Experience of Transition in Families with Terminal Illness.* Amityville, N.Y.: Baywood, 1996.

Kenneth J. Doka. *Living with Life-Threatening Illness: A Guide for Patients, Their Families, and Caregivers.* New York: Lexington, 1993.

📖 Herman Feifel, "Psychology and Death: Meaningful Rediscovery," pp. 19–28.

Susan Folkman and Steven Greer. "Promoting Psychological Well-Being in the Face of Serious Illness: When Theory, Research and Practice Inform Each Other," *Psycho-Oncology* 9, no. 1 (2000): 11–19.

Jerome Groopman. *The Measure of Our Days: New Beginnings at Life's End*. New York: Viking, 1997.

Marie de Hennezel. *Intimate Death: How the Dying Teach Us To Live*. New York: Alfred A. Knopf, 1997.

📖 Robert Kastenbaum, "Reconstructing Death in Postmodern Society," pp. 7–18.

📖 Joseph M. Kaufert and John D. O'Neil, "Cultural Mediation of Dying and Grieving Among Native Canadian Patients in Urban Hospitals," pp. 59–74.

📖 Alfred G. Killilea, "The Politics of Being Mortal," pp. 342–347.

📖 Janmarie Silvera, "Crossing the Border," pp. 301–302.

TREATMENT OPTIONS AND ISSUES

Lori Arviso Alvord and Elizabeth Cohen Van Pelt. *The Scalpel and the Silver Bear*. New York: Bantam, 1999.

Roger S. Cicala. *The Heart Disease Sourcebook*. Los Angeles: Lowell House, 1997.

C. Norman Coleman. *Understanding Cancer: A Patient's Guide to Diagnosis, Prognosis, and Treatment*. Baltimore: Johns Hopkins University Press, 1998.

Geoffrey M. Cooper. *The Cancer Book: A Guide to Understanding the Causes, Prevention, and Treatment of Cancer*. Boston: Jones and Bartlett, 1993.

Lesley F. Degner. "Treatment Decision Making," in *A Challenge for Living: Dying, Death, and Bereavement*, ed. Inge B. Corless, Barbara B. Germino, and Mary A. Pittman, 3–16. Boston: Jones & Bartlett, 1995.

Marcia K. Merboth and Susan Barnason. "Managing Pain: The Fifth Vital Sign," *Nursing Clinics of North America* 35, no. 2 (2000): 375-383.

📖 Stanley Joel Reiser, "The Era of the Patient: Using the Experience of Illness in Shaping the Missions of Health Care," pp. 106–115.

"What You Need to Know About Cancer" (Special Issue). *Scientific American* 275, no. 3 (September 1996).

Robert L. Wrenn, Dan Levinson, and Danai Papadatou. *End of Life Decisions: Guidelines for the Health Care Provider*. Tucson: University of Arizona Health Sciences Center, 1996.

Organizations and Internet Resources

Association of Oncology Social Work: <www.aosw.org/mission/ons-aosw.html>. 1211 Locust Street, Philadelphia, PA 19107. (215) 599-6093. Fax: (215) 545-8017. The resources here include a position paper advocating a proactive approach to all facets of end-of-life care and intending neither to hasten nor postpone death.

Cancer Information Service: <cis.nci.nih.gov/>. National Cancer Institute, Building 31, Room 10A24, 9000 Rockville Pike, Bethesda, MD 20892. (800) 4-CANCER; (800) 524-1234 (within Hawaii); (800) 638-6070 (within Alaska).

Center for Attitudinal Healing: <www.healingcenter.org>. 33 Buchanan Drive, Sausalito, CA 94965. (415) 331-6161. Fax: (415) 331-4545. Help for adults and children with life-threatening illnesses.

The Centre for Living with Dying: <www.thecentre.org>. 554 Mansion Park Drive, Santa Clara, CA 95050. (408) 980-9801. Volunteer organization for individuals facing life-threatening illness and their families.

Dream Foundation: <www.dreamfoundation.com>. Suite D, 621 Chapala Street, Santa Barbara, CA 93101. (805) 564-2131. Fax: (805) 564-7002. National organization granting wishes to terminally ill adults.

Elisabeth Kübler-Ross: <www.elisabethkublerross.com>. P.O. Box 6168, Scottsdale, AZ 85261. Information about the career and philosophy of Elisabeth Kübler-Ross.

Gilda's Club® Worldwide: <www.gildasclub.org>. Suite 609, 95 Madison Avenue, New York, NY 10016. (212) 686-9898. Fax: (212) 686-9290. Programs for people with cancer and their families and friends to join together to build social and emotional support.

Living/Dying Project: <www.livingdying.org>. P.O. Box 357, Fairfax, CA 94978. Education, counseling, and direct care offered within an Eastern spiritual framework to individuals and families living with life-threatening illness.

Shanti Project: <www.shanti.org>. 730 Polk Street, San Francisco, CA 94109. (415) 674-4700. Fax: (415) 674-0370. Counseling support service for persons with AIDS and their families and loved ones.

ToDo Institute: <www.todoinstitute.org/mlt.html>. P.O. Box 874, Middlebury, VT 05753. (802) 453-4440. Fax: (802) 453-2458. Describes the practice of Japanese therapies, including Meaningful Life Therapy (MLT).

National Women's Health Information Center: <www.4woman.gov/HealthPro/cultural>. 8550 Arlington Blvd., Suite 300, Fairfax, VA 22031. (800-994-9662). A project of the U.S. Department of Health and Human Service's Office on Women's Health, this section of the site discusses cultural responsiveness and ethnomedicine, including many resources.

&‌ Additional resources are available online at mhhe.com ‌&

Major Points in This Chapter

- When life-threatening illness is made to seem taboo, it creates difficulties in communication and hampers social support.
- Life-threatening illness is costly, personally as well as socially and spiritually.
- The adaptive response to losses associated with life-threatening illness changes as circumstances change.
- The awareness contexts relative to dying patients, families, and caregivers include closed awareness, suspected awareness, mutual pretense, and open awareness.
- The manner in which individuals cope with life-threatening illness is described in terms of Elisabeth Kübler-Ross's pioneering stage-based approach as well as more recent task-, phase-, and pattern-oriented approaches.
- Maintaining coping potency in the face of life-threatening illness requires access to both inner and external resources.

- The options for treatment of serious illness vary according to the illness and ongoing developments in medical knowledge; withholding or discontinuing treatment may also be an option.
- Alternative therapies encompass adjunctive or complementary therapies, as well as unorthodox therapies.
- Pain management is an essential component of a comprehensive treatment plan.
- Studies of the dying trajectory distinguish two main types: (1) a lingering trajectory whereby death takes place gradually and over an extended period of time, and (2) a quick trajectory whereby death is the outcome of an acute medical crisis.
- The social role of a dying patient differs between cultural groups and among individuals and families.

Observations and Reflections

This chapter emphasizes the importance of patient choice based on an individual's need to achieve a sense of self-control and empowerment. Notice if you find yourself judging too quickly or harshly the care options and dying styles chosen by someone who is terminally ill. Even though a patient's choices may seem wrong or odd to you for any number of reasons, it is important to acknowledge that a crucial aspect of such choices is that they not be made solely by health care providers or family members.

Use the space below to make notes about this chapter.

⇒ *Death Fears*

Directions: *Respond to each of the following statements with "yes," "no," or "maybe" in the blank spaces. After completing the questionnaire, use the following page to write about your experience of completing this activity.*

_____ 1. I am afraid of nothingness—the end of everything.

_____ 2. I am afraid of abandoning the people who depend on me.

_____ 3. I am afraid of making those who love me unhappy.

_____ 4. I am afraid of not having time to make amends for all my sins of commission and omission.

_____ 5. I am afraid that death will be the end of feeling and thinking.

_____ 6. I am afraid of losing control over what is being done to my body.

_____ 7. I am afraid of pain and dying.

_____ 8. I am afraid of punishment after death.

_____ 9. I am afraid of losing those I care about.

_____ 10. I am afraid of being helpless and having to depend completely on others.

_____ 11. I am afraid of dying because I don't know what happens after death.

_____ 12. I am afraid of dying before I am ready to go.

_____ 13. I am afraid of taking a long time to die.

_____ 14. I am afraid of dying suddenly and violently.

_____ 15. I am afraid of dying alone.

Adapted from *Nursing the Dying Patient,* by Charlotte Epstein (Reston, Va.: Reston Publishing Co., 1975), p. 122. Reprinted by permission.

Use the space below to write about the experience of completing the Death Fears questionnaire on the previous page:

_____

_____

_____

_____

_____

_____

_____

_____

_____

_____

_____

_____

_____

_____

_____

_____

_____

_____

_____

_____

_____

⟫➡ *Questionnaire: Life-Threatening Illness*

Directions: *Respond to each of the statements below by indicating one of the following:*

SA   = strongly agree
A   = agree
U   = undecided
D   = disagree
SD   = strongly disagree

_____   1. A physician's decision to inform a patient about his or her terminal illness should be made on a case-by-case basis.

_____   2. A close family member should be the one to inform the patient about his or her life-threatening illness.

_____   3. A patient who is prematurely informed about his or her terminal illness will lose the will to live.

_____   4. A child with a life-threatening illness should not be told about the possibility of his or her death.

_____   5. I would not want the responsibility of informing a member of my family about the nature of his or her life-threatening illness.

_____   6. If I had a life-threatening illness, I definitely would want to be informed by my physician.

_____   7. A person can make important changes in his or her life when given knowledge of impending death.

_____   8. Knowledge of impending death gives both the patient and his or her family an opportunity to communicate about important matters.

_____   9. Sudden death is much easier for an individual and his or her family than death resulting from a lingering degenerative illness.

_____ 10. Overwhelming and unrelenting physical pain would be the worst aspect of coping with a life-threatening illness.

Use this page to write about your reaction to completing the questionnaire. What other opinions or experience do you have with life-threatening illness?

_____

_____

_____

_____

_____

_____

_____

_____

_____

_____

_____

_____

_____

_____

_____

_____

_____

_____

_____

➠ *Signs and Symptoms Near Death*

Directions: *Read the following description of the physical, emotional, spiritual, and mental signs and symptoms of impending death and complete the questions that follow. They are designed to help you understand the natural changes that may occur during the dying process and how to best respond. All of these signs and symptoms will not occur with everyone, nor will they occur in this particular sequence. Each person is unique and needs to do things in his or her own way. In general, however, the body prepares itself for the final days of life in the following ways.*

DECREASING FLUID AND FOOD CONSUMPTION

There is usually little interest in eating and drinking. Allow the person to eat and drink whatever is appetizing. Nourishment should be taken slowly and in small amounts. Let the person decide how much and when to eat and drink. Reflexes needed to swallow may be sluggish. Do not force fluids if the person coughs soon after. Small chips of ice, frozen juices, or popsicles may be refreshing.

The body lets a person know when it no longer desires nor can tolerate food or liquids. The loss of this desire is a signal that the person is making ready to leave. This is not a painful process. Dehydration no longer makes them uncomfortable. Glycerin swabs may help keep the mouth and lips moist and comfortable. A cool, moist washcloth on the forehead may also be welcome.

DECREASING SOCIALIZATION

The person may want to be alone with just one person or with just a few people. Speech is often slow or difficult or the person may not have the ability to speak at all. It is natural to not like socializing when feeling weak and fatigued. It may be disturbing to the dying person to have more than a few people in the room. Consider taking shifts in order for different people to be with the person. Keep the environment quiet and calm. Reassure the person that it is okay to sleep.

SLEEPING

The person may spend an increasing amount of time sleeping and become uncommunicative, unresponsive, and difficult to arouse at times. This normal change is due partly to changes in the metabolism of the body. Sit with the patient. Hold his or her hand gently. Speak softly and naturally. At this point *being with* is more important than *doing for*. Do not assume that the person cannot hear. Hearing is said to be the last of the five senses to be lost. Hearing may still remain very acute even when the person may seem asleep. Therefore do not say anything you would not say when the person is awake.

RESTLESSNESS

The person may make restless and repetitive motions, such as pulling at sheets or clothing, or have visions of people or things that do not exist. These symptoms may result from a decrease in oxygen circulation to the brain or a change in the body's metabolism. Do not be alarmed or try to restrain such motions. Talk calmly and reassuringly with the person so as not to startle or frighten him or her further. Lightly massage the hands, feet, or forehead. Reading to the person or playing soft music can also have a calming effect.

DISORIENTATION

The person may seem confused about time, place, and the identity of people in the room, including close and familiar people. Identify yourself by name rather than asking the person to guess who you are. In conscious moments, the person may speak or claim to have spoken to people who have already died or to see places not presently accessible or visible to you. This is not necessarily a hallucination or a reaction to medication. It signifies a person beginning the normal detachment from this life.

Accept this transitional time. There is no need to contradict, explain away, belittle, or argue about what the person claims to see or hear. Respectfully listen to whatever the person has to say. Allow free expression of feelings and offer comfort through touching and talking reassuringly and calmly.

INCONTINENCE

The person may lose control of urine or bowels as the muscles begin to relax. Diapers or disposable pads can help protect the bed and assist in keeping the person clean and comfortable.

URINE DECREASE

Urine output normally decreases, becomes more concentrated, and may become the color of tea. This is due to decreased fluid intake and to a lessening of circulation through the kidneys.

BREATHING

The person's usual breathing patterns may change. Breathing can become abnormal, shallow, irregular, fast, or slow. A common pattern consists of breathing irregularly with shallow respiration or periods of no breaths for 5 to 30 seconds, followed by a deep breath. The person may also have periods of rapid and shallow panting. Sometimes there is a moaning-like sound on exhalation. This does not indicate distress, but rather the sound of air passing over relaxed vocal chords. Changed breathing patterns are very common for a person nearing death. They indicate decreased circulation in the internal organs and buildup of body waste products. Elevating the head and turning the patient onto his or her side may help to increase comfort.

CONGESTION

Oral secretions may become more profuse and collect in the back of the throat. The person may develop gurgling sounds coming from the chest. These sounds can become loud and may be distressing to hear. These normal changes come from fluid imbalance and an inability to cough up normal secretions. It is helpful to raise the head of the bed or use pillows to raise the person's head so that the secretions pool lower and do not stimulate the gag reflex. Turn the person's head to the side and allow gravity to drain the congestion. You can also gently wipe the person's mouth with a moist cloth.

COLOR CHANGES

Because of changes in circulation, the person's arms and legs may become cold, hot, or discolored. This may be especially noticeable in the extremities (arms or legs) where the color may change to a darker, bluish hue. This is a normal indication that the circulation is conserving energy to the core of the body to support the most vital organs.

Irregular temperatures can be the result of the brain sending unclear messages. Keep the person warm if he or she appears cold, but do not use an electric blanket. If the person continually removes the covers, use just a light sheet. Sweating may occur, and there may be an odor resulting from the many physiological changes taking place in the body. The heartbeat and pulses may become slower, weaker, and irregular.

PERMISSION TO GO

When someone enters the last days of dying, the body begins the process of shutting down, a process that ends when all the physical systems stop functioning. This is usually an orderly and non-dramatic series of physical changes. They are not medical emergencies and do not require invasive interventions. These physical changes are a normal, natural way in which the body prepares itself for death. This release may accompany the resolution of unfinished business. It may include seeking or receiving permission from family members to "let go."

A dying person may try to hold on, even though it brings discomfort, in order to be assured that those left behind will be all right. A family's ability to reassure and release the dying person from this concern is the greatest gift of love that can be given at this time.

SAYING GOODBYE

When the person is ready to die and the family is able to let go, this is the time to say good-bye in personal ways. It may be helpful to just lie in bed with the person, hold his or her hand, and say anything you need to say. Tears are a normal and natural part of saying good-bye and do not need hiding or apology. Tears express your love and help you to let go.

AT THE TIME OF DEATH

It may be helpful for family members to discuss ahead of time what to do when the final moments arrive. At the time of death breathing ceases, heartbeat ceases, the person cannot be aroused, the eyelids may be partially open with the eyes in a fixed stare, the mouth may fall open as the jaw relaxes. There is sometimes a release of bowel and bladder contents as the body relaxes.

The death of someone you are caring for, although an anxious event for family and friends, is not an acute medical emergency. It is not necessary to immediately call the medical examiner, the police, or 911. After the death has occurred, take the time needed to call a supportive person or adjust to the situation. There is no rush. Taking care of yourself is more important now.

The physical and emotional, spiritual, and mental signs and symptoms of impending death described here are intended to help you understand what may happen as a person's body completes the natural process of shutting down and the person completes the natural process of dying. Ideally, these processes happen in a way that is appropriate and unique to the values, beliefs, and life-style of the individual and his or her family.

After reading this information answer the following questions.

1. With which of the signs and symptoms of dying would you feel most comfortable observing and providing assistance?

   _____

   _____

   _____

2. Which of the signs and symptoms create anxiety or fear?

   _____

   _____

   _____

3. How comfortable are you responding to a dying person's version of reality? (For example, seeing people in the room or asking, "Have you got the tickets for my trip?")

   _____

   _____

   _____

   _____

4. Describe the most important information you have gained from reading this article.

   _____

   _____

   _____

   _____

Adapted from *On Our Own Terms: Moyers on Dying Discussion Guide* (New York: Educational Broadcasting Corporation and Public Affairs Television, Inc., 2000). Original Copyright © 2000 Metropolitan Hospice of Greater New York. Reprinted by permission.

End-of-Life Issues and Decisions

Chapter Summary

Chapter 7 deals with issues and decisions that pertain to the end of life. Many of these are central concerns in medical ethics and have become prominent with advances in biomedical technology. Medical technologies such as CPR (cardiopulmonary resuscitation) allow for life-sustaining interventions that were not available just a few decades ago. Yet such technological advances raise questions about how they should be used. The medical obligation to keep people alive can lead to confusing consequences in the modern era. Coming to terms with these consequences and finding a satisfactory guide to behavior requires familiarity with fundamental ethical principles such as autonomy, beneficence, and justice.

Although philosophers have discussed these principles for thousands of years, their application in medical practice has varied, reflecting changes in public attitudes and social situations. For example, studies done in the 1960s showed that most physicians tended to withhold information about a terminal illness. Telling the plain truth was viewed as possibly harmful to a patient's best interest. Instead, patients with incurable cancer were told that they had a "lesion" or "mass." Adjectives such as "suspicious" or "degenerated" were used to temper the impact of a disturbing diagnosis. Over the next couple of decades, however, a different climate of truth telling emerged, with physicians becoming much more likely to reveal the true nature of a terminal diagnosis.

In tracing the reasons for this change, we can note the influence of consumer attitudes as well as improvements in the medical outlook for patients with life-threatening disease. Excessive paternalism, wherein doctors assume responsibility for making medical decisions, tends to create problems when outcomes differ from expectations. In addition, newer therapies often require more knowledgeable cooperation from patients if treatment regimes are to be followed successfully.

Informed consent is based on three principles: First, the patient must be competent to give consent. Second, consent must be given voluntarily. Third, consent must be based on an adequate understanding of the proposed treatment program. Because individual and cultural attitudes toward autonomy or self-determination as applied to medical care differ, the process of giving information and obtaining consent to a treatment plan must be flexible. Shared decision making places special emphasis on the process of communication between caregivers and patients. Not simply a laundry list of risks to be recited in an effort to avoid potential complaints or legal problems, the process of informed consent can be a mechanism for facilitating communication between patient and physician, leading to greater cooperation toward the common goal of optimal health care. Good communication between caregiver and patient helps motivate the patient's own healing system, creating the potential for a positive outcome regardless of the ultimate prognosis. Total care encompasses the patient's physical, mental, emotional, and spiritual needs.

In recent years, the most emotionally charged issues in medical ethics have been those concerning decisions about end-of-life choices, including euthanasia (intentionally and actively bringing about the death of a terminally ill person) and forgoing life-sustaining treatment (either by withholding or withdrawing treatment). Debate about a "right to die" has been prominent since the landmark case involving Karen Ann Quinlan during the mid-1970s. What is the proper balance between sustaining life and preventing suffering in cases where further treatment is likely to be futile? What is the effect of life-sustaining medical technologies on the quality of patients' lives?

The belief that human beings have an inherent "right to die" and that physicians should be allowed to assist terminally ill patients in voluntarily ending their lives has received widespread support. Yet critics of euthanasia and physician-assisted suicide express concerns that a legally sanctioned "right" to die could become an "obligation" to die because of subtle pressures to lessen the burden on loved ones or lessen the economic impact of terminal care on society as a whole. Where would one draw the line, they ask, once we embark upon the "slippery slope" of physician-assisted suicide? They also argue that requests for physician-assisted suicide or euthanasia usually are not made when pain and depression are adequately treated.

Owing to the efforts of right-to-die organizations, as well as the highly publicized activities of Michigan pathologist Jack Kevorkian, considerable attention has been drawn to an ongoing debate about the ethical and legal issues involved in physicians providing aid in dying. At present in the United States, such aid can be legally provided in only one state, Oregon, where physicians are allowed to prescribe lethal medications to terminally ill patients who satisfy the law's requirements. Although the U.S. Supreme Court has ruled that there is no constitutional right to physician-assisted suicide, the debate about legalization of aid-in-dying and its acceptance within medical practice continues.

In contrast to the ongoing debate about euthanasia and physician-assisted suicide, the practice of withholding or withdrawing treatment that is considered medically useless has become increasingly well-established and accepted. For virtually any life-threatening condition, some medical intervention is capable of delaying the moment of death (or, as some would say, prolonging dying). Although there is general agreement among medical practitioners as well as the general public that extraordinary interventions are not required when a patient is hopelessly ill, gray areas remain. One such area involves the meaning of the term "extraordinary." For example, is artificial provision of nutrition and hydration an extraordinary intervention or ordinary care? Discussions about such issues often revolve around conceptual ambiguities—in this case, those involving the artificial delivery of food and fluids. The symbolic significance of providing nutrition and the specter of "starving a person to death" are deeply rooted in the human psyche.

In 1990, the U.S. Supreme Court ruled on a petition to end the artificial feeding of Nancy Beth Cruzan, a Missouri woman who had been in a persistent vegetative state resulting from an automobile accident in 1983. The Court said that a competent person has a right to refuse life-sustaining medical treatment but also ruled that states (in this case, Missouri) had the right to establish procedural requirements for "clear and convincing evidence" about an incompetent patient's wishes. Cases like this have brought public attention to *advance directives*, a category that encompasses living wills, natural death directives, and durable powers of attorney for health care. Advance directives express a person's desire that medical heroics be avoided when death is imminent, that life-sustaining or extraordinary procedures not be used when there is no chance of recovery. Such directives are completed while the person is able to make informed decisions and can be important in shaping the circumstances of a person's dying.

Wills provide a legal means for expressing a person's intentions regarding the disposition of his or her property after death. As such, the will is a valuable tool for planning one's estate and for conveying property to one's beneficiaries. The conventional document for specifying such intentions is the formally executed will, which is usually completed in consultation with an attorney who knows the requirements established by the laws of the state in which the will is executed. The making and probating of a will can be symbolically significant for both the testator and his or her survivors.

During the course of probate, the validity of the will is proved, the matters necessary to settling the estate are carried out by the executor or administrator, and, with the probate court's approval, the decedent's property is distributed to his or her beneficiaries. In the absence of a will, the distribution will be made according to the applicable laws of intestate succession.

Life insurance can provide a basic estate for one's beneficiaries, or it may be part of a more comprehensive estate. Insurance plans can be designed in a variety of ways to suit many different purposes. Unlike some other assets, life insurance benefits usually become available to beneficiaries immediately following the insured's death, thus providing funds and perhaps a sense of security to survivors. Other death benefits may be payable through governmental programs, such as Social Security and the Veterans Administration, or through pension plans resulting from employment.

Ethical issues in medicine have increasingly come to the forefront owing to rapid and innovative advances in medical technologies. There is now a "booming business" for ethicists and others—both professionals and laypeople—who seek to provide answers (at least tentative ones) to hard questions. As Leon Kass observes, however, theorizing has its place, but the "morality of ordinary practice" is where the rubber meets the road. When it comes to ethical issues, our choices result not only from the unique blend of our own personal values but also from values present within our particular cultural group and community. It is important to reflect on the reality that decisions about medical ethics have an impact not only on some vague realm of public policy "out there" but also, often poignantly, on the lives of individuals and families.

Objectives

- To explain how the fundamental ethical principles of autonomy, beneficence, and justice apply to medical ethics.
- To assess patients' rights with respect to self-determination and informed consent.
- To describe the factors affecting truth telling in cases involving terminal illness.

- To identify the consequences of withholding the truth from the point of view of both patient and physician.
- To describe the characteristics of an optimal patient-caregiver relationship.
- To evaluate modes of communication that facilitate being with someone who is dying.
- To evaluate the ethical issues involved in euthanasia.
- To explain how issues regarding competency affect decisions to withhold treatment from infants or comatose patients.
- To appraise one's own death in terms of advance directives.
- To evaluate the arguments for and against physician-assisted suicide.
- To identify the types, content, and purposes of wills.
- To explain the processes of probate and to evaluate the consequences of dying intestate.
- To assess the value to survivors of a comprehensive plan that includes trusts, life insurance, and other death benefits.

Key Terms and Concepts

active euthanasia
advance directive
Aesculapian authority
allowing to die
artificial nutrition and hydration
autonomy
beneficence
beneficiary
bequest
CMO (comfort measures only)
codicil
CPR (cardiopulmonary resuscitation)
death benefits
Death with Dignity Act (Oregon)
DNR (do not resuscitate)
double effect
durable power of attorney for health care
end of life
estate
ethics
executor
extraordinary measures
futile treatment
health care proxy
Hippocratic oath

iconics
informed consent
intestate succession
justice
life insurance
life-sustaining treatment
living will
neonatal intensive care
passive euthanasia
paternalism
Patient Self-Determination Act
physician-assisted suicide (PAS)
placebo
probate
prognosis
proximics
right to die
slippery slope
surrogate
testator
viatical settlement
whole patient care
will
withholding vs. withdrawing treatment

Questions for Guided Study and Review

1. What is the relationship among the fundamental ethical principles of autonomy, beneficence, and justice?
2. What are some reasons for limiting the ethical principle of autonomy?

3. What is *informed consent*, and what three legal principles are involved?
4. How do today's attitudes among physicians toward disclosing a terminal diagnosis differ from attitudes prevalent in the 1950s?
5. What personal and social factors should be considered in the context of informing patients about a terminal prognosis?
6. What five strategies for responding to a dying patient's communication are discussed in the text?
7. How might the impact of medical technology tend to prolong the dying process as opposed to extending the living process?
8. Why is the case of Karen Ann Quinlan important in medical ethics?
9. Why is the case of Nancy Beth Cruzan important in medical ethics?
10. What three options have medical ethicists outlined when a patient is hopelessly ill?
11. What is the distinction between allowing to die and helping to die?
12. What is the difference between withholding and withdrawing treatment?
13. What is "terminal sedation"?
14. What is the principle of "double effect"?
15. What criteria have been established in the Netherlands concerning euthanasia and physician-assisted suicide?
16. What is the "wedge" or "slippery slope" argument?
17. What is the difference between *ordinary care* and *extraordinary measures*?
18. What "conceptual ambiguity" is evoked in ethical issues involving artificial nutrition?
19. With respect to forgoing life-sustaining treatment, what factors were emphasized by the President's Commission as important?
20. What is the purpose of an advance directive?
21. What are the different types of advance directives?
22. What is a living will, and what is it meant to accomplish?
23. What is an advance proxy directive, or durable power of attorney for health care?
24. How do advance proxy directives differ from living wills?
25. What is the purpose of the Patient Self-Determination Act, and what does it require of health care providers?
26. What is the current legal standing of physician-assisted suicide?
27. What are the requirements of the Oregon Death with Dignity Act?
28. Summarize the U.S. Supreme Court's 1997 ruling on physician-assisted suicide.
29. What is the purpose of making a will?
30. What are the requirements for making a will?
31. What is the meaning of the terms *codicil, intestate, executor, administrator*?
32. Can a legally executed will be amended or revoked?
33. How does an executor differ from an administrator?
34. What is probate?
35. How do laws of intestate succession function?
36. In what way is life insurance a death benefit?
37. What is a *viatical settlement*?
38. What are some of the main categories or types of death benefits that may be available to survivors?
39. Why is attention to the legal aspects of death and dying important for the bereaved?

40. What issue does Leon Kass address in speaking about "the morality of ordinary practice"?

Practice Test Questions

MULTIPLE CHOICE

1. In which case is the individual's right to autonomy violated?
   a. a small baby whose parents elect for surgery to correct a congenital heart defect
   b. an older woman who refuses to undergo back surgery
   c. an athlete who seeks a second opinion concerning knee surgery
   d. an older man whose physician and family coerce him to have foot surgery

2. How might the prescribing of placebos violate good medical ethics?
   a. Prescribing placebos violates the medical principle of beneficence—that is, the doctor doing what is best for the patient.
   b. Prescribing placebos violates the principle of justice—that is, fairness to the patient.
   c. Prescribing placebos violates the principle of autonomy—that is, allowing the patient to decide the type and course of treatment.
   d. Prescribing placebos violates the principle of health care—that is, it provides no benefit to the patient.

3. Which of the following statements supports "passive euthanasia"?
   a. "Seriously ill individuals who prefer to end it quickly and painlessly should be allowed to receive a fatal injection."
   b. "Individuals exhibiting no normal signs of human life should be quickly euthanized with their family's consent."
   c. "Whenever we allow a person to die by withholding or withdrawing life-sustaining means, we are moving in a dangerous direction."
   d. "Seriously ill patients should have the right to refuse treatment that only prolongs their dying."

4. Which of the following best describes a *covenantal relationship?*
   1. shared decision making
   2. physician's authority
   3. mutuality of interests
   4. patient's participation

   a. 1, 3, and 4
   b. 1 and 3
   c. 2 and 4
   d. 1, 2, and 4

5. The concept of a living will was initially developed with the aim of allowing individuals to
   a. avoid being kept alive against their wishes.
   b. declare what they wanted to accomplish while living.
   c. encourage health professionals to try every possible means to keep them alive.
   d. communicate to their beneficiaries after death through the use of videotapes.

TRUE/FALSE

_____ 1. Ethical concerns regarding the "normal" dying process center mainly upon physicians' efforts to keep people alive.

_____ 2. The SUPPORT study shows that physicians tend to be very aware of their patients' preferences about resuscitation.

_____ 3. The Supreme Court ruled in 1997 that *double effect* is permissible if the harm is not intended.

_____ 4. During the course of probate, the deceased's property is distributed to the beneficiaries.

_____ 5. The quote in the text titled *Death of a Son* is used to illustrate how money is poor compensation for the loss of a loved one.

MATCHING

Match each of the following definitions with its appropriate term.

_____ 1. the appointed decision maker in a health care proxy

a. will

_____ 2. legal instrument expressing a persons intentions for the disposition of his or her property after death

b. DNR order

_____ 3. written to avoid the use of artificial resuscitation

c. surrogate

_____ 4. when a terminally ill person sells his or her life insurance policy

d. viatical settlement

✎ Answers to practice questions can be found in Part IV ✎

Related Readings

📖 Indicates selection from *The Path Ahead: Readings in Death and Dying,* ed. Lynne Ann DeSpelder and Albert Lee Strickland (Mountain View, Calif.: Mayfield, 1995).

ETHICAL PRINCIPLES

📖 Daniel Callahan, "The Limits of Medical Progress: A Principle of Symmetry," pp. 103–105.

Albert R. Jonsen. *The New Medicine and the Old Ethics.* Cambridge, Mass.: Harvard University Press, 1990.

📖 Robert Kastenbaum, "Reconstructing Death in Postmodern Society," pp. 7–18.

Ruth Macklin. "Ethical Relativism in a Multicultural Society," in *Medical Ethics: Applying Theories and Principles to the Patient Encounter,* ed. Matt Weinberg, 52–68. Buffalo, N.Y.: Prometheus, 2001.

Edmund D. Pellegrino and David C. Thomasma. *The Virtues in Medical Practice.* New York: Oxford University Press, 1993.

📖 Stanley Joel Reiser, "The Era of the Patient: Using the Experience of Illness in Shaping the Missions of Health Care," pp. 106–115.

David C. Thomasma. "Early Bioethics," *Cambridge Quarterly of Healthcare Ethics* 11, no. 4 (2002): 335–343.

Robert M. Veatch. *Cross Cultural Perspectives in Medical Ethics.* Boston: Jones and Bartlett, 1989.

INFORMED CONSENT

📖 William Bartholome, "Care of the Dying Child: The Demands of Ethics," pp. 133–143.

📖 Margot L. White and John C. Fletcher, "The Story of Mr. and Mrs. Doe: 'You Can't Tell My Husband He's Dying; It Will Kill Him,'" pp. 148–153.

THE CAREGIVER-PATIENT RELATIONSHIP

Merrill Collett. *Stay Close and Do Nothing: A Spiritual and Practical Guide to Caring for the Dying at Home.* Kansas City, Mo.: Andrews McMeel, 1997.

Dale G. Larson. *The Helper's Journey: Working with People Facing Grief, Loss, and Life-Threatening Illness.* Champaign, Ill.: Research Press, 1993.

📖 Stanley Joel Reiser, "The Era of the Patient: Using the Experience of Illness in Shaping the Missions of Health Care," pp. 106–115.

Howard Spiro, Mary G. McCrea Curnen, Enid Peschel, and Deborah St. James, eds. *Empathy and the Practice of Medicine: Beyond Pills and the Scalpel.* New Haven, Conn.: Yale University Press, 1993.

PHYSICIAN-ASSISTED SUICIDE, EUTHANASIA, AND ALLOWING TO DIE

Margaret Pabst Battin. *The Least Worst Death: Essays in Bioethics on the End of Life.* New York: Oxford University Press, 1994.

Lisa Belkin. *First, Do No Harm.* New York: Simon & Schuster, 1993.

Howard Brody. "Assisted Death: A Compassionate Response to Medical Failure." *New England Journal of Medicine* 327, no. 19 (5 November 1992): 1384–1388.

📖 Charles J. Dougherty, "The Common Good, Terminal Illness, and Euthanasia," pp. 154–164.

Herbert Hendin. *Seduced by Death: Doctors, Patients, and the Dutch Cure.* New York: Norton, 1996.

Thane Josef Messinger. "A Gentle and Easy Death: From Ancient Greece to Beyond Cruzan Toward a Reasoned Legal Response to the Societal Dilemma of Euthanasia." *Denver University Law Review* 71, no. 1 (1993): 175–251.

Fiona Randall and R. S. Downie. *Palliative Care Ethics: A Good Companion.* New York: Oxford University Press, 1996.

📖 Richard S. Sandor, "On Death and Coding," pp. 144–147.

Marilyn Webb. *The Good Death: The New American Search to Reshape the End of Life.* New York: Bantam, 1997.

WILLS AND ESTATE PLANNING

Paul P. Ashley. *You and Your Will: The Planning and Management of Your Estate*, rev. ed. New York: New American Library, 1985.

S. Badreshia, V. Bansal, P. S. Houts, and N. Ballentine. "Viatical Settlements: Effects on Terminally Ill Patients," *Cancer Practice* 10, no. 6 (2002): 293–296.

Joseph M. Belth. *Life Insurance: A Consumer's Handbook*, 2nd ed. Bloomington: Indiana University Press, 1985.

Carole Shammas, Marylynn Salmon, and Michel Dahlin. *Inheritance in America from Colonial Times to the Present*. New Brunswick, N.J.: Rutgers University Press, 1987.

Edward F. Sutkowski. *Estate Planning: A Basic Guide*. Chicago: American Bar Association, 1986.

Organizations and Internet Resources

DeathNET: <www.rights.org/lowband.shtml>. Resources about "choice in dying" issues, including physician-assisted suicide and euthanasia.

Family Caregiver Alliance: <www.caregiver.org/caregiver/jsp/content_node.jsp?nodeid=39>. 7690 Market Street, Suite 600, San Francisco, CA 94104. (800) 445-8106. Information for caregivers, ranging from public policy and research issues to practical caregiving information and advice. This section of the site provides facts about CPR and DNR orders.

Five Wishes: <www.agingwithdignity.org>. Source for forms for an advanced directive that is currently valid in thirty-three states.

Hemlock Society: <www.hemlock.org/physician.html> P.O. Box 101810, Denver, CO 80250. (303) 639-1202 or (800) 247-7421. Fax: (303) 639-1224. Information and advocacy for physician-assisted suicide and euthanasia.

Informed Consent, Medicine: <http://reference.allrefer.com/encyclopedia/I/informed.html>. An online encyclopedia description of informed consent with links to articles from eLibrary.

Karen Ann Quinlan: <www.who2.com/karenannquinlan.html>. Information and links to resources about the famous "right-to-die case."

Longwood College Library/Doctor Assisted Suicide—A Guide to Websites and the Literature: <www.longwood.edu/library/suic.htm>. Covers print and electronic sources of information on physician-assisted suicide.

Nolo Press—Wills and Estate Planning: <www.nolo.com>. Provides answers to questions about planning for death, from writing a basic will to organ donation, as well as information about probate, methods for eliminating or reducing death taxes, funeral planning, and choosing someone to handle your affairs if you become incapacitated.

Oregon Health Division, Center for Health Statistics and Vital Records: <www.ohd.hr.state.or.us/chs/pas/pas.cfm>. Information about Oregon's Death with Dignity Act, which allows physician-assisted suicide in certain cases.

❧ Additional resources are available online at mhhe.com ❧

Major Points in This Chapter

- As medical technologies evolve, assuming greater importance in health care, individuals are confronted by situations that involve difficult ethical issues.

- Autonomy, beneficence, and justice are ethical principles that apply to decision making in health care.

- Informed consent requires that the patient is competent, understands the treatment options, and freely and voluntarily makes choices.

- In the context of health care, a covenantal relationship implies a mutuality of interest between health care providers and patients; it encourages clear communication and promotes sharing of decision making.

- Health care institutions are increasingly oriented toward providing "total" or "whole-person" care (physical, emotional, and spiritual) and social support.

- The high-profile cases of Karen Ann Quinlan and Nancy Cruzan have provoked public debate about dying in an era of sophisticated medical technology.

- Right-to-die advocates view euthanasia as a basic human right, an alternative to needless suffering. Opponents argue that it is often difficult or impossible to obtain a patient's clear consent to euthanasia, that there is always a risk of faulty diagnosis, that a timely cure may be found, that palliative care can ease pain and discomfort, and that opening the door to euthanasia will inevitably lead down a "slippery slope" toward inhumane and unethical practices.

- Euthanasia (a "good" or gentle and painless death) encompasses a range of medical decisions: choosing to withhold a particular treatment; withdrawing artificial life support or nutrition and hydration; administering high doses of pain medication that have the "double effect" of hastening death; providing a terminally ill person with the means to end his or her own life; and actively assisting in causing death (as in the case of a lethal injection administered by a physician).

- Neonatal intensive care frequently involves painful decisions with respect to life-sustaining medical interventions.

- Advance directives such as living wills and durable powers of attorney for health care provide a means for individuals to express their wishes about the use of life-sustaining treatment.

- The Patient Self-Determination Act, enacted into law by Congress in 1990, requires health care providers who receive federal funds to give information to patients concerning advance directives.

- Physician-assisted suicide, as exemplified in the highly publicized actions of Dr. Jack Kevorkian, is increasingly an issue for national debate and legislative initiatives. In 1994, Oregon voters passed the Oregon Death with Dignity Act, making that state the first to legalize aid-in-dying. In March 1998, an elderly woman with breast cancer became the first known person to die under the law, having taken a lethal dose of barbiturates prescribed by her doctor.

- A will is a legal document expressing an individual's wishes and intentions with respect to the disposition of his or her property after death.

- Probate is the legal process whereby a will is proved valid and an estate is distributed to its beneficiaries; it is conducted by an administrator or executor under supervision of a court.

- Life insurance and other death benefits provide funds to survivors who have been named by the decedent as beneficiaries or who are otherwise entitled to the proceeds from such benefits.

Observations and Reflections

After reading the section about wills, you now have more information about their importance. Making a will may be viewed as a task restricted to later life. You are now aware of the form and content of a will. You also understand the potential ramifications of dying intestate, even at a young age. Think about the importance of the nonmaterial aspects of will-making, as well as those involving the distribution of material goods. In this way, you can understand that it is not merely the amount of wealth you have to distribute that might motivate you to make a will.

If you already have a will, consider reviewing it in light of the information you now have. Is it time for a change?

The discussion and consideration of ethical issues may bring up past experiences that determine your present stands. Take a moment to relate your experiences to your beliefs.

Use the space below and on the following page to record your thoughts and feelings about end-of-life issues and decisions.

130 ～ Chapter 7

Journey Through The Last Dance, 7th ed.
Activities and Resources

⟫➡ *End-of Life Issues: Withdrawing Life Support*

Directions: *Read the following scenario and complete the assignment.*

Your closest relative is in a hospital, hooked up to life-sustaining machinery. First, in the space to the right of the numbers, make a list of all of the factors you would need to consider before you formed an opinion about his or her care, or your position about turning off the machines.

Ranking   Factors to consider

____   1. _____

____   2. _____

____   3. _____

____   4. _____

____   5. _____

____   6. _____

____   7. _____

____   8. _____

____   9. _____

____   10. _____

____   11. _____

____   12. _____

Now, in the space to the left of the numbers, rate each of these factors on a scale of 1–5 (1 as very important to 5 as not important at all).

After completing this portion of the activity, continue by responding to the questions on the following page.

If it were totally your decision and the doctors said that there was no hope of recovery, what would you do?

_____

_____

_____

_____

_____

_____

_____

_____

_____

_____

Explain your decision:

_____

_____

_____

_____

_____

_____

_____

_____

_____

_____

_____

_____

⟫➡ *Final Wishes*

Directions: *Fill out the following information.*

- I have signed an advance directive (also known as a living will or durable power of attorney for health care): _____ It is located at _____

  _____

- The individuals to be contacted regarding this document are _____

  _____

  _____

- I would most like to die at _____

  And I would like (who) _____

  _____

  _____ there.

- If this isn't possible, I would like to die _____

  _____

  _____

- To prepare before my death, I would like (clergy, close friend, special reading, service, or . . .) _____

  _____

  _____

- My family (or loved one) may need extra support. Please contact (agency or individual) _____

  _____

- I have a donor card. I would like to donate _____

  _____

  _____

- If given a choice, I would (approve/not approve) of an autopsy _____

- Immediately after my death, please notify _____

  _____

- As soon as possible, please notify _____

  _____

- Later, please notify _____

  _____

- For my children, I have requested (who) to be their guardian _____

  _____

- My important papers (vital statistics, veteran's papers, life insurance and other benefits, financial records, will, safe deposit box key) are located at

  _____

  _____

- Other important information is _____

  _____

  _____

  _____

  _____

  _____

  _____

  _____

  _____

  _____

  _____

  _____

  _____

Date: _____ Signed: _____

⇒ *Attorney Interview*

Directions: *Locate an attorney who specializes in estate planning and probate. Tell him or her about the course that you are taking and ask if you may conduct an interview, either in person or over the phone. During the interview, you will be concentrating on dying intestate, probate, durable power of attorney, education, and personal experience. Sample questions follow:*

- I've read about a number of different kinds of wills in our text. Some students in the class have made wills, but, statistically, seven out of ten people die intestate. Perhaps some of us have not made a will because we have little property to leave our friends and loved ones and so believe that wills are for others and not for us. Would you describe the average person for whom you draw up a formally executed will? For instance, what is his or her socioeconomic status?

_____

_____

_____

_____

_____

_____

_____

- What is contained in a typical will, with respect to both material and nonmaterial considerations? Besides the distribution of the testator's property, what are the benefits of drawing up a will? Is there an emotional value for the testator and for his or her survivors?

_____

_____

_____

_____

_____

_____

_____

- Under what circumstances would a mutual will or a conditional will be executed? What about a holographic or a nuncupative will? When would it be appropriate to make one of these types of wills?

_____

_____

_____

_____

_____

_____

_____

_____

- What occurs in this state when a person dies without leaving a will? In other words, what are the laws of succession? Let's take a hypothetical case: Suppose a middle-aged corporation officer with two grown children divorces his wife to marry another woman. Then he adopts the new wife's two children from her previous marriage. The next year he dies of a heart attack, intestate. How would his estate be divided? For instance, would the line of succession go from his present spouse to the four children? What about the former wife to whom he may have been married for more than twenty years? If a former spouse is not included in the laws of succession, does she or he have any recourse? How would a court determine the distribution of property in such cases?

_____

_____

_____

_____

_____

_____

_____

_____

_____

- In turning to the subject of probate, would you describe the legal procedures that occur when a client dies? What actions do you take? Under what circumstances might you be named as executor? What does an executor do? What is the cost of probate and is there any way to reasonably avoid it? Are there any pitfalls in trying to avoid probate?

_____

_____

_____

_____

_____

_____

- Are you familiar with living wills or advance death directives? Have you been asked to draw one up? Under what circumstances do you find them to be valuable? Do you believe that having an advance directive will result in an individual experiencing a "better" death? Is the living will legally enforceable? Are individuals truly able to exercise choice about life support? What do you think are some problems with advance directives and similar documents?

_____

_____

_____

_____

_____

_____

- What was the most complicated or difficult will for you to draw up? Why?

_____

_____

_____

_____

_____

_____

- As a professional, how do you cope with the loss when a client dies? Can you describe any particularly difficult experiences related to the issue of loss?

_____

_____

_____

_____

_____

_____

_____

_____

_____

- In your experience, does law school prepare attorneys for dealing with survivors? One might imagine a course called "Survivors 102." If there is some preparation, how is the topic of death dealt with? Has this aspect of your work ever been a problem to you?

_____

_____

_____

_____

_____

_____

_____

_____

_____

_____

_____

_____

Survivors: Understanding the Experience of Loss

Chapter Summary

Chapter 8 provides a comprehensive inquiry into the human experience of loss. We are all survivors of loss, whether of "little deaths," exemplified by endings and changes that occur throughout the normal course of life, or of more significant losses related to the deaths of loved ones. Although the terms are often used more or less interchangeably, it can be helpful to define *bereavement* as the objective event of loss, *grief* as the response to loss, and *mourning* as the process by which a survivor incorporates the experience of loss into his or her ongoing life.

Various models have been proposed to explain patterns of grief and mourning. Such models are useful in providing an overview, or "snapshot," of a living process, but they tend to oversimplify and may distort the reality experienced by the bereaved. The well-known "five stages" model, described by Elisabeth Kübler-Ross, has become almost a modern mythology of how grieving should be done, and the concept of "working through" a loss is important in the standard theoretical formulations on grief. Such models can be useful as part of a comprehensive understanding of grief. Problems arise, however, when they lead to the notion that "one size fits all," that everyone must cope with grief the same way for successful "recovery" from loss.

Learning about other models of grief and bereavement expands understanding and brings us closer to an accurate representation of the various ways human beings actually cope with loss. Task-oriented models, such as those proposed by William Worden and Therese Rando, are valuable in this regard, as are recent insights about ways that individuals maintain bonds with deceased loved ones. Our understanding of grief has been expanded by the recent contributions of researchers and clinicians like Dennis Klass, Phyllis Silverman, and Margaret Stroebe, to name just a few.

Indeed, it is useful to consider grief from a number of viewpoints. We can observe various physical, emotional, and behavioral reactions associated with grief. We can look at how the experience of grief changes over time. We can investigate the effects of grief on the bereaved's physical and psychological functioning. We can examine situations that make the bereaved more prone to complicated grief. Each of these approaches adds detail to the portrait of grief.

Many variables must be considered in developing an adequate understanding of grief. These variables include the survivor's model of the world (personality, social roles, perceived importance of the deceased, and value structure), mode of death (natural, accidental, homicide, or suicide), circumstances of the death (whether it occurred suddenly or was anticipated), perceptions (whether the death is seen as having been preventable or unavoidable), the relationship of the survivor to the deceased (central or peripheral), the presence of unfinished business between the deceased and the survivor, any conflict between intellectual and emotional responses to the death, and the amount of social support available to the bereaved.

Bereavement usually creates significant change in many aspects of a person's life. The family unit is different, social realities have changed, legal and financial matters require attention. In all these areas, survivors are challenged. In the midst of a burden of loss and grief, it may be difficult to recognize that bereavement can be an opportunity for growth. In coping with loss, creative energy is generated. The tragic event can become a stepping stone to new opportunities. Without dismissing or diminishing the impact of the loss, many bereaved people describe themselves as stronger, more competent, more mature, more independent, and better able to face other crises in life because of their journey through grief. For these survivors, grief becomes a unifying rather than alienating experience. By making space in one's life to accommodate loss, grief is seen as part of the warp and weft of human experience.

Objectives

- To define *bereavement*, *grief*, and *mourning*.
- To describe the experience of grief.
- To list the somatic, perceptual, and emotional manifestations of grief and to assess its impact on morbidity and mortality.
- To evaluate the concept of complicated mourning.
- To describe and evaluate different models of grief.
- To explain the variables that influence grief.
- To list various coping mechanisms and assess the value of each.
- To draw conclusions regarding bereavement support.
- To assess how bereavement may provide an opportunity for growth.

Key Terms and Concepts

acute grief
anticipatory grief
attachment theory
bereavement
bereavement burnout
"broken heart" phenomenon
central vs. peripheral relationship
complicated mourning
deathbed promises
directive mourning therapy
disenfranchised grief
dual-process model of grief

linking objects
"little deaths"
loss
loss-oriented coping
maintaining bonds
mourning
pathological grief
perceived similarity
restoration-oriented coping
secondary morbidity
separation distress
survivor guilt

grief
"grief work"
high grief vs. low grief
inner representation
intuitive vs. instrumental grieving

tasks of mourning
traumatic grief
trigger events
unfinished business

Questions for Guided Study and Review

1. How can we distinguish between the terms *grief, bereavement*, and *mourning*?
2. How do social and cultural norms influence mourning practices?
3. What is the "grief work" model?
4. How does *attachment theory* relate to understanding the dynamics of grief?
5. In what way is bereavement a type of *psychosocial transition*?
6. What are the four tasks of mourning described by William Worden?
7. What are the six Rs described by Therese Rando?
8. Is it necessary to "break the bonds" to adjust to grief?
9. In what way is the notion of "maintaining bonds with the deceased" a useful addition to our understanding of grief?
10. How do bereaved people in different cultures maintain connections with deceased loved ones?
11. How is "telling the story" related to coping with grief?
12. What is the dual process model of grief, and what are the two processes?
13. How does the dual-process model show grief as a dynamic process?
14. How does grief manifest in various ways?
15. How does grief tend to progress in phases?
16. What special issues are typically associated with the acute, middle, and final phases of grief?
17. What kinds of events may reactive grief for a loss previously mourned?
18. What factors potentially result in complicated grief?
19. What factors potentially influence the "mortality of bereavement," and why is it a concern?
20. How might conflict occur between emotional versus intellectual responses to grief?
21. What are some of the main variables influencing the experience of grief, and how might they affect the bereaved?
22. How do personality and social roles influence grief?
23. How is grief likely to be affected by factors such as the nature of the relationship (i.e., central versus peripheral) and beliefs about the circumstances of the death (i.e., preventable versus unavoidable)?
24. What effect might *perceived similarity* have on grief?
25. How does the *mode of death* influence grief?
26. What is *anticipatory grief*?
27. In what ways might suicide and homicide effect the course of grief?
28. What is *disenfranchised grief*?
29. What is the role of social support in coping with grief?
30. What is *unfinished business*, and under what circumstances might it be a factor in grief?

31. How do funerals and other leave-taking rituals and activities provide a framework for social support?
32. What are *linking objects*?
33. In what ways might bereavement lead to personal growth?

Practice Test Questions

MULTIPLE CHOICE

1. The word bereavement comes from a root word meaning
   a. shorn off.
   b. empty.
   c. sieve-like.
   d. left alone.

2. A widower of two months decides to marry again. His friends are split as to whether this is appropriate. How might this controversy best be explained?
   a. In modern society there are no strict social definitions of what is appropriate mourning behavior.
   b. Cultural norms are being violated that for some are important and for others less important.
   c. Society is split on the issue of whether or not individuals are capable of making sound decisions on important matters shortly after the death of a significant other.
   d. In modern society, people are expected to remain in mourning for one year following the death of a spouse.

3. Changing language usage from present to past tense is a signpost from which of William Worden's tasks of mourning?
   a. accepting the reality
   b. working through the pain
   c. adjusting to a changed environment
   d. emotionally relocating the deceased and moving on with life

4. Which of the following tasks of mourning are included in Therese Rando's "Six Rs"?
   1. reinvest
   2. redefine one's existence
   3. recognize the loss
   4. react to the separation

   a. 1, 2, and 3
   b. 1, 3, and 4
   c. 2, 3, and 4
   d. 3 only

5. In dealing with grief and survivorship, which of the following is FALSE?
   a. The emotional response to grief is so varied, one should be careful about judging whether particular emotions and actions are appropriate.
   b. Grief can be a unifying human experience that promotes growth and maturity.
   c. Pathological grief can be easily identified, but it is difficult to treat.
   d. Funeral rites provide social support for the bereaved.

TRUE/FALSE

_____ 1. In U.S. culture we maintain rigid social definitions of appropriate mourning behavior.

_____ 2. Although the most intense feelings of grief occur in the first few days after a death, the grieving process is measured in years rather than weeks or months.

_____ 3. The African concept of the "living dead" is an example of the value of maintaining bonds with the "deceased."

_____ 4. It is humanly impossible to feel deep grief for individuals we do not know personally.

_____ 5. Whether the lost relationship is perceived as either ended or changed has no effect on the likelihood of experiencing bereavement as a process of growth.

MATCHING

Match each of the following terms on the left with the most appropriate description on the right. Each description may be used only once.

_____ 1. Grief

a. can occur when high-risk factors are present in the bereaved's experience of loss

_____ 2. Complicated mourning

b. can be felt by parents who survive the death of a child

_____ 3. Traumatic grief

c. Can involve conflicting feelings like sorrow, sadness, relief, and anger

_____ 4. Survivor guilt

d. if common grief reactions persist longer than two months and there is a clinically significant impairment in a persons occupation, then this diagnosis could be made

❧ Answers to practice questions can be found in Part IV ❧

Related Readings

📖 Indicates selection from *The Path Ahead: Readings in Death and Dying*, ed. Lynne Ann DeSpelder and Albert Lee Strickland (Mountain View, Calif.: Mayfield, 1995).

THE EXPERIENCE OF GRIEF

Thomas W. Attig. *How We Grieve: Relearning the World.* New York: Oxford University Press, 1996.

📖 Sandra L. Bertman, "Bearing the Unbearable: From Loss, the Gain," pp. 348–354.

Lynne Ann DeSpelder and Albert Lee Strickland. "Loss," in *Encyclopedia of Death and Dying*, ed. Glennys Howarth and Oliver Leaman, 288–289. New York: Routledge, 2001.

📖 Kenneth J. Doka, "Disenfranchised Grief," pp. 271–275.

Kenneth J. Doka and Joyce D. Davidson, eds. *Living with Grief: Who We Are, How We Grieve.* Washington, D.C.: Hospice Foundation of America, 1998.

Charles R. Figley, Brian E. Bride, and Nicholas Mazza, eds. *Death and Trauma: The Traumatology of Grieving.* Washington, D.C.: Taylor & Francis, 1997.

Jeffrey Kauffman, ed. *Loss of the Assumptive World: A Theory of Traumatic Loss.* New York: Brunner-Routledge, 2002.

📖 John D. Kelly, "Grief: Re-forming Life's Story," pp. 242–245.

Dennis Klass. "Developing a Cross-Cultural Model of Grief: The State of the Field," *Omega: Journal of Death and Dying* 39, no. 3 (1999): 153–178.

Louis E. Lagrand. *Gifts from the Unknown: Using Extraordinary Experiences to Cope with Loss and Change.* New York: Authors Choice Press, 2001.

William M. Lamers, Jr. "On the Psychology of Loss," in *Grief and the Healing Arts: Creativity As Therapy,* ed. Sandra L. Bertman, 1–18. Amityville, N.Y.: Baywood, 1998.

Ruth Malkinson, Simon Shimshon Rubin, and Eliezer Witztum, eds. *Traumatic and Nontraumatic Loss and Bereavement: Clinical Theory and Practice.* Madison, Conn.: Psychosocial Press, 2000.

Therese Rando. *Grieving: How to Go on Living When Someone You Love Dies.* Lexington, Mass.: Lexington Books, 1988.

Paul C. Rosenblatt. *Bitter, Bitter Tears: Nineteenth-Century Diarists and Twentieth-Century Grief Theories.* Minneapolis: University of Minnesota Press, 1983.

📖 Margaret Stroebe, Mary M. Gergen, Kenneth J. Gergen, and Wolfgang Stroebe, "Broken Hearts or Broken Bonds: Love and Death in Historical Perspective," pp. 231–241.

Margaret S. Stroebe, Wolfgang Stroebe, and Robert O. Hansson, eds. *Handbook of Bereavement: Theory, Research, and Intervention.* New York: Cambridge University Press, 1993.

Vamik D. Volkan and Elizabeth Zintl. *Life After Loss: The Lessons of Grief.* New York: Collier, 1994.

SPECIFIC TYPES OF BEREAVEMENT

📖 Dennis Klass, "Solace and Immortality: Bereaved Parents' Continuing Bond with Their Children," pp. 246–259.

Sandra Jacoby Klein. *Heavenly Hurts: Surviving AIDS-Related Deaths and Losses.* Amityville, N.Y.: Baywood, 1998.

Charles P. McDowell, Joseph M. Rothberg, and Ronald J. Koshes. "Witnessed Suicides," *Suicide and Life-Threatening Behavior* 24, no. 3 (1994): 213–223.

Therese A. Rando. *Loss and Anticipatory Grief.* Lexington, Mass.: Lexington Books, 1986.

Lula M. Redmond. *Surviving When Someone You Love Was Murdered.* Clearwater, Fla.: Psychological Consultation and Education Services, 1989).

Paul C. Rosenblatt. *Parent Grief: Narratives of Loss and Relationship.* Philadelphia: Brunner/Mazel, 2000.

Catherine M. Sanders. *Grief, The Mourning After: Dealing with Adult Bereavement.* New York: John Wiley and Sons, 1989.

📖 Nancy Scheper-Hughes, "Death Without Weeping: The Violence of Everyday Life in Brazil," pp. 41–58.

📖 Phyllis R. Silverman, Steven Nickman, and J. William Worden, "Detachment Revisited: The Child's Reconstruction of a Dead Parent," pp. 260–270.

📖 Avery D. Weisman, "Bereavement and Companion Animals," pp. 276–280.

SOCIAL SUPPORT AND FAMILIES

📖 Stephen J. Fleming and Leslie Balmer, "Bereaved Families of Ontario: A Mutual-Help Model for Families Experiencing Death," pp. 281–288.

Onno van der Hart. *Coping with Loss: The Therapeutic Use of Leave-Taking Ritual.* New York: Irvington, 1988.

Organizations and Internet Resources

Anticipated Losses and Anticipatory Grief: <www.indiana.edu/~famlygrf/units/anticipated.html>. Kathleen Gilbert's online component for a course, Grief in a Family Context, at Indiana University. Thorough discussion of these topics.

Bereavement Organization: <www.bereavement.org>. This is an "e-book" created to help those who grieve and those who provide support for the bereaved. Material is suitable for use at the college level. Here you will find information on the theorists in the field of grief; see especially Eric Lindemann.

Concerns of Police Survivors (COPS): <www.nationalcops.org>. P.O. Box 3199, South Highway 5, Camdenton, MO 65020. (573) 346-4911 or (800) 784-COPS (2677). Fax: (573) 346-1414. Provides support to families of police officers who have died in the line of duty.

GriefNet: <www.griefnet.org>. A site where participants communicate with others via e-mail support groups in the areas of death, grief, and major loss, including life-threatening and chronic illness.

Journey of Hearts Organization: <www.journeyofhearts.org>. Education about bereavement, grief, and mourning, including healthy coping.

National Self-Help Clearinghouse: <www.selfhelpweb.org>. Suite 330, 365 Fifth Avenue, New York, NY 10036. (212) 817-1822. Maintains current information on self-help groups.

❧ Additional resources are available online at mhhe.com ❧

Major Points in This Chapter

- Surviving a loss, whether a "little death" or a major bereavement experience, brings with it the possibility of grief and mourning.
- Awareness of cultural context and the multiplicity of mourning behaviors is essential to understanding the range of human responses to bereavement.
- The human response to loss is complex; it encompasses a multitude of personal, familial, and social factors.
- Manifestations of grief include both physical and psychological distress.

- Complicated mourning may occur when certain high-risk factors are present in the bereaved's experience of loss.
- Various models of grief—including Kübler-Ross's five stages, Lindemann's "working through" grief, Worden's tasks of mourning, and Rando's 6R processes of mourning—have guided the search for patterns in bereavement.
- The notion that resolving grief means "letting go" is being revised in light of the recognition that people generally "relocate" the deceased in some fashion into their ongoing lives.
- Narrative approaches to grief employ an important component: talking about the death and the deceased.
- Variables influencing grief include the survivor's model of the world (including his or her values, personality, social roles, and perception of the deceased's importance), the mode of death (e.g., sudden, anticipated, suicide, or homicide), the nature of the survivor's relationship to the deceased, the presence of social support, and whether the survivor has a sense of "unfinished business" with the deceased.
- Disenfranchised grief typically occurs when the significance of a loss is not socially recognized or when the relationship between the deceased and the survivor is not socially sanctioned.
- Funerals and other leave-taking rituals, along with survivor support groups, can be important aids to coping with bereavement.
- Bereavement can be an opportunity for personal growth.

Observations and Reflections

The possibility of evoking strong emotions exists during activities and discussions and bereavement and grief. Voices may become choked. Tears may be shed. Keep in mind that there is no need to become alarmed simply because someone is expressing difficult or emotions or painful memories. Pause and take a couple of slow, deep breaths. The rest of the story will come out.

Use the space below to make notes about the material covered in this chapter.

⟫➔ *The 5L Model for Companioning the Bereaved*

Directions: Read Patrick Dean's 5L Model. Answer the questions in the space provided.

Love. Ultimately, when all is said and done, love is the only happiness. While we can and do come to terms with the death of someone we love, in our own ways and our own time spaces, we need to remember that, while people die, love does not. Vincent van Gogh said it wonderfully when he taught that the best way to know life was to love many things.

Laugh. Numerous studies have shown the powerful healing and palliative effect of a good laugh or, even better, a shared laugh. A hallmark of the grief and healing process is the ability, in the midst of intense feelings of loss, to be able to find humor or allow the presence of laughter to balance sadness. Bereaved people will often deny themselves the pleasure that accompanies laughing in an unhealthy attempt to show the outside world the fact of their mourning. They may even deny themselves the gift of feeling pleasure as a way to stay connected to their sadness and to the deceased.

Live. As companions to the bereaved, it is critical that we model an "attitude of gratitude" toward the gift that is life. In so doing, we honor not only the death that has happened but also the life that was lived. When we couple this attitude with the religious or secular beliefs of our bereaved companion, we are modeling a truly high level of spirituality.

Learn. We need to learn to cultivate curiosity. This "client as teacher" attitude allows the narrative that is every bereaved person's story of loss to unfold from and by the expert—that is, the person surviving any particular loss. This frees us as companions to the bereaved from having to say the right thing or to be some particular way that we may or may not be comfortable with when we assume total responsibility for "fixing" the necessary sadness that is grief.

Listen. We have been given two ears and one mouth and we ought to use them in that proportion, listening more than talking. We need to listen with our head and our heart. Listening with our head is an important "academic part" of helping. Equally important, and the perfect compliment to the academic, is listening with the heart. Finding the balance between the science of head knowledge and the art of listening with the heart is a skill developed with practice, patience, and prayer.

1. Is "companioning the bereaved" the same thing as being with a person who is grieving? Why or why not?

   _____

   _____

   _____

   _____

2. When Dean talks about a "client," do you think this would also apply to a friend or family member? Explain.

_____

_____

_____

_____

3. Which is your favorite "L"?_____. Describe your interest.

_____

_____

_____

_____

4. Rank order the "5 Ls" from 1–5 (1 being the most important to 5 the least important). Notice how your ranking is related to your own coping skills.

_____

_____

_____

_____

_____

5. Can you think of any other "L" that belongs on this list? What would it be? Explain why it should be included.

_____

_____

_____

_____

_____

_____

_____

_____

➠ *Survivor Interview*

Directions: *Find a person who has experienced a death and who is willing to share his or her experience. The interviewee need not share anything that makes him or her uncomfortable. The person may become emotional at times. Begin the interview by asking the following questions:*

Who was the person who died? _____

_____

When did the death occur? _____

_____

Where did the death occur? _____

_____

How did you react at first? _____

_____

_____

_____

_____

_____

_____

How did this initial reaction change over time? _____

_____

_____

_____

_____

_____

_____

What helped you cope with your grief? _____

_____

_____

_____

_____

_____

_____

_____

What didn't help?_____

_____

_____

_____

_____

_____

_____

_____

What did you learn from the experience? _____

_____

_____

_____

_____

_____

_____

_____

_____

_____

➠ 📖 *Internet Survivor Support*

Directions: *The Internet functions, on some level, as a survivor support group. There are numerous web pages designed to memorialize and many of them have resources about a particular type of loss. Other sites contain opportunities for survivors to tell the stories of their loss. Here, you will search the web to identify five "survivor sites." Please rate each listing from 1 (very good) to 5 (useless) and give a summary of the information to be found on the site.*

You may begin your Internet web search at:<http://www.webhealing.com/honor.html> or the homepage of The Ring of Death, which is a network of death, dying, and bereavement pages on the web at <http://www.alsirat.com/silence/ring/>.

1. URL _____ Rating _____

_____

_____

_____

_____

_____

_____

_____

_____

2. URL _____ Rating _____

_____

_____

_____

_____

_____

_____

_____

_____

3. URL _____ Rating _____

_____

_____

_____

_____

_____

_____

_____

4. URL _____ Rating _____

_____

_____

_____

_____

_____

_____

_____

5. URL _____ Rating _____

_____

_____

_____

_____

_____

_____

_____

Last Rites:
Funerals and Body Disposition

Chapter Summary

Chapter 9 examines the structure, symbolic content, and function of funeral rituals. In a broad sense, funerals are rites that denote a change in status of both the deceased and his or her survivors. In modern societies, funerals have come to be seen largely as a means whereby social support is made available to survivors. The social aspects of last rites begin with notification of the death, a process that extends from relatives and close friends to those who were less intimately related to the deceased. Gathering together to comfort the bereaved during the various events associated with the funeral provides reassurance that the death of an individual—and the survivors' grief—are part of a larger whole. In this sense, funerals and other such rites of passage are seen as occurring within a caring community.

Although funerals typically fulfill an important function as a means for coping with loss, the modern funeral has been criticized for its cost as well as its tendency to "prettify" or deny death by cosmetically restoring the corpse, engaging in euphemistic language to describe the facts of death, and creating a "staged" ceremony. Studies have shown that most people are satisfied with current funeral practices and feel they have been treated fairly by funeral-service personnel. Still, because most people are unfamiliar with the various choices and costs surrounding funeral and mortuary services, there is lingering concern that customers could be taken advantage of by the funeral industry.

Becoming familiar with the historical evolution of funeral practices aids our understanding of the shape of present-day practices. Undertakers were initially trades people who supplied funeral paraphernalia to families, usually as a sideline to some other business. Undertakers essentially provided a service to families who were, in effect, their own funeral directors. Over time, urbanization and other social changes altered this traditional relationship, with professional morticians taking on an ever-larger role in caring for the dead as family involvement diminished.

Even when individuals do not wish to assume a larger role in designing their own funerals or creating appropriate farewells for their deceased loved ones, it is still worthwhile to become acquainted with the options available in funeral services. The purpose of the funeral—as an occasion for acknowledging publicly that a member of the community has died and to effect closure on that person's life for the bereaved—can be realized whether it is garnished with diamonds and rubies or with poetry and a song. As a transaction unique in commerce, the contract for funeral services is usually entered into during a time of crisis. Preparing oneself in advance by learning about the various funeral service charges and their approximate costs can be helpful when the time comes for making meaningful decisions.

Funeral service charges typically include categories for professional services (covering mortuary staff services and general overhead), intake charges (for transporting remains), embalming or refrigeration of the body, other body preparation (cosmetology, hairstyling, dressing the corpse, and the like), the casket (of which there is a wide range of choices), facilities (use of a visitation or viewing room, or the mortuary chapel), vehicles (hearse, family cars), and a miscellaneous category that may include the costs of newspaper death notices, acknowledgment cards, floral arrangements, honoraria for pallbearers or clergy, and burial garments purchased from the mortuary.

Purchasers of mortuary services also benefit from being aware of the various options for body disposition—burial, entombment, and cremation being the most common in North America. The options and costs associated with placing grave markers or erecting more elaborate memorials at the gravesite also need to be considered, along with any fees for "perpetual care" that may be assessed by cemeteries or mausoleums.

As a response to death, funerals range from simple to elaborate, from the few essentials needed for proper disposal of the body to ornate ceremonies that span several days, or even longer. Some people prefer minimal involvement in caring for their deceased loved ones; others seek more active participation. There are many ways of dealing meaningfully with death. Becoming aware of our choices enables us to make more informed, and more gratifying, choices about last rites.

Objectives

- To describe the function of funeral rituals, including their psychosocial aspects.
- To describe the historical changes in funeral rituals and assess the relevance of criticisms about current practices.
- To examine practices and costs of various mortuary and cemetery options.
- To identify the elements of last rites and design a personally meaningful funeral ritual.

Key Terms and Concepts

aftercare	crypt
body disposition	cybermourners
burial	death notification
casket	direct cremation
cemetery	embalming
coffin	entombment
columbarium	FTC Funeral Rule
committal	funeral
cremation	funeral director
cryogenic suspension	funeral home

funerary artifacts	mortician
grave goods	mortuary
grave liner	niche
grave marker	procession
immediate burial	undertaker
intake fee	vault
itemized pricing	viewing room
last rites	vigil
mausoleum	virtual cemeteries
memorial service	visitation
memorial society	wake
memorialization	water burial

Questions for Guided Study and Review

1. According to Vanderlyn Pine, what are the four major social functions historically associated with funerals?
2. What purpose did embalming and preservation of the body have for the ancient Egyptians?
3. What are the main purposes—socially and psychologically—of last rites?
4. How does the gathering of the community serve the psychosocial aspects of last rites?
5. What seven elements of funeral rituals are described in the text?
6. How does notification of a death take place?
7. Why is death notification and the manner in which it occurs important?
8. How are themes of separation and integration evident in funeral rites?
9. How does the notion of a "change of status" apply to funeral rites?
10. How are funeral rites an impetus to cope with a loss?
11. What are the main criticisms voiced about funerals?
12. What major changes occurred in funerals during the twentieth century?
13. How has the role of the undertaker changed since the end of the nineteenth century?
14. How did the term "funeral parlor" come into being?
15. In what way is the purchase of funeral goods and services a unique commercial transaction?
16. What are the four categories of costs related to a standard funeral as outlined by the National Funeral Directors Association?
17. What is the Funeral Rule, and what does it require?
18. How did the practice of embalming develop in the United States?
19. In modern usage, how is embalming done?
20. What is the purpose of embalming, and when is it required?
21. What types of caskets are generally available?
22. What are the requirements for using a casket when a body is to be cremated?
23. How do direct cremations and immediate burials differ from the standard funeral?
24. What are the main choices for body disposition?
25. How do religious beliefs potentially affect the method of body disposition?
26. What is *cryogenic suspension*?

27. How is the process of cremation accomplished?
28. What are the choices for disposition of cremated remains?
29. What is *memorialization?*
30. What are some recent innovations in funeral and memorialization practices?
31. Does the definition of funerals as "an organized, purposeful, time-limited, flexible, group-centered response to death" apply to current approaches to caring for the dead?

Practice Test Questions

MULTIPLE CHOICE

1. The ceremonies a community enacts to mark the passing of one of its members are expressed through
   a. symbols and metaphor.
   b. prayer and solemnity.
   c. mourning and grief.
   d. acceptance and transition.

2. Funerals or last rites essentially
   a. celebrate an individual's achievement in life.
   b. mark the transition of an individual's status as a member of the community.
   c. focus on the void left because of the individual's absence.
   d. increase surviving family members' anxiety toward death because they must deal directly with it.

3. Which of the following criticisms did Jessica Mitford express about funeral practices in the United States?
   1. euphemistic language
   2. bizarre and morbid funeral practices
   3. efforts to disguise death
   4. efforts to make death more realistic

   a. 1, 2, and 3
   b. 1, 2, and 4
   c. 1, 3, and 4
   d. 1 and 2 only

4. The Federal Trade Commission's Funeral Rule requires
   a. pricing methods that limit profit on funerals.
   b. telephone hotlines that provide funeral information.
   c. disclosure of itemized price information.
   d. all funeral workers to pass a written test and be certified.

5. In most states, the final disposition of the body is the responsibility of the
   a. physician's assistant.
   b. coroner.
   c. medical examiner.
   d. deceased's next of kin.

TRUE/FALSE

_____ 1. Death notification provides a potent psychological impetus for coping with loss.

_____ 2. Decisions about one's own last rites are ideally made with a view to the needs and wishes of one's survivors.

_____ 3. Spending a large sum of money is necessary to positively effect closure on the deceased's life and comfort the bereaved.

_____ 4. Body disposition can have symbolic meaning to the followers of a religious tradition.

_____ 5. A mausoleum is an above-ground structure of concrete, marble, or other stone in which one or more bodies are entombed.

MATCHING

Match each of the following funeral ritual elements with its appropriate description.

_____ 1. Deathwatch   a. the "centerpiece" of the ritual surrounding death

_____ 2. Wake   b. relatives and friends gather to say farewells and show respect for the dying

_____ 3. Funeral   c. the conveyance of the corpse from the site of the funeral to the place of burial

_____ 4. Procession   d. offers opportunities for social interactions that can be healing in the aftermath of loss

❧ Answers to practice questions can be found in Part IV ❧

Related Readings

📖 Indicates selection from *The Path Ahead: Readings in Death and Dying,* ed. Lynne Ann DeSpelder and Albert Lee Strickland (Mountain View, Calif.: Mayfield, 1995).

FUNERAL PRACTICES: GENERAL

Douglas J. Davies. *Death, Ritual, and Belief,* 2nd ed. London: Continuum, 2002.

📖 Stephen J. Fleming and Leslie Balmer, "Bereaved Families of Ontario: A Mutual-Help Model for Families Experiencing Death," pp. 281–288.

Kenneth T. Jackson and Camilo José Vergara. *Silent Cities: The Evolution of the American Cemetery.* New York: Princeton Architectural Press, 1989.

Jessica Mitford. *The American Way of Death Revisited.* New York: Alfred A. Knopf, 1998.

Ernest Morgan. *Dealing Creatively with Death: A Manual of Death Education and Simple Burial.* 11th ed. Burnsville, N.C.: Celo Press, 1988.

Phyllis Theroux. *The Book of Eulogies.* New York: Simon & Schuster, 1997.

Alan Wolfelt. *Creating Meaningful Funeral Ceremonies: A Guide for Families.* Fort Collins, Colo.: Companion Press, 1999.

FUNERAL PRACTICES: CULTURAL STUDIES

Vernel Bagneris. *Rejoice When You Die: The New Orleans Jazz Funerals.* Baton Rouge: Louisiana State University Press, 1998.

📖 Ronald K. Barrett, "Contemporary African-American Funeral Rites and Traditions," pp. 80–92.

James K. Crissman. *Death and Dying in Central Appalachia: Changing Attitudes and Practices.* Urbana: University of Illinois Press, 1994.

Robert W. Habenstein and William M. Lamers. *The History of American Funeral Directing.* Milwaukee: Bulfin Printers, 1962.

📖 Christopher L. Hayes and Richard A. Kalish, "Death-Related Experiences and Funerary Practices of the Hmong Refugee in the United States," pp. 75–79.

Karla F. C. Holloway. *Passed On: African American Mourning Stories.* Durham, N.C.: Duke University Press, 2002.

Richard E. Meyer, ed. *Ethnicity and the American Cemetery.* Bowling Green, Ohio: Bowling Green State University Popular Press, 1993.

Thierry Secretan. *Going into Darkness: Fantastic Coffins from Africa.* London: Thames and Hudson, 1995.

Organizations and Internet Resources

American Casket Retailers Association: <www.acra.org>. 177 Riverside Avenue, Suite 902, Newport Beach, CA 92633. Information to assist consumers in purchasing caskets.

American Cryonics Society: <http://pweb.jps.net/~cryonics/>. 1901 Middlefield Way, Suite 1, Mountain View, CA 94043. (650) 254-2001 or (800) 523-2001. Information about cryonics as a method of body disposition.

Batesville Casket Company: <www.batesville.com>. One Batesville Blvd., Batesville, IN 47116. (812) 934-7500 or (800) 622-8373. Literature for the bereaved about funerals and grief.

Internet Cremation Society: <www.cremation.org>. A website that screens local cremation societies to provide information on the least expensive alternative for body disposition in various locations in the United States and Canada.

Jewish Funeral Directors of America: <www.jfda.org>. 150 Lynnway, Suite 506, Seaport Landing, Lynn, MA 01902. (781) 477-9300. Fax: (781) 477-9393. Information about customs and traditions associated with Jewish funerals.

National Funeral Directors Association (NFDA): <www.nfda.org>. 13625 Bishops Drive, Brookfield, WI 53005. (262) 789-1880 or (800) 228-6332, Fax: (262) 789-6977. Resources related to funerals and funeral costs, body disposition, and bereavement support.

Neptune Society: <www.neptunesociety.com>. 4321 Woodman Avenue, 3rd Floor, Sherman Oaks, CA 91423. (818) 953-9995 or (888) 637-8863. Fax: (818) 953-9844. Cremation service company.

New Orleans Jazz Club: <www.nojazzclub.com> 828 Royal Street, Suite 265, New Orleans, LA 70116. (504) 455-6847. Devoted to historical preservation and performance of jazz developed from the music accompanying African American funeral processions.

❧ Additional resources are available online at mhhe.com ❧

Major Points in This Chapter

- The choices people make involving funeral rituals and body disposition reflect their attitudes and beliefs about death.
- The psychosocial aspects of funeral rites include death notification (including obituaries and death notices) as well as mutual support as an impetus for coping with loss.
- The American funeral has evolved from handmade coffins and wakes held in the parlor of the family home to ornate caskets and ceremonies managed by funeral directors. Critics maintain that modern funerals are prone to unnecessarily high costs.
- Well-informed consumers of funeral services are knowledgeable about costs and are able to compare prices and evaluate the variety of services offered in the marketplace.
- Funeral and memorial societies are organized to serve their members or customers by negotiating reduced prices for basic services.
- The laws regulating the disposition of human remains generally specify where and how burials and disposal of cremated remains can be accomplished.

Observations and Reflections

Many local funeral directors will be happy to meet with you individually to answer your questions and give you a tour of the facilities. Some students express discomfort about visiting a mortuary. If you are uncomfortable, it is good to realize that the experience probably will not match your worst expectations. The visit should be arranged with the funeral director ahead of time so that you can have choices about what you will see. You may be afraid of seeing a dead body, embalming equipment, or the like. In fact, it is unlikely that you will see any dead bodies since mortuary personnel are careful to protect the rights of the families using their facilities. Be aware that mourners may be present during your visit.

Use the space below and on the following page to make notes about what you have learned about funerals and body disposition.

⇒ *Creating a Funeral Home*

Directions: *To your surprise you have just found out that you have inherited the funeral home of a long-lost relative. The will states that, if you can keep the funeral home business for five years and make a profit, you will receive an inheritance of $1,000,000! You now have some decisions to make about your new business:*

1. You must hire five new funeral directors. What characteristics do you want them to have?

_____

_____

_____

_____

_____

_____

2. What would your casket selection room look like?

_____

_____

_____

_____

_____

_____

3. What would the entryway of your mortuary look like?

_____

_____

_____

_____

_____

_____

4. Would your funeral home provide "aftercare"? Describe your aftercare services.

_____

_____

_____

_____

_____

5. How would you be personally active in the business (for example, being present at funerals)?

_____

_____

_____

_____

_____

6. How would you try to reduce criticisms of the funeral industry?

_____

_____

_____

_____

_____

7. What innovations would you bring to your new enterprise to make it the "best funeral home in the nation"?

_____

_____

_____

_____

_____

➠ *Questionnaire: Funeral Planning*

Directions: Indicate your funeral wishes by completing the following sentences:

- I would like my body to be (embalmed, viewed at home, not viewed, cremated, buried, entombed) _____

_____

_____

- I'd like to be wearing _____

- Please transport my body in a _____

- The mortuary, crematory, or memorial society I prefer is _____

_____

- The price range I would want spent on my funeral is

_____

- I would like the final disposition of my body to be

_____

_____

- If I were cremated, I would want my ashes _____

_____

_____

- I'd like a tombstone or marker that reads _____

_____

_____

_____

- I (would/would not) like flowers sent

  _____

  and/or donations made to _____

  _____

  _____

- I would like a funeral or memorial service led by

  _____

  at _____

- I'd like a (religious/secular) service that would include (open casket, flowers, music, quotes, speakers) _____

  _____

  _____

  _____

  _____

  _____

  _____

  _____

- I'd prefer to leave the arrangements for my funeral to

  _____

  _____

  _____

  _____

  _____

  _____

⟫⟫➡ *Interview with a Funeral Director*

Directions: *Make arrangements to visit a funeral home and talk to one of the funeral directors. This interview is designed to give you firsthand knowledge about the business of funeral directing, including the services offered by a mortuary. The following interview pertains to three areas: personal history, services offered, and business realities. Add any additional questions you may have. Report on the learnings from your interview.*

- Many children talk about what they want to be when they grow up. I would imagine they don't often say "a mortician." When did you know that you wanted to be a mortician? What prompted you to choose this career over, say, being a firefighter or a doctor?

- Will you tell me about the first time you saw a dead body? What were the circumstances and how did you feel?

- What allows you to handle so much exposure to death? How do you cope?

- How does the public perceive you? For example, how do children react to your occupation? What about acquaintances, close friends, and relatives?

- What training did you receive for your job?

- Did you receive training in grief counseling?

- Would you describe the embalming process? Is it required by law and, if so, under what circumstances?

- Can refrigeration substitute for embalming? How do the costs compare?

- What is the longest period of time you've kept a body before final disposition?

- Would you say something about body viewing? For example, under what circumstances would you recommend not viewing a body? When do you think body viewing is most beneficial for survivors? What are your feelings about the importance of viewing the body?

- Should children view a dead body? Have there been situations when you thought they should not have viewed the body? What were the circumstances?

- What about cosmetics? Are they required? What do you think are the advantages? Any disadvantages?

- Making funeral rituals personally meaningful can be valuable for survivors. What requests do people make? What would be an unconventional request?

- Could survivors handle all the details of a funeral themselves? How would it be done? What would be the costs?

- What do you find to be the most difficult deaths? How do you personally cope?

- What are some of the costs in operating this business?

- Do you think the stereotype of the rich mortician making money from others' pain is ever accurate?

- What kinds of malpractice claims might be filed against mortuaries?

- How do funeral directors build their businesses?

ADDITIONAL QUESTIONS

_____

_____

_____

_____

_____

_____

_____

_____

REPORT ON INTERVIEW

Use this space (and additional sheets if needed) to make notes from your interview.

_____

_____

_____

_____

_____

_____

_____

_____

_____

_____

_____

_____

Death in the Lives of Children and Adolescents

Chapter Summary

Chapter 10 looks at experiences of loss in the lives of children and adolescents. In making use of a lifespan approach, this chapter builds on material presented in earlier chapters—particularly those dealing with how children are socialized about death, how individuals cope with serious illness, and how survivors' cope with loss and bereavement. Change is a common component of children's lives. They may experience separations from friends and neighborhoods to which they have become attached. Changes in the composition of the family unit—through death, divorce, or the departure of a sibling—require children to adapt to unfamiliar and sometimes painful circumstances.

When a child is diagnosed with a serious and possibly life-threatening illness, confusion and emotional upheaval usually result—for the child as well as his or her family. A child's natural curiosity about the seriousness of his or her condition sometimes meets with silence or attempts to mask the truth on the part of adults. Being subjected to a discomforting medical regimen can add to a child's fears and anxieties. As with adults, children use a range of coping strategies as they adjust to difficult and painful circumstances. How a child perceives an illness and the manner in which he or she responds to it depends on such factors as age and developmental level, patterns of social interaction, family relationships, and past experiences, as well as the nature of the illness and its treatment.

Caring for a seriously ill child involves attending not only to physical needs but also to emotional and psychological needs. While trained personnel are best equipped to provide the technical aspects of medical care, family members can participate in the crucial non-technical aspects of care, such as those involving emotional support and encouragement.

Although not all children experience serious injury or illness, most do experience themselves as survivors of a death—whether it is the death of a pet, a parent or grandparent, a sibling, or other close relation or acquaintance. A child's response to loss reflects such factors as his or her stage of mental and emotional development as well as previous experiences with death. Children of the same age may exhibit significant differences in their abilities to comprehend death and cope with its effects on them as survivors. Experiencing a close death may stimulate the development of more mature concepts about death as a child copes with the fact of loss in his or her life.

Children typically look to parents and other adults for examples of how to deal with loss. Children should be given opportunities to express their grief. Their feelings need to be openly explored in a supportive atmosphere. Children seem to cope more easily with their feelings about a close death or other traumatic event when they are allowed to participate in the unfolding experience. When children are excluded, or when their questions go unanswered, they are likely to experience more confusion and pain.

Foremost among the guidelines for helping a child cope with crisis is a willingness to listen. Acknowledge the child's feelings. Discover what he or she thinks and feels. Questions should be answered honestly and directly, without overwhelming the child with information beyond his or her ability to comprehend. Age-appropriate books dealing with situations involving dying and death provide opportunities to explore issues and experiences with children. A variety of organizations provide social support to children who are coping with life-threatening illness or with a significant death. As much as we might wish it were otherwise, children cannot ultimately be shielded from painful experiences involving loss.

Children are naturally curious and inquisitive about death. The material covered in this chapter can provide a basis for helping children cope with their experiences of change and loss. Adults who are prepared to discuss the subject openly and honestly, and in a way appropriate to the child's level of understanding, can play a crucial supportive role in the child's efforts to come to terms with the reality of death and the emotions engendered by loss.

Objectives

- To describe the child's perception of illness.
- To explain how a terminally ill child's fears and anxieties are developmentally related.
- To identify the various coping mechanisms used by terminally ill children and to assess the value of each.
- To identify factors influencing a child's experience of grief.
- To illustrate ways of helping children cope with death.

Key Terms and Concepts

bibliotherapy
distancing strategies
mental first aid
parent death
pet death

prothanatic behavior
selective forgetting
"should haves"
sibling death
sublimation

Questions for Guided Study and Review

1. What are some of the ways that young children encounter loss and death?
2. When do children generally become aware of death?
3. How does the "peekaboo" game or a child's statement "no more" reflect death-related understandings?
4. How do play activities help children reach some understanding of death?
5. At what age do children begin to make efforts to come to terms with death-related experiences?
6. How might "mental first aid" be offered to help a seriously ill child?
7. How does development of a "death concept" relate to the concerns expressed by seriously ill children?
8. What methods of coping are typically used by seriously ill children?
9. How are distancing and sublimation used as coping mechanism?
10. What are some issues that deserve consideration in caring for a seriously ill or dying child?
11. What factors influence a bereaved child's experience of grief?
12. How might guilt complicate childhood grief?
13. Why is the death of a pet often experienced as a significant loss?
14. What are some ways that children can be helped in coping with the death of a parent?
15. What is an "inner representation of the deceased," and how is it related to a child's grief for a parent's death?
16. What are some issues that should be considered in a child's experience of a parent's death?
17. How does the death of a sibling potentially affect the surviving child's sense of vulnerability?
18. What are some issues that should be considered in a child's experience of a sibling's death?
19. How might parental responses influence a child's ability to cope with a sibling's death?
20. Why is it important to share information about change and loss with children?
21. What are the main guidelines for sharing information about death with children?
22. What are some of the important considerations in talking with children about death before a crisis occurs, when a family member is seriously ill, and in the aftermath of a loss?
23. When discussing death with children, why is listening often more important than speaking?
24. Why is it important to verify what a child understands about what you've said about death?
25. What are some factors to consider when discussing *beliefs* with children?
26. How might books be used with children as an aid to their understanding of and coping with death?
27. What are some of the support groups for ill and bereaved children?
28. How do you interpret Erik Erikson's statement "Healthy children will not fear life if their parents have the integrity not to fear death"?

Practice Test Questions

MULTIPLE CHOICE

1. Research conducted by Mark Speece showed that children between the ages of one and three
   a. are unable to deal with death-related experiences.
   b. are unable to respond to death-related experiences.
   c. come to terms with death-related experiences.
   d. pretend that they understand death.

2. When a seriously ill child uses distancing strategies, it is usually because he or she
   a. has concerns about spreading the illness.
   b. wants to psychologically deny the illness.
   c. requires complete isolation from other people.
   d. wants to limit the number of close relationships.

3. A parent's death is perceived as a loss of all of the following EXCEPT
   a. security.
   b. nurture.
   c. affection.
   d. memories.

4. According to David Balk, which of the following is most likely to cause adolescents to ask questions about the nature of life and death, about good and evil, and about the meaning of life?
   a. death of brother or sister
   b. death of pet
   c. death of teacher
   d. death of child

5. In situations involving a seriously ill child, a lack of communication between parent and child
   a. sustains the child's emotional stability.
   b. thwarts needs for affection and reassurance.
   c. exemplifies child preceding parent in death.
   d. harms because of mutual resentment in final days.

TRUE/FALSE

_____ 1. Games like cowboys and indians reflect a child's efforts to understand the place of death in his or her world.

_____ 2. Myra Bluebond-Langner observed that sick children usually were able to guess their condition by interpreting how people behaved toward them.

_____ 3. Recent studies show that children are NOT capable of experiencing grief because their level of cognitive development does not allow them to fully understand death.

_____ 4. It is best to wait to introduce the topic of death to a child until after the death of someone close occurs so that the child will understand the conversation better.

5. In using bibliotherapy as an aid in coping, books that use euphemisms are ideal for young children.

MATCHING

Match each type of loss with the corresponding characteristic.

_____ 1. Death of a pet

_____ 2. Death of a parent

_____ 3. Death of a sibling

_____ 4. Change in family relationship(s)

a. may be experienced as a "little death"

b. grieving openly may elicit ridicule from others

c. may involve mourning the years of "lost relationship"

d. minimizing contact or overprotection may result

❧ Answers to practice questions can be found in Part IV ❧

Related Readings

📖 Indicates selection from *The Path Ahead: Readings in Death and Dying,* ed. Lynne Ann DeSpelder and Albert Lee Strickland (Mountain View, Calif.: Mayfield, 1995).

CHILDREN: GENERAL WORKS

Charles A. Corr and David E. Balk, eds. *Handbook of Adolescent Death and Bereavement.* New York: Springer, 1996.

Charles A. Corr and Donna M. Corr, eds. *Handbook of Childhood Death and Bereavement.* New York: Springer, 1996.

CHILDREN AND GRIEF

Myra Bluebond-Langner. *In the Shadow of Illness: Parents and Siblings of the Chronically Ill Child.* Princeton, N.J.: Princeton University Press, 1996.

Betty Carmack. *Grieving the Death of a Pet.* Minneapolis: Augsburg, 2003.

Mary Ann Emswiler and James P. Emswiler. *Guiding Your Child Through Grief.* New York: Bantam, 2000.

Linda Goldman. *Life & Loss: A Guide to Help Grieving Children,* 2nd ed. Philadelphia: Accelerated Development, 2000.

Dianne McKissock. *The Grief of Our Children.* Sidney: Australian Broadcasting Commission, 1998.

Dan Schaefer and Christine Lyons. *How Do We Tell the Children? A Step-by-Step Guide for Helping Children Two to Teen Cope When Someone Dies.* New York: Newmarket Press, 2002.

Wallace Sife. The *Loss of a Pet,* rev. ed. New York: Howell, 1998.

📖 Phyllis R. Silverman, Steven Nickman, and J. William Worden, "Detachment Revisited: The Child's Reconstruction of a Dead Parent," pp. 260–270.

📖 Avery D. Weisman, "Bereavement and Companion Animals," pp. 276–280.

J. William Worden. *Children and Grief: When a Parent Dies.* New York: Guilford, 1996.

CHILDREN AND LIFE-THREATENING ILLNESS

📖 William G. Bartholome, "Care of the Dying Child: The Demands of Ethics," pp. 133–143.

Robert W. Buckingham. *Care of the Dying Child: A Practical Guide for Those Who Help Others.* New York: Continuum, 1989.

Shelley Geballe, Janice Gruendel, and Warren Andiman, eds. *Forgotten Children of the AIDS Epidemic.* New Haven, Conn.: Yale University Press, 1995.

Anne Hunsaker Hawkins. *A Small. Good Thing: Stories of Children With HIV and Those Who Care for Them.* New York: Norton, 2000.

Leigh A. Woznick and Carol D. Goodheart. *Living with Childhood Cancer: A Practical Guide to Help Families Cope.* Washington, D.C.: American Psychological Association, 2002.

CHILDREN AND OTHER ENCOUNTERS WITH DEATH

📖 Zlata Filipovic, "Zlata's Diary: A Child's Life in Sarajevo," pp. 175–178.

📖 James Garbarino, "Challenges We Face in Understanding Children and War: A Personal Essay," pp. 169–174.

James Garbarino, Nancy Dubrow, Kathleen Kostelny, and Carole Pardo. *Children in Danger: Coping with the Consequences of Community Violence.* San Francisco: Jossey-Bass, 1992.

📖 Ice T, "The Killing Fields," pp. 178–181.

Organizations and Internet Resources

All Kids Grieve: <www.allkidsgrieve.org/home.html>. This website has numerous resources for understand children and teens. See especially the literature review titled, "How children understand death and loss," which focuses on the development of the concept of death.

American Library Association: <www.ala.org>. 50 East Huron, Chicago, IL 60611-2795. (800) 545-2433. Fax: (312) 944-7671. The Association for Library Service to Children, a division of the ALA, produces listings of books and web sites for children, teens, parents, and teachers.

Big Brothers/Big Sisters of America: <www.bbbsa.org>. 230 North 13th Street, Philadelphia, PA 19107. (215) 567-7000. Fax: (215) 567-0394. E-mail: <national@bbbsa.org>. Help for children who are without a parent because of divorce, death, or other losses.

Helping Children Deal with Grief: <http://users.erols.com/lgold>. Information from Linda Goldman designed to assist grieving children. Site also has a section "for kids only."

Kansas City Hospice: <www.kansascityhospice.org>. 9221 Ward Parkway, Suite 100, Kansas City, MO 64114. (816) 363-2600. This organization's "Safe Passage Series" includes a booklet available online covering various aspects of talking to children about death, including a listing of children's books.

Kids in the Middle: <www.kidsinthemiddle.org>. 121 West Monroe, St Louis, MO 63122. (314) 909-9922. Resources for children and adults experiencing loss owing to family transitions such as divorce, separation, or remarriage.

Starlight Children's Foundation: <www.starlight.org>. International Headquarters, Suite 2530, 5900 Wilshire Blvd., Los Angeles, CA 90036. (323) 634-0080. Fax: (323) 634-0090. Helps fulfill the wishes of terminally and chronically ill children. Administers programs in 50 states and internationally through various chapters.

Sunshine Foundation: <www.sunshinefoundation.org>. 1041 Mill Creek Drive, Feasterville, PA 19053. (215) 396-4770 or (800) 767-1976. Fax: (215) 396-4774. Volunteer organization dedicated to fulfilling the wishes of dying children.

Sunshine Foundation of Canada: <www.sunshine.wwdc.com>. 1710-148 Fullerton Street, London, Ontario, Canada N6A 5P3. (519) 642-0990 or (800) 461-7935. With over 30 chapters across Canada, "Sunshine Dreams for Kids" fulfills wishes for children living with severe physical disabilities or life-threatening illnesses.

❧ Additional resources are available online at mhhe.com ❧

Major Points in This Chapter

- Children with life-threatening illness are usually able to guess their condition by observing and interpreting the behavior of adults in their environment.
- Sick children use a variety of coping mechanisms to deal with anxiety, confusion, and the sometimes painful treatments that accompany life-threatening illness.
- A child's experience of grief is influenced by such factors as age, stage of mental development, patterns of family interaction and communication, the nature of the relationship with the person (or pet) who has died, and previous experiences with death.
- Grief in response to the death of a pet is normal for adults as well as children.
- Studies of children who have experienced a parent's death reveal that children typically construct an "inner representation" (manifested in memories, feelings, and actions) that is used to maintain a relationship with the dead parent. The nature of this relationship changes as the child grows older and acute grief diminishes.
- Books for children and adolescents are a source of information and insight about dying, death, and bereavement; they offer opportunities for sharing between adults and young people.
- Honest communication tailored to a child's level of comprehension can promote healthy coping with life-threatening illness and grief.
- In discussing death with children, it is important to listen carefully and verify what they understand. Accept the reality of the child's grief and answer questions honestly and directly.
- Social support for children includes many of the same kinds of options available to adults who are coping with life-threatening illness or bereavement. Besides peer-oriented support groups, there are programs that focus on the needs of specific populations (such as inner-city children bereaved as a result of drive-by shootings and other types of violence) and programs that seek to grant the wishes of children with serious illness.

Observations and Reflections

Support groups for bereaved children and families are becoming more widespread. Check the resources in your community to determine the availability and type of support. You may find peer support, open-ended, drop-in, structured, volunteer-based, professionally facilitated, free or fee-for-service programs. If you had a loss during your childhood, were any of these services available in your community? Would you, or did you, take advantage of these support programs? Check for similar resources for children with life-threatening illnesses.

Use the space below to record your notes and responses to the topics covered in this chapter.

➠ *Explaining Death to Children: An Example from the Popular Press*

Directions: *As you read the following excerpt from a contemporary paperback horror novel, think about your readings from* The Last Dance. *After you read the excerpt, respond to the review questions in the spaces provided on the following page.*

Tuck wiped the tears from his eyes as he pondered this. "Daddy?"

"Yes, Tuck?"

"Are we still going to move?"

"Not for the time being. Maybe in a little while."

Tuck fiddled with a button on his shirt. "I'm glad we didn't leave," he returned. "You know why."

"Why?"

"Because that would have meant that we were leaving Ben behind." After this remark Tuck continued to fumble distractedly with his shirt button, gazing meditatively off into space. David drew in his breath, grateful at least that Tuck had not phrased the remark in the form of a question, and hugged his son tighter. Nonetheless, a moment later David noticed that Tuck's expression had taken on a darker cast, and as he continued to stare off into the distance some inner voice seemed to be speaking to him, prodding him with things he found painful.

"Daddy?"

"Yes, Tuck?"

"Is Ben ever coming back?"

David closed his eyes as he embraced his son tighter still. It was the question he had been dreading. As long as he himself had been ignorant of Ben's fate it had been easy to be evasive, to postpone confronting the matter. But now that he knew the truth he was left in a quandary. The last thing in the world he wanted to do was tell Tuck the truth, for he feared it would send Tuck even further into his ever-increasing depressions. But after what he had said about Mrs. Comfrey he felt he had no right to lie. He took a deep breath.

"No, Tuck. Ben isn't coming back."

Tuck remained absolutely motionless, absorbing the information with no visible sign of distress.

"Why not?" he asked.

David took another deep breath. "Do you know how every fall the flowers die and the leaves fall off the trees? Do you know why they do that?"

Tuck shook his head in the negative. "Cause winter's coming?" he offered tentatively.

"Partly because the winter's coming," David returned. "But partly because they have to make room for the new flowers and leaves. You see, that's the way nature works. Everything has a beginning and an end. If it didn't the world would become stagnant, like a bucket of water that you just let sit and sit. Can you imagine what the world would be like if everything lasted forever? Just think about it. Every bee that ever lived, every tree and every person would still be here, and what a crowded place it would be. The only problem is that it's painful when things we love go away. We miss them and that's okay. But what's not okay is to think that it's bad that things have to go away, because it's not bad. It's a very important thing. It's what allows new flowers to grow, and new leaves to replace the old, and the world to renew itself."

"And Ben went away?"

"Yes, Ben went away."

"Where did he go?"

"To heaven," David replied.

Tuck's lower lip started to quiver. "But why did he have to go to heaven?"

"Because it was his time to go."

A large tear rolled down Tuck's cheek and hit David's arm, and he gave his son another reassuring hug. "Hey, now, I don't want you to be upset about this. I told you the truth about Ben because I don't want you to be afraid when things have to go to heaven. Too many people in this world spend too much time being afraid of that, and it's just silly. When something goes to heaven it's a scary thing, and it's a painful thing. But you've got to be brave about it. Things don't go to heaven very often, but when they do, you've got to face it like a man."

Tuck wiped the tear from his eye. "I've got to have moxie, huh, Dad?"

David smiled. He had forgotten about that. "Yes, Tuck. You've got to have moxie."

⟶ *Review Questions for* **The Bog.**

1. Which euphemism does the father use when describing what happened to Ben?

   _____ (Underline each appearance in the excerpt.)

2. Review Table 1.2 in Chapter 1 of *The Last Dance.* Pick another euphemism and substitute it for the one in the story excerpt. How does the discussion read now?

   _____

   _____

3. Using Piaget's model of cognitive development, discussed in Chapter 2, what

   developmental phase is presumed in the father's explanation? _____

   What age range is associated with this developmental phase? _____

   What are the characteristics of this phase? _____

   _____

   _____

4. What is the parental message about death that is being communicated in this story? _____

   _____

   _____

5. Based on the information given in the text and in class, evaluate the parental communication. Using specific examples, which elements of the communication do you believe are appropriate? _____

   _____

   _____

   Which are inadequate? _____

   _____

   _____

   _____

6. Given that the child in this story is a survivor of a high-grief death, what are at least five possible benefits to him that might result from this conversation?

_____

_____

_____

_____

_____

_____

_____

7. Does it seem that descriptions of talking with children about death are rare in contemporary paperback novels? _____

_____

_____

_____

8. What editorial advice would you give to the author if you knew that the child in this story was five years old? _____

_____

_____

_____

_____

_____

_____

_____

_____

178 ～ Chapter 10

Journey Through The Last Dance, 7th ed.
Activities and Resources

⟫➡ *Factors and Variables That Influence Grief Reactions in Bereaved Children*

Directions: *Read Carol Berns's list of factors that can influence a child's grief. Circle the numbers of those you identify as particularly important. In the space provided following this text, add your own factors to the list.*

1. **Age, cognitive development, and life experiences**: Can the child verbalize his or her sense of what has occurred? Does the child have a mature understanding of death?

2. **Early attachment patterns**: Researchers identify early patterns of attachment as determinants of whether a child may be resilient or vulnerable to later stressful life events.

3. **Genetic factors and medical history**: The role of genetic factors is difficult to determine; however, children with genetic susceptibility, such as depression, may have their vulnerability triggered by bereavement.

4. **Previous losses**: Has the child experienced prior losses? If those losses have been unaddressed or poorly managed, the risk of poor resolution in this loss may be increased.

5. **The role of the child's personality prior to bereavement**: How does this child see himself or herself? Children who perceive themselves as capable and take responsibility for themselves after a death often gain mastery over their environment. Having *acted* on rather than *reacted* to the loss, they can develop self-esteem, strength, and confidence that helps with later stresses.

6. **The preexisting relationship between the bereaved and the deceased**: The more ambivalent or dependent the relationship, the more complex the mourning and greater probability of a poor outcome. The level of intimacy and the complexity of the relationship will affect grief.

7. **The amount of "unfinished business" between the bereaved and the deceased**: Unfinished business refers to those issues left unsettled or never addressed.

8. **The type of death**: Sudden, unexpected, and untimely deaths are more likely to be associated with difficult outcomes than are anticipated deaths. However, death from a lingering, terminal illness may also lead to difficult outcomes. Is this death viewed as preventable, as with an accidental poisoning or suicide?

9. **The circumstances and nature of the death**: How, when, and where did the person die? Is the death in the natural order of expected deaths in the family? Have older members already died? Was the child present at the time of death? Did the deceased suffer in dying, or was he or she disfigured in death? Was this loss violent, the result of suicide or murder? Did it occur in wartime, or in a faraway location? Was the body found? If the death was caused by homicide, the child can have vengeful thoughts, intense anger, and revenge fantasies towards the killer. When the killer cannot be identified, the fantasies may be greater and the grief more difficult.

10. **Intensity of guilt or responsibility**: What intensity of guilt or responsibility is the child experiencing? Children often ask, "Could I have saved him/her?" Magical thinking and confused notions of what happened will need clarification.

11. **Change in child's role**: To what extent has the child's role changed since the death? The child whose only sibling dies becomes an only child, perhaps having to take on more responsibility in his or her parents' eyes. The child may place added pressure on himself or herself. Can the child be helped to move through the grief naturally, rather than be subject to unnecessary pressure?

12. **Current stress or crises**: Stress, crises, or other losses occurring during bereavement may demand the child's resources, thereby creating extra pressure and impeding healing.

13. **Sanctioned by society**: Is this a disenfranchised grief, or does society or the social/cultural group sanction this loss? When a loss is not socially validated—that is, not acknowledged by society as an important loss to be mourned—the child is put in a difficult situation. This may be the case when the relationship is unrecognized, not understood, or largely unaccepted by society. Examples may include a child losing a pet, a grandparent, a newborn sibling to Sudden Infant Death Syndrome, a best friend or classmate, a parent's former live-in mate, a nanny, or a non-relative caregiver.

14. **Availability of community support**: Is there an aftercare program or school awareness program? Is there a church, community, or school bereavement group?

15. **Coincidental deaths or losses**: Were there simultaneous deaths in a family or community? For example, a multiple car accident or major disaster? In such cases, the grief is more complex and there may be less comfort and support available. Coincidental losses render the child especially vulnerable because the different losses each need to be individually grieved and support may not be available.

16. **The responses of the family and social network**: A poor outcome is more likely when the child perceives his or her family and social network as not supportive in terms of sharing in or allowing for expression of grief, or when there is chaos in the family and members fail to support each other. Enmeshed or disengaged family patterns, in which individuals lack tolerance for different responses or cohesion for mutual support, is problematic. Is there healthful family modeling? Is there support for emotional expression?

17. **Religious-cultural-ethnic influence and accessibility**: Does the religious, cultural, or ethnic identification affect how grief is acknowledged? The child's responses to loss and death generally reflect the norms, mores, and sanctions of the immediate sociocultural environment. Religious faith or belief may increase the comfort, support, and hope, or may instead increase guilt, regret, and despair. Is a spiritual leader available?

18. **Successive deaths or losses**: When losses, death, or disaster follow in quick succession, the grief over one may be distracted or disturbed by the shock and grief over the next. "Bereavement overload" can occur when an individual has experienced too many deaths, either as serial losses or simultaneous losses.

19. **The behavior, attitudes, and responsiveness of parents and other significant adults in the child's environment**: Is an open display of emotions allowed? Is communication encouraged? Are there secrets, myths, or taboos surrounding death? Does the family belief system invoke blame, shame, or guilt surrounding death? Is healing, growth, laughter encouraged?

20. **Sociodemographic factors**: Chronological and developmental age, gender, religion, culture, and parental occupation and economic position are factors that influence outcome.

21. **Environmental factors**: Is the child in a dangerous home environment or neighborhood? Does he or she see movies or television programs that show destruction and violence? Is the household unstable?

22. **New losses or changes**: What other losses or changes might occur because of this death? "Secondary losses" are those losses that develop as a consequence of a loved one's death. Will a surviving parent have to work away from home or be away longer hours? Will the child's extracurricular activities be changed or terminated? Will family activities be altered? Will there be a change in economic status?

23. **Subsequent life circumstances for the child**: Have siblings or friends reacted by withdrawing from the child? Will there be a change in schools? Is the surviving parent dating or thinking of remarriage?

24. **Involvement by the media**: Children may experience discomfort when what is private for them is made public.

Use the space below and on the following page to list and describe additional factors that you think are important in dealing with a child's grief.

_____

_____

_____

_____

_____

_____

_____

_____

_____

_____

_____

⇒ *Tools for Helping Bereaved Children*

Directions: *Read each of the items below. (Note how most also apply to children who have a life-threatening illness or who have a seriously ill loved one.) In the blank next to each statement, use the following codes to indicate your opinion.*

SA = Strongly Agree

A = Agree

NA = No Opinion

D = Disagree

SD = Strongly Disagree

_____ 1. Know your own feelings.

_____ 2. Know your expectations. What do you expect to give? What do you expect in return? Why are you offering it?

_____ 3. Be guided by the child's needs, not your own.

_____ 4. Be a good observer. Watch body language and emotional expression.

_____ 5. Listen to unspoken as well as verbal language. Listen for themes, cues, fantasies, and feelings.

_____ 6. Realize that responses may not be obvious and immediate.

_____ 7. Give permission for the child to feel anything. Allow him/her to hurt, grieve, and express grief.

_____ 8. Don't rush through the "stages." Keep in check your impulse to guide the grief process. Each child grieves at his/her own pace and in his/her own way.

_____ 9. Remember that there are no right or wrong ways to grieve.

_____ 10. Help find constructive outlets for energy, anger, fears, and tears.

_____ 11. Maintain discipline. Consistency and strong guides are comforting in a world where everything else seems shattered, confused, and chaotic.

_____ 12. Regressive to aggressive behavior is common. Be supportive rather than punitive.

_____ 13. Do not condone misbehavior. Change or grief should never be excuses for antisocial conduct.

_____ 14. Continue to expect appropriate behaviors. Temper your expectations with kindness and understanding, but continue to expect functioning and participation.

_____ 15. Help a child find a supportive peer group. Children sharing with children works wonders.

_____ 16. Become part of a caring team by communicating with school, family, religious group, and community.

_____ 17. If the child's or family's religious beliefs are strong, use the teachings and faith. Faith may be very valuable in giving the child hope and reinvigorating inner resources.

_____ 18. Grieving children need to establish their roles and current identity. Help them in their search.

_____ 19. Remember that children and young people will continue to deal with their loss as they mature. The loss will be revisited as they gain new understandings, life experiences, and insights. Continue to be available long after you think they "should be over it."

_____ 20. Recognize that no one lives forever. Nothing lasts or stays the same. Acknowledge this and provide support and guidance.

_____ 21. Be open and honest. Create an atmosphere of acceptance that invites questions and fosters confidence and trust.

_____ 22. Be available for continued support. Have some fun.

Use the space below to add several items to this list.

_____ 23. _____

_____ 24. _____

_____ 25. _____

_____ 26. _____

_____ 27. _____

_____ 28. _____

_____ 29. _____

_____ 30. _____

_____ 31. _____

_____ 32. _____

_____ 33. _____

_____ 34. _____

Death in the Lives of Adults

Chapter Summary

Chapter 11 continues the lifespan perspective of the previous chapter by focusing on loss experiences during adulthood. As with the years of childhood, particular psychosocial concerns—or developmental crises—are emphasized during the various stages of adulthood. Young adulthood is characterized by concerns involving intimacy versus isolation, middle adulthood by concerns involving generativity versus stagnation, and maturity by concerns involving integrity versus despair. The meaning given to a loss event—that is, how it is interpreted—depends in significant measure on the nature of the developmental issues being dealt with by the individual experiencing the loss.

In the normal course of events, the incidence of loss increases as we grow older. Besides confronting the prospect of our own mortality as a result of aging, growing older increases the chances that we will experience the deaths of our parents, and, conversely, that, as parents, we may experience the death of a child. For most parents, a child's death is devastating. It represents not only a loss of the potential and unique future envisioned for the child, but also the loss of a kind of genetic and social immortality for the parent.

In coping with the death of a child, the individuals within a couple relationship may have different styles of grieving the loss, and both may be overwhelmed by a sense of general chaos, confusion, and uncertainty. Each partner may feel isolated and unsupported by the only other person who shares the magnitude of the loss. Behavior that is meant to be supportive may be interpreted by one's mate as being otherwise. Conflict is reduced and positive interaction promoted when couples engage in open and honest communication, share emotional responses as well as information, and validate one another's perception of the loss.

Miscarriage, induced abortion, stillbirth, and neonatal death are examples of childbearing losses that sometimes go unrecognized, unsupported, and unresolved. Yet the grief experienced by parents following such losses may be just as devastating as that resulting from the death of an older child. This is true also of individuals who give up a child for adoption or who find themselves unable to have children because of sterility or infertility. In mourning *unlived lives*, grief is felt not only for the physical loss but also for the symbolic loss. When a person's identity as a nurturing parent is thwarted, healing the grief requires honoring the archetypal bonds between parent and child. It also requires that the wider community acknowledge the loss so that the necessary solace and social support can be offered to the bereaved person.

Adult survivors of a parent's death often encounter not only the loss of security represented by a parent's love and support but also a reminder of their own mortality. Studies indicate that, for most midlife adults, the death of a parent is an important symbolic event, one that triggers a period of self-examination accompanied by a transition to a more mature stance toward life.

Spousal bereavement has been termed the most disruptive of all the transitions in the life cycle. The aftermath of a mate's death requires a multitude of adjustments. What were once shared pleasures become occasions for individual pain. Age, gender, and the nature of the relationship are among important factors that influence the experience of spousal bereavement. Research indicates that individuals who have lived out traditional sex roles may find the transition especially difficult. New skills must be learned to manage the needs of daily life. The availability of a stable social network appears to be crucial in determining how bereaved spouses adjust to their changed status. Besides maintaining the continuity of relationships with friends, neighbors, and family, one of the most valuable resources for the recently widowed is contact with other bereaved persons who have lost a mate and who can serve as role models.

For the older adult, the experience of aging typically involves losses related to a variety of physical and mental declines. Although the debilitating effects of aging are being steadily pushed toward the end of the human lifespan, thus "compressing" morbidity and extending "active" life expectancy, the processes of senescence—the aging of the human organism—eventually result in greater frailty and susceptibility to illness and injury. To receive adequate care, many frail older people require institutional or community support, such as that provided by personal care homes, skilled nursing facilities, and home health care agencies. Yet, growing old is not essentially a medical problem. The latter part of life has its own distinct challenges. Facing death has been characterized as the final developmental task of old age.

Objectives
- To list and describe Erik Erikson's psychosocial stages of adult development.
- To identify the kinds of losses adults experience.
- To distinguish the characteristics of parental bereavement and to identify the types of support available.
- To compare and contrast the emotional responses to miscarriage, abortion, stillbirth, neonatal death, sudden infant death syndrome, and loss of the "perfect" child.
- To describe disenfranchised grief, with examples of its occurrence, and to identify how grief resulting from such losses can be facilitated.
- To explain family interaction patterns that may be observed when a child is seriously or terminally ill.
- To compare and contrast ways of caring for a child who is seriously or terminally ill.
- To identify the factors influencing grief in response to the death of an adult child.

- To describe the factors influencing spousal bereavement and to summarize the types of social support available.
- To distinguish the factors influencing the response to the death of a parent.
- To identify the factors influencing grief in response to the death of a friend.
- To summarize the physiological and psychological changes that typically occur with aging.

Key Terms and Concepts

adoption loss
adulthood
childbearing losses
developmental push
induced abortion
infertility
maturity
miscarriage
mizuko
neonatal death
parent death
parental bereavement

postneonatal death
reframing
senescence
spontaneous abortion
spousal bereavement
sterility
stillbirth
sudden infant death syndrome (SIDS)
symbolic loss
widowhood
wished-for child

Questions for Guided Study and Review

1. How do the psychosocial stages of adulthood relate to coping with death?
2. What are some of the common features as well as unique features of the various types of parental bereavement?
3. What are the characteristics that tend to make the death of a child a high-grief death?
4. What factors influence conflict and cooperation in coping with parental bereavement as a couple?
5. What is *reframing,* and why is it important?
6. What are the various childbearing losses?
7. What is the difference between *miscarriage* and *stillbirth?*
8. How might the birth of a severely disabled child evoke grief in terms of the concept of a "wished-for" child?
9. What are the dynamics of blame and anger in childbearing losses?
10. How does disenfranchised grief relate to childbearing losses?
11. What are some ways that hospitals can help parents cope with stillbirth?
12. What is SIDS?
13. What factors tend to complicate grief from a SIDS death?
14. How might different reasons for abortion lead to different loss reactions?
15. What are "water children"?
16. What are the major causes of death for school-age children?
17. What special factors in parental bereavement are likely to accompany the death of an adult child?
18. What kind of social support is available for bereaved parents?
19. How does the death of a parent affect the survivor?

20. What factors are important in affecting the outcome of spousal bereavement?
21. What kind of social support is available for widows and widowers?
22. When does aging begin?
23. What is *senescence*?
24. How does the National Council on Aging categorize older people?
25. In what ways do stereotypes of older people differ from the reality?
26. What are the steps to be considered in choosing a nursing care facility?
27. What is the meaning of the statement "Growing old is not essentially a medical problem?"

Practice Test Questions

MULTIPLE CHOICE

1. According to Erik Erikson, the different stages of psychosocial development are
   a. unrelated and separate.
   b. connected and evolutionary.
   c. specific to childhood and adolescence.
   d. parallel and unconnected.

2. When a child dies, parents usually feel
   a. anxious because they have not discussed death with the child.
   b. sad because they have not spent enough time with the child.
   c. regret because they have been unable to protect the child.
   d. resigned because they could do nothing about it.

3. Conflicting views about which type of childbearing loss may place the bereaved in a dilemma?
   a. spontaneous abortion
   b. induced abortion
   c. neonatal death
   d. postneonatal death

4. Which of the following support groups would likely be most appropriate for a parent whose child has been diagnosed with cancer?
   a. Candlelighters
   b. Compassionate Friends
   c. Parents of Children with Cancer
   d. The Cancer Foundation

5. Which of the following are among the reasons typically given by older people for accepting death?
   1. Death is preferable to losing one's friends.
   2. Death is preferable to loss of mental faculties.
   3. Death is preferable to loss of ability to be useful.
   4. Death is preferable to becoming a burden.

   a. 1, 3, and 4
   b. 1, 2, and 3
   c. 1, 2, and 4
   d. 2, 3, and 4

TRUE/FALSE

_____ 1. Differing interpretations of their partner's behavior may cause conflict between bereaved couples.

_____ 2. A childbearing loss during the early stages of pregnancy usually evokes feelings of disappointment but not grief.

_____ 3. The death of a father is generally a "higher-grief" loss than the death of a mother

_____ 4. Peer contact is one of the most valuable resources for the recently widowed.

_____ 5. According to the text, there are few opportunities to openly mourn the death of a friend.

MATCHING

Match each of the following terms with the appropriate definition.

_____ 1. Neonatal death   a. occurs prior to the twentieth week of pregnancy

_____ 2. Postneonatal death   b. occurs between the twentieth week of pregnancy and birth

_____ 3. Miscarriage   c. occurs during the first four weeks after birth

_____ 4. Stillbirth   d. occurs after the first four weeks and up to eleven months after birth

❧ Answers to practice questions can be found in Part IV ❧

Related Readings

📖 Indicates selection from *The Path Ahead: Readings in Death and Dying,* ed. Lynne Ann DeSpelder and Albert Lee Strickland (Mountain View, Calif.: Mayfield, 1995).

GENERAL READINGS

📖 Thomas Attig, "Coping with Mortality: An Essay on Self-Mourning," pp. 337–341.

📖 Sandra L. Bertman, "Bearing the Unbearable: From Loss, the Gain," pp. 348–354.

Charles W. Brice. "Mourning Throughout the Life Cycle," *American Journal of Psychoanalysis* 42, no. 4 (1982): 320–321.

📖 Kenneth J. Doka, "Disenfranchised Grief," pp. 271–275.

📖 John D. Kelly, "Grief: Re-forming Life's Story," pp. 242–245.

📖 Alfred G. Killilea, "The Politics of Being Mortal," pp. 342–347.

DEATH OF A CHILD

Glen W. Davidson, "Stillbirth, Neonatal Death, and Sudden Infant Death Syndrome." In *Childhood and Death,* edited by Hannelore Wass and Charles A. Corr, 243–260. Washington, D.C.: Hemisphere, 1995.

📖 Stephen J. Fleming and Leslie Balmer, "Bereaved Families of Ontario: A Mutual-Help Model for Families Experiencing Death," pp. 281–288.

Kathleen R. Gilbert and Laura S. Smart. *Coping with Infant or Fetal Loss: The Couple's Healing Process.* New York: Brunner/Mazel, 1992.

Henya Kagan-Klein. *Gili's Book: A Journey into Bereavement for Parents and Counselors.* New York: Teachers College Press, 1998.

📖 Klass, "Solace and Immortality: Bereaved Parents' Continuing Bond with Their Children," pp. 246–259.

Dennis Klass. *Parental Grief: Solace and Resolution.* New York: Springer, 1988.

Ronald J. Knapp. *Beyond Endurance: When a Child Dies.* New York: Schocken, 1986.

Hannah Lothrop. *Help, Comfort, and Hope After Losing Your Baby in Pregnancy or the First Year.* Tucson, Ariz.: Fisher Books, 1997.

Donald M. Murray. *The Lively Shadow: Living with the Death of a Child.* New York: Ballantine, 2003.

Judith A. Savage. *Mourning Unlived Lives: A Psychological Study of Childbearing Loss.* Wilmette, Ill.: Chiron Publications, 1989.

Kay Talbot. *What Forever Means After the Death of a Child.* New York: Brunner-Routledge, 2002.

DEATH OF A PARENT

Andrew E. Scharlach and Karen I. Fredriksen. "Reactions to the Death of a Parent During Midlife," *Omega: Journal of Death and Dying* 27, no. 4 (1993): 307–319.

📖 Janmarie Silvera, "Crossing the Border," pp. 301–302.

Harold Ivan Smith. *Grieving the Death of a Mother.* Minneapolis: Augsburg, 2003.

SPOUSAL BEREAVEMENT

Susan Heinlein, Grace Brumett, and Jane Tibbals, eds. *When a Lifemate Dies: Stories of Love, Loss, and Healing.* Minneapolis: Fairview Press, 1997.

Phyllis R. Silverman. *Widow to Widow.* New York: Springer, 1986.

📖 Margaret Stroebe, Mary M. Gergen, Kenneth J. Gergen, and Wolfgang Stroebe, "Broken Hearts or Broken Bonds: Love and Death in Historical Perspective," pp. 231–241.

Jill Truman. *Letter to My Husband: Notes About Mourning and Recovery.* New York: Viking Penguin, 1987.

AGING

Pamela T. Amoss and Steven Harrell, eds. *Other Ways of Growing Old: Anthropological Perspectives.* Palo Alto, Calif.: Stanford University Press, 1981.

Stanley Brandes. *Forty: The Age and the Symbol.* Nashville: University of Tennessee Press, 1985.

📖 Allan B. Chinen, "The Mortal King," pp. 335–336.

Jane W. Peterson. "Age of Wisdom: Elderly Black Women in Family and Church." In *The Cultural Context of Aging: Worldwide Perspectives,* edited by Jay Sokolovsky, 213–227. New York: Bergin & Garvey, 1990.

Organizations and Internet Resources

American Association of Retired Persons (AARP): <www.aarp.org/griefandloss>. 601 E. Street, NW, Washington, DC 20049. (800) 424-3410. Resources and information about the death of a spouse, including caregiving issues and phone support.

American Life League: <www.all.org>. P.O. Box 1350, Stafford, VA 22555. (540) 659-4171. Advocates "Human Life Amendment" to U.S. Constitution to legally recognize personhood of the unborn.

American SIDS Institute: <www.sids.org>. 2480 Windy Hill Road, Suite 380, Marietta, GA 30067. (770) 612-1030 or (800) 232-7437. Fax: (770) 612-8277. Resources for families affected by Sudden Infant Death Syndrome.

Hospice Foundation of America: <www.hospicefoundation.org>. 2001 S Street NW, Suite 300, Washington, DC 20009. (800) 854-3402. Fax: (202) 638-5312. Excellent resources on grief and the loss of a partner. Includes extensive listing of bereavement resources.

LAMDA Institute of Gay and Lesbian Studies: <www.ualberta.ca/~cbidwell/cmb/lambda.htm>. 10654 82nd Avenue NW, Edmonton, Alberta T6E 2A7, Canada. (780) 988-2194. Fax: (780) 988-2112. Promotes research into lesbian and gay issues and lifestyles. Provides education about the loss of a partner.

People Animals Love (PAL): <www.tidalwave.net/~pal>. Suite N, 14101 Parke Long Court, Chantilly, VA 20151. (703) 968-5744 or (888) 400-WAVE. Fax: (703) 803-0377. Provides pets (including veterinary care and food) to elderly, widowed, and institutionalized persons.

September Smiles: <www.septembersmiles.com>. 182 East 79th Street, Suite C2, New York, NY 10021. (203) 856-7917. Support for families in New York City dealing with tragic death, especially young families.

Share Pregnancy and Infant Loss Support: <www.nationalshareofffice.com>. 300 First Capitol Drive, St. Charles, MO 63301. (636) 947-6164 or (800) 821-6819. Fax: (636) 947-7486. Support groups and education regarding childbearing losses.

SIDS Alliance: <www.sidsalliance.org>. 1314 Bedford Avenue, Suite 210, Baltimore, Maryland 21208. (410) 653-8226. Fax: (410) 653-8709. Promotes infant health and survival through advocacy, education, and research. Also includes bereavement services for SIDS and other infant deaths.

USAA Educational Foundation: <www.uasadedfundation.org>. 9800 Fredericksburg Road, San Antonio, TX 78288. (800) 531-8159. Fax: (210) 498.9590. Information about coping with the loss of a spouse.

❧ Additional resources are available online at mhhe.com ❧

Major Points in This Chapter

- The meaning of death is interpreted differently as a person grows older. Erikson's model of psychosocial development identifies three stages of adulthood: young adulthood, adulthood, and maturity.

- Many issues of parental bereavement span the adult life cycle. They are present for twenty-year-old parents, forty-year-old parents, and eighty-year-old parents. To understand the nature of a particular parent's grief and the specific losses involved, both the parent's age and the child's age must be taken into account.

- The death of a child places considerable stress on the marital relationship; thus, it is important to be aware of ways to minimize potential conflict between grieving parents and to promote positive interactions that aid in coping with the tragedy of a child's death.

- Childbearing losses typically involve the sense of "mourning an unlived life."

- Perinatal bereavement support can be helpful to parents who experience childbearing loss. Support programs typically offer a variety of ways to recognize and affirm the loss, thereby facilitating healthy coping by the bereaved parent.

- Among children between the ages of five and fourteen, accidents are the leading cause of death.

- When a young person's life is threatened by serious illness, it affects the whole of family life. In families that deal openly with crisis, the parents tend not to derive their personal identity solely from the role of "being a parent."

- The death of a parent can have a lasting impact as a bereaved adult child mourns the loss of the special bond that had been shared with the deceased parent. The death of a parent can also evoke a "developmental push" as parentally bereaved adults no longer think of themselves as children.

- Because spousal bereavement often follows years of shared experience and mutual commitment, the death of a mate can disrupt the very meaning of the surviving partner's existence. The transition from being a couple to being single can be especially difficult when the surviving spouse is also a parent, because it involves the added burden of making a transition to single parenthood.

- The death of a close friend is a significant loss that can evoke grief similar to that experienced following the death of a relative. For older adults, friendships are sometimes more important than family relationships.

- The processes of aging may lead to a variety of debilitating conditions that are experienced as losses of various kinds. Older people may require assistance with many activities of daily life. Making appropriate care available and affordable is important not only to older people themselves and their relatives but also to society as a whole.

Observations and Reflections

It is likely that as an adult you have had some experience in dealing with the loss issues presented in this chapter—death of a mate or intended mate, miscarriage, abortion, perinatal death, death of a child, or death of a parent.

If this is the case, think about your experience and the issues involved. What information presented in this chapter allows you to understand your grief in a different way?

Consider also the issue of social support. Did you make use of a survivor support group of some kind? What other forms of social support have been useful to you in coping with loss and grief?

Use the space below and on the following page to make notes about the topics covered in this chapter and your own experiences.

⇒ *For an Adult Who Had a Parent Die in Childhood or Adolescence: An Assessment*

Directions: As a quick exercise to see how your experience compares to that of others who had a parent die in childhood or adolescence, check off any of the following statements which are true for you. (Adapted from Never the Same: Coming to Terms with the Death of a Parent, *by Donna Schuurman. [New York: St Martin's, 2003.])*

❏ When my parent died, no one really included me or explained everything that had happened or what was happening.

❏ For a long time after my parent's death, I felt alone and isolated, different.

❏ My family and other adults didn't talk together much about my deceased parent in the months following his or her death.

❏ My family members still don't talk about it much.

❏ Since the time my parent died, I've always felt different.

❏ No one gave me all the facts and information or answered all my questions. In fact, I still have unanswered questions, and there are many things I don't know that I'd like to know about what happened.

❏ I wasn't given a choice about attending the memorial service, funeral home, or cemetery.

❏ No one explained what decisions were being made about what we'd call the "disposition of the body." I had no opportunity to say how I felt about burial versus cremation, where my parent would be buried, the type of service, or participation in the service.

❏ Everyone in my family handled my parent's death in a different way. . . and still does.

❏ It was hard going back to school.

❏ I had many difficult times around holidays and the anniversary of my parent's death.

❏ I still have difficulties with holidays and the anniversary time of my parent's death.

❏ I didn't talk about it much to anyone back then.

❏ I haven't really talked all that much to others as an adult about the impact of my parent's death on me.

❏ I wanted to "protect" my surviving parent, so I didn't talk about it much with him or her.

❏ I felt different from other kids after my parent died.

❏ I didn't really know many, if any, other kids who'd had a parent die.

❏ There are parts of what happened when my parent died that I remember like they happened yesterday.

❏ I remember having some experiences or feelings that made me wonder if I was going crazy, or if something was wrong with me.

❏ There are parts of what happened when my parent died that remain a blur.

❏ For a long time I put it out of my mind and didn't think about it.

❏ We didn't do much as a family around the anniversary date of my parent's death.

❏ I sometimes wonder how things would have been different if my parent hadn't died.

❏ At some point in my adult life I realized my parent's death had a great impact on me.

❏ I suspect in some ways that my adult relationships have been affected by how I responded to my parent's death.

Scoring:

Now, count how many boxes you have checked: _____

Here's what your responses indicate:

If you checked 0–5 boxes:
If few of the 25 statements above are true for you, your experience is extremely rare. The adults around you apparently handled the aftermath of your parent's death in a supportive way and you have completed some significant work in your adult psychological life. Or you're in major denial!

If you checked 6–10 boxes:
Sounds like there was a great deal of support for you when your parent died and that you feel fairly resolved about how it affected you. You're in the minority here, but there still may be some avenues left for you to explore.

If you checked 11–15 boxes:
You're on the fence as far as your awareness of the impact of your parent's death on you as a child and what work you have left to do. There are still some important roads you have not walked along. Your sense of self and your relationships can be strengthened by applying the ideas and information in the book by Donna Schuurman, *Never the Same: Coming to Terms with the Death of a Parent.*

If you checked 16–20 boxes:
You will benefit tremendously from reading Donna Schuurman's *Never the Same*, hearing about the experiences of others, and exploring what your parent's death means for you now. You've likely had difficulty with intimacy in your relationships and have felt like something is disconnected inside you.

If you checked 21–25 boxes:
Stop whatever you have planned for the next several days, carve out some time alone, and read *Never the Same*. It could help you make significant positive changes in your life. The quality of all of your relationships is related to your relationship with yourself, and there are parts—important parts—you have not explored.

However many of these statements are true for you, take heart in the belief that you're exploring these issues at this time in your life because you're ready to do so. Experiencing your parent's death changed the course of your life in some good ways and in some ways that have not served you well. Your parent's death forced a premature maturity on you compared to your peers. As a result, you have a deeper inner knowing about what matters in life and how quickly people who matter can be taken away from us.

After completing this activity from Donna Schuurman's book, use the space below and on the following page to reflect on your experience.

_____

_____

_____

_____

_____

_____

_____

_____

_____

_____

_____

_____

_____

_____

_____

_____

_____

_____

_____

⌨ *Children and Life-threatening Illness: Internet Support*

Directions: *There is Internet support and information for adults dealing with the life-threatening illness of a child. In this activity, you will search and report on five websites. Rate each of the five sites from 1 (excellent) to 5 (very poor).*

Some places to start:

Pediatric Pain: Professional and Research Resources
<http://is.dal.ca/%7Epedpain/prohp.html>

Candlelighters Childhood Cancer Foundation
< www.candlelighters.org/>

HealthWeb: Pediatrics
< www.galter.nwu.edu/hw/ped/>

1. URL _____ Rating_____

   _____

   _____

   _____

   _____

   _____

   _____

   _____

2. URL _____ Rating_____

   _____

   _____

   _____

   _____

   _____

   _____

   _____

3. URL _____ Rating _____

_____

_____

_____

_____

_____

_____

_____

4. URL _____ Rating _____

_____

_____

_____

_____

_____

_____

_____

5. URL _____ Rating _____

_____

_____

_____

_____

_____

_____

_____

⤳ 🖥 *Death of a Child: Internet Support*

Directions: *There are many Internet sites devoted to information and support for adults grieving the death of a child. In this activity you will search and report on five websites. Rate each of the five sites from 1 (excellent) to 5 (very poor).*

Some places to start are:

> Bereaved Families Online
> <www.inforamp.net/~bfo/index.html>

> The Compassionate Friends

> SIDS Network
> <http://sids-network.org/>

1. URL _____ Rating_____

_____

_____

_____

_____

_____

_____

_____

2. URL _____ Rating_____

_____

_____

_____

_____

_____

_____

_____

3. URL _____ Rating _____

_____

_____

_____

_____

_____

_____

_____

4. URL _____ Rating _____

_____

_____

_____

_____

_____

_____

_____

5. URL _____ Rating _____

_____

_____

_____

_____

_____

_____

_____

Suicide

Chapter Summary

Chapter 12 examines suicidal behavior by focusing on theoretical explanations of suicide, types of suicide, risk factors influencing suicide, patterns of suicidal behavior during different stages of the lifespan, methods used in suicide, suicide notes, and efforts related to suicide prevention, intervention, and postvention. Until the late 1960s, suicide rates generally increased directly with age, with the lowest rates among the young and the highest among the aged. More recently, this pattern has shifted, with a decrease in the suicide rate among older persons being offset by an increase among adolescents and young adults. Both of these trends are due largely to changes in the behavior of white males, a group that accounts for the majority of suicides in the United States.

Generally speaking, suicide is listed as the cause of death only when circumstances are clear and unequivocal. Hesitancy about classifying a death as suicide is due largely to the social stigma of suicide, which is commonly viewed as a failure on the part of the person who dies by suicide, his or her family and friends, and society as a whole. Some automobile fatalities, for example, are believed to be suicides in disguise, as are some victim-precipitated homicides. Thus, the actual extent of suicide is likely to be greater than official statistics suggest.

One of the methods devised to improve the accuracy of suicide statistics is the *psychological autopsy*, which involves gathering information about the lifestyle of the victim, any stresses that he or she may have been experiencing, and any suicidal communications made prior to death. In addition to being an investigative tool for correctly classifying deaths, the psychological autopsy is a valuable research tool that can help to identify risk factors for suicide.

Efforts to explain suicidal behavior have generally examined either the social context in which it occurs or the mental and emotional dynamics within the life of the individual. Whereas the sociological model focuses on the relationship between the individual and society, the psychological model focuses on the individual's conscious as well as unconscious motivations. Both of these approaches contribute to our understanding of suicide. Suicide is best understood as behavior influenced by both culture and personality, as well as by the unique circumstances of an individual's situation.

Our understanding of suicide is also broadened by examining it from various perspectives, such as types of suicide, the nature of risk factors influencing it, and patterns of suicidal behavior throughout the lifespan. When we examine the characteristics of suicidal behavior, we can distinguish, for example, (1) suicide as escape (as with terminally ill persons who see no other exit from unremitting suffering), (2) subintentional and chronic suicide (in which the victim plays a partial or subliminal role in his or her own demise, perhaps over a period of time due to an unhealthy lifestyle), and (3) suicide as a "cry for help" (a form of communication intended to elicit some change, but that can have lethal consequences).

Examining risk factors for suicide, we find that they generally involve four broad areas—culture, personality, the individual situation, and biological factors—some or all of which may overlap when we consider an individual instance of suicidal behavior. Our understanding of risk factors is broadened by looking at suicide from a lifespan perspective. Different motives and influences are found to be more or less important at different stages of life—childhood, adolescence and young adulthood, middle adulthood, and late adulthood.

To gain a comprehensive understanding of suicide, it is also useful to consider how a person progresses from thought to action, from contemplating suicide to obtaining the means of suicide, thereby setting into motion the logistics that make suicide a real possibility. Although the steps toward lethality can be presented in an orderly sequence, a suicidal person is likely to experience them very differently. Suicide typically involves an array of conflicting thoughts and emotions. The particular method chosen to carry out a suicidal intention may be based on personality factors, as well as ease of access. There is an "order of lethality" in the various methods. Some have a greater risk of lethality than others.

Suicide notes, which have been called "cryptic maps of ill-advised journeys," are studied with the aim of better understanding the factors and circumstances that lead to suicide. Such notes usually display a variety of messages and intentions. Often, they express confused logic and an intense love-hate ambivalence that points up the dyadic nature of many suicidal acts. Suicide notes can provide clues about a person's intentions and emotional state, but they rarely tell the whole story. Their effect on survivors, however, can be significant. Whether the final message is one of affection or blame, survivors have no opportunity to respond.

Much can be done to reduce suicide risk. Education is an essential element in any program of suicide prevention. Such education generally emphasizes two key points: (1) Since life is complex, all of us will inevitably experience disappointment, failure, and loss in our lives; (2) we can learn to deal with such experiences by developing appropriate coping techniques, including a healthy sense of humor. Whereas the goal of suicide prevention is primarily to eliminate or minimize suicide risk, the goal of suicide intervention is to reduce the lethality of a particular suicidal crisis. The emphasis of intervention is on short-term care and treatment of persons in crisis. The cardinal rule is to do something—take the threat seriously, answer cries for help by offering support and compassion, and provide constructive alternatives to suicide. Suicide postvention refers to the assistance given to survivors, including those who survive suicide attempts as well as the families, friends, and associates of those who die by suicide.

Objectives

- To identify potential suicide populations.
- To construct a comprehensive definition of suicide.
- To describe the sociological and psychological models of suicide.
- To list and describe four types of suicide and to give examples of each.
- To explain the risk factors influencing suicide through the lifespan.
- To describe methods of suicide and to analyze them for information regarding the suicidal person's intent.
- To create a model of suicide intervention.
- To plan a suicide postvention strategy.

Key Terms and Concepts

acute suicidal crisis
altruistic suicide
ambivalence
anomie
attempted suicide
biological markers
chronic suicide
cluster suicides
crisis suicide
cry for help
depression
double suicides
dyadic event
egoistic suicide
equivocal death
fatalistic suicide
hopelessness
intervention

level of lethality
mass suicide
middlescence
postvention
psych-ache
psychodynamics of suicide
psychological autopsy
rational suicide
referred suicide
seppuku
social context of suicide
subintentional death
suicide notes
suicide pacts
suicide prevention
suttee
victim-precipitated homicide
Werther effect

Questions for Guided Study and Review

1. What is the definition of suicide?
2. What do statistics tell us about suicide?
3. Why is discussion of suicide sometimes considered taboo?
4. What are two examples of the possible underreporting of suicide?
5. What is victim-precipitated homicide?
6. What is a *psychological autopsy?*
7. When and why is a psychological autopsy done?
8. What are two major theoretical models for explaining suicide?
9. How does Durkheim's model of the social context of suicide add to our understanding?
10. What are the differences between anomic suicide, fatalistic suicide, egoistic suicide, and altruistic suicide?
11. What are *seppuka* and *suttee*, and what category of suicide do they fit into?
12. What are the key features of the psychodynamic model of suicide?

---

13. What are the roles of aggression and ambivalence in the psychological model of suicide?
14. How long does the acute suicidal crisis generally last?
15. In what way can suicidal events be described as *dyadic*?
16. What is *psychache*, and why is it important in understanding suicide?
17. What are the types of suicide discussed in the text, and how do they differ?
18. List and describe at least three cultural and three individual meanings of suicide.
19. What is the relationship between depression and suicide?
20. Why is some suicidal behavior described as a "cry for help"?
21. What gender differences have been noted between attempted and completed suicides?
22. Differentiate between intentioned, unintentioned, and subintentioned deaths, and identify at least two specific patterns in each category.
23. How do culture, personality, individual situation and biologic factors influence suicide risk?
24. How does Brian Barry's model of "pro-life" and "pro-death" forces relate to cultural factors that may increase suicide risk?
25. How might reducing the fear of death facilitate suicidal behavior?
26. How are stress and suicide correlated?
27. How does a lifespan perspective add to our understanding of suicide?
28. What is the effect of the different developmental periods on suicide?
29. Why is labeling a young child's death as suicide problematic?
30. How serious a problem is suicide during the teen and early adult years?
31. What are some of the risk factors for suicide during adolescence and young adulthood?
32. What are *cluster suicides*?
33. What are *suicide pacts*, and at what ages do they occur?
34. Which age group has the highest risk for suicide?
35. What are the three most commonly used methods for suicide?
36. How does the "order of lethality" relate to suicide?
37. What do suicide notes tell us about suicide?
38. What are the goals of suicide prevention, intervention, and postvention?
39. What are the four main ways people express suicidal intent?
40. What are some warning signs of suicide?
41. List and refute the myths about suicide.
42. What are some ways for helping a person who is suicidal?

Practice Test Questions

MULTIPLE CHOICE

1. Edwin Shneidman's definition of suicide emphasizes
   a. specific acts.
   b. feelings.
   c. intention and action.
   d. resolving problems.

2. Which of the following are limitations of the *psychological autopsy?*
    1. retrospective nature
    2. lack of standardized procedures
    3. not admissible in court
    4. the individual of interest is not available for examination

    a. 1, 2, and 4
    b. 1, 2, and 3
    c. 1, 3, and 4
    d. 2, 3, and 4

3. According to the sociological model, egoistic suicide
    a. results when individuals have excessive pride.
    b. occurs when individuals are disenfranchised or alienated from society.
    c. results when individuals have a diminished sense of personal identity.
    d. occurs when individuals are overly patriotic.

4. For most suicides, the goal is to
    a. end one's life.
    b. solve some problem.
    c. hurt others.
    d. relieve pressure.

5. Which of the following factors is NOT cited in the text as a contributor to suicide risk?
    a. lifestyle
    b. stressful life events
    c. environment
    d. direction

TRUE/FALSE

_____ 1. Suicide has been seen as a way of expressing the ultimate commitment to a moral or philosophical principle.

_____ 2. Sudden wealth can potentially stimulate suicidal behavior.

_____ 3. The suicide rate among white Americans is lower than among black Americans because white Americans consider suicide a cowardly way out of problems.

_____ 4. Positive self-esteem is a preventative against suicide.

_____ 5. Suicide postvention is a type of assistance given to individuals who attempt suicide.

Matching

Match each of the types of suicide on the left with the appropriate description on the right.

_____ 1. Anomie

_____ 2. Altruistic

_____ 3. Seppuku

_____ 4. Suttee

a. ritual disembowelment to show devotion upon the death of a superior

b. reluctance to enact this ritual might cause a widow to be "helped" onto her husband's cremation pyre

c. related to social instability and disruptive change

d. self-destruction as the price for being a member of a particular society

✎ Answers to practice questions can be found in Part IV ✍

Related Readings

📖 Indicates selection from *The Path Ahead: Readings in Death and Dying,* ed. Lynne Ann DeSpelder and Albert Lee Strickland (Mountain View, Calif.: Mayfield, 1995).

GENERAL STUDIES

Glen Evans and Norman L. Farberow. *The Encyclopedia of Suicide.* New York: Facts on File, 1988.

Antoon A. Leenaars, ed. *Suicidology: Essays in Honor of Edwin Shneidman.* Northvale, N.J.: Jason Aronson, 1993.

Georges Minois. *History of Suicide: Voluntary Death in the Western World.* Baltimore, Md.: Johns Hopkins University Press, 1999.

Edwin S. Shneidman. "Suicide As Psychache," *Journal of Nervous and Mental Disease* 181, no. 3 (1993): 147–149.

📖 Judith M. Stillion, "Premature Exits: Understanding Suicide," pp. 182–197.

LIFESPAN AND CULTURAL PERSPECTIVES

📖 Kevin E. Early and Ronald L. Akers, "'It's a White Thing'—An Exploration of Beliefs About Suicide in the African-American Community," pp. 198–210.

Kevin E. Early. *Religion and Suicide in the African-American Community.* Westport, Conn.: Greenwood, 1992.

📖 Kathleen Erwin, "Interpreting the Evidence: Competing Paradigms and the Emergence of Lesbian and Gay Suicide as a 'Social Fact,'" pp. 211–220.

Carolyn S. Henry and others. "Adolescent Suicide and Families: An Ecological Approach," *Adolescence* 28 (Summer 1993): 291–308.

Israel Orbach. *Children Who Don't Want to Live: Understanding and Treating the Suicidal Child.* San Francisco: Jossey-Bass, 1988.

Jack Seward. *Hari-Kiri: Japanese Ritual Suicide.* Rutland, Vt.: Charles E. Tuttle, 1968.

The Psychological Autopsy

David A. Brent. "The Psychological Autopsy: Methodological Considerations for the Study of Adolescent Suicide," *Suicide and Life-Threatening Behavior* 19 (Spring 1989): 43–57.

James R. P. Ogloff and Randy K. Otto. "Psychological Autopsy: Clinical and Legal Perspectives," *Saint Louis University Law Journal* 37, no. 3 (Spring 1993): 607–646.

Shneidman, Edwin S. "The Psychological Autopsy," *Suicide and Life-Threatening Behavior* 11 (1981): 325–40.

Avery D. Weisman. *The Realization of Death: A Guide for the Psychological Autopsy*. New York: Aronson, 1974.

Organizations and Internet Resources

American Association of Suicidology: <www.suicidology.org>. Suite 408, 4201 Connecticut Avenue NW, Washington, DC 20008. (202) 237-2280. Fax: (202) 237-2282. Nonprofit organization dedicated to understanding and preventing suicide.

American Foundation for Suicide Prevention: <www.afsp.org>. 120 Wall Street, 22d Floor, New York, NY 10005. (212) 363-3500 or (888) 333-2377. Fax: (212) 363-6237. Research, education, and information about suicide.

Befrienders International: <www.befrienders.org>. 26/27 Market Place, Kingston-upon-Thames, Surrey, U.K. KT1 1JH. (20) 8541-4949. Fax: (20) 8549-1544. Composed of volunteers from forty-one countries who befriend suicidal and other lonely, anxious, or depressed people, and who distribute information about suicide.

Centre for Suicide Prevention: <www.suicideinfo.ca> 1202 Centre Street S.E., Calgary, AB T2G 5A5, Canada. (403) 245-3900. Fax: (403) 245-0299. Provides information and conducts training and research about suicide. This is not a crisis center.

Emile Durkheim Archive: <http://durkheim.itgo.com>. A resource created for undergraduate students of sociology (navigate on this site to "suicide").

Indian Health Service: <www.ihs.gov>. Room 5A-43, 5600 Fishers Lane, Rockville, MD 20857. (301) 443-2546. Fax: (301) 594-3146. Information related to concerns about high suicide rate among some Native American populations.

National Center for Injury Prevention and Control: <www.cdc.gov/ncipc>. Mailstop K60, 4770 Buford Highway, Atlanta, GA 30341. (770) 488.4362. Fax: (770) 488-4349. This branch of the Centers for Disease Control provides information about suicide in the United States.

National Institutes of Mental Health—Suicide Facts: <www.nimh.nih.gov/research/ suifact.cfm>. A U.S. government site that provides suicide statistics and trends.

SAVE: Suicide Awareness\Voices of Education: <www.save.org>. Provides education and information about suicide and suicide prevention, as well as outreach and grief support for those whose loved ones died by suicide. Includes recent statistics on death by suicide, frequently asked questions about suicide, book reviews, and other resources about suicide.

❧ Additional resources are available online at mhhe.com ❧

Major Points in This Chapter

- It is generally agreed that official suicide statistics understate the actual number of suicides, perhaps by as much as fifty percent. Such underrepresentation is due to social stigma against suicide, the need for unequivocal proof before classifying a death as suicide, suicides that masquerade as accidents or victim-precipitated homicides, and sensitivity to survivors' concerns, as well as to differences in the manner in which coroner's and medical examiner's investigations of possible suicides are conducted in different jurisdictions.

- The psychological autopsy is a potent investigative tool for improving suicide statistics as well as enhancing knowledge about the factors that influence suicidal behavior.

- Theoretical approaches to explaining suicide are based mainly on a sociological model (focusing on the relationship between the individual and society) and a psychological model (focusing on the dynamics of an individual's mental and emotional life). A comprehensive understanding of suicide makes use of both models.

- Typologically, suicidal behavior can be classified as an escape from some mental or physical pain, as the result of impaired logic caused by clinical depression or psychosis, as the unconscious result of chronic or subintentional factors hastening death, and as a "cry for help" in alleviating some problem.

- There may be two fairly distinct populations of people engaging in suicidal behaviors: attempters and completers. It must be recognized, however, that any suicide attempt can end in death.

- Culture, personality, mental status, and the unique combination of circumstances affecting a particular individual's life each play a role in determining the degree to which a person may be at risk of suicide.

- The varying risk of suicide also corresponds to changes in outlook and circumstance that occur throughout the lifespan. Suicide among adolescents and young adults is viewed as a major public health problem.

- The likelihood of a fatal outcome increases as a suicidal person plans his or her demise and acquires the means to carry out the plan; as the potential lethality of the method increases, the more likely the outcome will be death. There is an "order of lethality" among the various methods people employ when engaging in suicidal behavior.

- Suicide notes reflect a range of concerns by people who die by suicide, from simple reminders directed to survivors about carrying out ordinary tasks to complex explanations about why the person ended his or her life. Ambivalence is a hallmark of many suicide notes.

- Suicide prevention, intervention, and postvention are important in reducing the incidence of suicidal behavior and easing the pain of loss for people who are bereaved as a result of a loved one's suicide.

Observations and Reflections

Your responses to suicide—for instance, whether a particular suicide evokes feelings of anger or forgiveness—will depend partly on your cultural, religious, and psychological background. Can you distinguish between these components of understanding? Take time to identify from which part of your belief system and background your response to suicide arises.

Use the space below and on the following page to record your notes and responses to the topics covered in this chapter.

212 ⌒ Chapter 12

Journey Through The Last Dance, 7th ed.
Activities and Resources

⇒ *Suicidal Behavior*

Directions: *Indicate your beliefs about the suicidal intent of the following persons in the situations described. Rank each item on a scale of 1 to 5 (with 1 indicating no suicidal intent whatsoever, 2 probably not suicidal, 3 could be either, 4 likely suicidal, 5 definitely suicidal).*

A person who . . .

_____　1.　Drives 10 miles over the speed limit on a winding mountain road.

_____　2.　Assassinates a world leader.

_____　3.　Sacrifices his or her life to protest a political cause.

_____　4.　Suffers from a terminal illness and refuses medical treatment.

_____　5.　Points a loaded gun at his or her head and pulls the trigger.

_____　6.　Knowingly drinks poison when directed to by an authority figure.

_____　7.　Takes a drug overdose.

_____　8.　Refuses to change his or her lifestyle despite two previous heart attacks.

_____　9.　Consumes alcohol to the point of intoxication and then drives a car.

_____　10.　Goes on an extended hunger strike in order to force a particular issue.

_____　11.　Uses a motorcycle to jump long distances (over cars, over canyons, etc.)

_____　12.　Gains a large amount of weight.

_____　13.　Talks constantly about what a drag life is and frequently says: "I feel like ending it all."

_____　14.　Pours gasoline upon himself or herself and lights a match.

_____　15.　Walks into a post office, randomly firing a gun, killing many people.

⇒ *Suicidal Tendencies*

Directions: *Respond to the following statements, indicating true or false, and explain the reason for your answer:*

_____   1. People who talk about suicide do not commit suicide.

_____

_____

_____   2. Improvement in a suicidal person means the danger has passed.

_____

_____

_____   3. Once a suicide risk, always a suicide risk.

_____

_____

_____   4. Suicide is inherited.

_____

_____

_____   5. Suicide affects only a specific group or class of people.

_____

_____

_____   6. Suicidal behavior is insane.

_____

_____

_____   7. Suicidal people are fully intent on dying.

_____

_____

_____   8. The motive for suicide is always clearly evident.

_____

_____

Risks of Death
in the Modern World

Chapter Summary

Chapter 13 examines a broad range of encounters with death, including occupational, environmental, and other risks; accidents; disasters; violence; war; terrorism; and emerging diseases, such as AIDS. Some of these encounters seem remote from our own lives; others are pervasive, though we may give little conscious attention to them. News reports are filled with accounts of disasters—natural as well as human-caused. But, until we ourselves confront such a threat to well-being, we may not comprehend all the dimensions of loss such events represent. Even so, consciously or not, we risk subtle, and sometimes dramatic, encounters with death as we engage in our life's pursuits.

All life involves risk, although the degree of risk we are willing to assume is often subject to personal choice. Individuals can exercise control over risks related to smoking, driving habits, and the kinds of recreational activities they pursue. In many areas of life, steps can be taken to minimize our exposure to risk. Simply ignoring or denying the risk inherent in an activity does not make the danger disappear, but it may result in our failure to take adequate steps to counteract the risk.

Although accidents are commonly viewed as events that "just happen," deeper analysis reveals that many accidents are preventable. Instead of being unavoidable, accidents frequently result from carelessness, lack of awareness, or ignorance. Thus, accidents are often events over which individuals do have varying degrees of control. For example, about half the drivers involved in fatality accidents are under the influence of alcohol. Such accidents represent tragedies that could have been avoided.

Accidents are influenced both by intrinsic factors—a person's own physical and mental qualities—and by extrinsic factors—conditions in the environment. Unsafe conditions in the environment are sometimes called "accidents waiting to happen." These conditions often exist because of negligence. If we view accidents as caused solely by chance or fate, then we ignore the significant role of carelessness and neglect. Attention to such factors could lead to constructive actions toward prevention. Although life can never be completely free of risk, steps usually can be taken to minimize it.

Disasters, which can be defined as life-threatening events that affect many people within a relatively brief period of time and that bring sudden and great misfortune, result from both natural phenomena and human activities. Floods and earthquakes are examples of natural disasters; fires, airplane crashes, and chemical spills are examples of disasters resulting from human activities. Population growth, urbanization, and industrialization have increased exposure to disasters related to human activities. Individuals and communities can often decrease the risk of injury and death by taking measures to lessen the impact of a potential disaster, but the effects of a disaster are difficult to fully anticipate. Although adequate warnings of an impending disaster can save lives, necessary information may be withheld because of greed or political expediency, or simply because of uncertainty about the nature and extent of the threat, or because of concern about causing panic. Even with an adequate warning system, however, people do not always respond to the threat prudently. Just as some people ignore the risks associated with smoking or place themselves in situations prone to risks or accidents, individuals frequently view themselves as immune to the effects of a disastrous situation.

In the aftermath of disaster, meeting the immediate needs of survivors, such as food and shelter, medical care, vital services, is essential. Important, too, is attending to survivors' emotional needs. Although efforts directed toward coping with disaster tend to focus on the initial period of emergency, the return to financial and emotional stability may take years. In addition, the needs of caregivers who provide support services to survivors also need to be acknowledged as part of a comprehensive program of disaster postvention.

Violence, one of the most potent and frightening encounters with death, can affect our thoughts and actions even when we have not been victimized ourselves. Special emphasis is placed on the prevalence of interpersonal violence.

Within the framework of the U.S. judicial system, the circumstances of a particular killing, the relationship between killer and victim, and the killer's motivation and intent are all considered in assessing a homicidal act. Research shows that the legal outcome for a person who kills a relative is usually quite different from the outcome for a person who combines killing with theft, robbery, or other such criminal or antisocial acts. The most severe penalty is usually reserved as punishment for killing a stranger. The killer who chooses a stranger as his or her victim overtly threatens the preservation of the social order.

Within the context of ordinary human interaction, our moral as well as legal codes stand in strict opposition to killing. In war, however, killing is not only acceptable and necessary but possibly heroic. Yet, despite society's efforts to convert civilians into warriors, those who face the prospect of kill-or-be-killed in war often pay a high emotional and psychological price due to the traumatic effects of combat. War also creates a "phantom army" of spouses, children, parents, and friends who serve invisibly at home.

To prepare the way for war, individuals and societies engage in a psychological process of creating the enemy. Dividing the world into "us" and "them" devalues and dehumanizes members of the outgroup, paving the way for hostile acts. In seeking ways to civilize hostilities, we need to focus on processes that promote or deter war in both the individual psyche and social institutions.

In considering threats to well-being resulting from violence and warfare, terrorism combines aspects of both to generate fear and accomplish political or other aims. It can involve carefully planned as well as indiscriminate killing. Because it typically occurs outside the boundaries of the social sanctions intended to regulate conduct between individuals and between groups, terrorism is an affront to civilization.

The terrorist attack on the United States on September 11, 2001, took place in a "global public space" created by extensive media coverage as millions of people worldwide saw disturbing images of destruction and death. Official rescue and recovery operations were accompanied by a search for the missing conducted by relatives and friends, a search that became a poignant memorialization of the losses suffered as a result of the terrorists' actions.

Another kind of terror occurs in the context of emerging infectious diseases, which often appear to strike without warning and randomly. Although progress against such diseases has created a widespread sense of complacency, AIDS became a wake-up call about the worldwide threat of emerging diseases, and it continues to have a devastating impact on individuals and societies. Many friends, neighbors, mates, and relatives of people with AIDS have experienced multiple losses. The greatest impact of AIDS at present is in the developing world, particularly in sub-Saharan Africa. As options for treating AIDS lead to better outcomes for many individuals, the focus is changing from "dying with AIDS" to "living with AIDS." Some believe that AIDS is part of a series of emerging diseases that will threaten people on a global scale in coming decades. There have been localized epidemics of hermorrhagic fever viruses such as the Marburg, Ebola, Lassa, and hantaviruses, as well as yellow fever, swine flu, Legionnaires' disease, and cholera. Expansion of human population, forest clearing, and other human-initiated activities disturb previously stable ecosystems, thereby facilitating contact with pathogenic viruses that threaten life and health.

Risks of various kinds—accidents, disasters, violence, war, terrorism, epidemic diseases—affect us to varying degrees as we go about our daily lives. Sometimes the encounter is subtle; at other times it is overt, requiring concerted action to counter the threat. Understanding the nature of such risks is a first step toward successfully coping with the range of encounters with death that can threaten both societies and individuals.

Objectives

- To assess one's level of risk-taking activities.
- To describe the incidence and extent of accidents and to compare the factors influencing accidents in specific populations.
- To identify helping strategies for survivors of disaster.
- To define homicide and distinguish various categories and types.
- To identify and explain the cultural standards by which homicidal acts are judged.
- To evaluate the effects of capital punishment.
- To develop an alternative model for punishment.
- To name and give examples of the factors increasing the likelihood of violence.
- To differentiate between the moral standards of war and peacetime relative to the taking of life.

- To assess the effects of war and its aftermath on both combatants and non-combatants.
- To identify the needs and motives that give rise to war and evaluate strategies for reducing conflict.
- To develop a working definition of terrorism.
- To explain how the *amplification effect* assists terrorists in achieving their aims.
- To identify issues that arise in the context of rescue and recovery efforts in the aftermath of terrorist acts.
- To assess how memorialization aids survivors in coping with the effects of terrorism.
- To describe social and psychological factors that motivate terrorists and suggest ways of reducing the influence of these factors.
- To identify and explain the impact of AIDS and other emerging diseases.
- To describe a healthy response in coping with risks of death in the modern world.

Key Terms and Concepts

accident-prone
acquired immunodeficiency syndrome (AIDS)
amplification effect
capital punishment
conversion of the warrior
death penalty
disaster
emerging diseases
genocide
"haiku obit"
homicide
horrendous death
human immunodeficiency virus (HIV)
karoshi

manslaughter
medical-legal investigation
militarism
murder
posttraumatic stress disorder (PTSD)
psychic maneuvers
psychic numbing
risk
social thanatology
technological alienation
terrorism
urban desertification
violence
war

Questions for Guided Study and Review

1. What are some of the different kinds of risks of death?
2. In what ways is the degree of risk a person faces subject to his or her own choices?
3. What is *karoshi* and what causes it?
4. How do accidents sometimes occur as a result of something besides chance?
5. What factors influence "accident proneness"?
6. How might gender affect risk-taking and accidents?
7. What is the definition of *disaster*?
8. What accounts for the increased risk of disaster in the United States in recent years?
9. How can the impact of disasters be reduced?
10. What role do warning systems play in managing the threat of disasters?
11. What needs must be addressed in disaster relief, and what are some shortcomings in most relief efforts?
12. How is "survivor guilt" a factor in grief reactions following disasters?

13. Why is violence now considered a public health problem?
14. What are the circumstances that led one commentator to say that "Being a child in America can be deadly"?
15. What factors are correlated with violence?
16. What are the two main categories of criminal homicide?
17. How do the legal system and community standards affect the way an act of homicide is judged?
18. What are the three components of a medical-legal investigation of homicide?
19. Assess the differences between homicidal acts directed toward strangers and homicidal acts that occur within the family unit or between individuals known to one another.
20. In considering the impact of violence on children, who are the "silent victims"?
21. What are the arguments for and against capital punishment?
22. What are the *psychic maneuvers* that lead to violence?
23. Evaluate the argument that violence is endemic in American society.
24. How are conventional sanctions against killing altered in war?
25. What is *genocide*?
26. What is the relationship between "technological alienation" and "psychic numbing"?
27. What is *posttraumatic stress disorder*, and how is it related to warfare?
28. How does war create a "phantom army"?
29. Review the steps toward civilizing hostilities.
30. How do the various definitions of terrorism help provide a comprehensive view of the nature of terrorist acts?
31. What role does the *amplification effect* play in helping terrorists achieve their aims?
32. Distinguish between *rescue* and *recovery* efforts in the aftermath of terrorist acts.
33. Assess the manner in which social, psychological, and religious factors influence the mindset of terrorists.
34. Why are newly emerging diseases a cause for concern?
35. In what ways is AIDS a challenge socially, politically, culturally, and individually?
36. How is AIDS transmitted, and how does it affect the body's immune system?
37. What is the typical progression of infection with human immunodeficiency virus (HIV)?
38. Assess the current status of AIDS in both developed and developing countries?
39. What are three of the important lessons from AIDS with respect to similarly threatening diseases?
40. Why are hemorrhagic fever viruses such as Ebola and Lassa becoming of increasing concern?
41. What infectious disease episode occurred in 1918, and what were its effects?
42. What are some typical examples of "horrendous death"?

Practice Test Questions

MULTIPLE CHOICE

1. Accidents are events that
   a. are subject to varying degrees of control.
   b. are subject to no control.
   c. specific individuals are more prone to.
   d. can be prevented.

2. The most threatening acts of violence
   a. occur within a family.
   b. result in a death.
   c. involve victims seemingly selected at random.
   d. involve influential or famous people.

3. Which of the following is true of the statement that a person who says "You haven't got the guts!" during an argument is "asking for it"?
   1. Victims may increase the potential for violent acts against themselves.
   2. Labeling victims denies the reality that everyone is vulnerable to victimization.
   3. Blaming the victim is a convenient way to overcome one's own sense of vulnerability and thereby regain a sense of personal security.
   4. Placing a stigma of blame on victims is an effective way to understand and explain violence.

   a. 1, 2, and 3
   b. 1, 2, and 4
   c. 2, 3, and 4
   d. 1, 3, and 4

4. Which of the following key points are part of a comprehensive definition of *terrorism?*
   1. It is intended to influence an audience.
   2. It is perpetrated only against military or police forces.
   3. It is perpetrated by states as well as subnational groups.
   4. It is intended only to express religious fervor.

   a. 1 and 2
   b. 1 and 3
   c. 1 and 4
   d. 2 and 4

5. Daniel Leviton's use of the term *horrendous death* describes categories of death that affect
   a. certain age groups.
   b. large numbers of people.
   c. certain cultures.
   d. selected groups of people.

TRUE/FALSE

_____ 1. By increasing an individual's stress, work potentially increases the risk of death.

_____ 2. A person who murders his or her spouse is likely to receive a harsher punishment than a person who murders a stranger.

_____ 3. Capital punishment may reinforce hostile fantasies and murderous tendencies.

_____ 4. Terrorists rely on amplification effect to achieve their goals.

_____ 5. The main message of the UNAIDS report is that the AIDS epidemic is close to being over.

MATCHING

Match each of the topics on the left with the appropriate supporting statement on the right.

_____ 1. Factors favoring violence   a. us versus them

_____ 2. Lessening the potential for violence   b. champion the good guys

_____ 3. Faces of the enemy   c. scope and extent of physical and emotional devastation

_____ 4. Factors increasing the impact of terrorism   d. anything encouraging a person to feel above or outside the law

❧ Answers to practice questions can be found in Part IV ❧

Related Readings

📖 Indicates selection from *The Path Ahead: Readings in Death and Dying,* ed. Lynne Ann DeSpelder and Albert Lee Strickland (Mountain View, Calif.: Mayfield, 1995).

ENCOUNTERS WITH DEATH

📖 Thomas Attig, "Coping with Mortality: An Essay on Self-Mourning," pp. 337–341.
📖 Robert Kastenbaum, "Reconstructing Death in Postmodern Society," pp. 7–18.
📖 Alfred G. Killilea, "The Politics of Being Mortal," pp. 342–347.
Harvey M. Sapolsky. "The Politics of Risk," *Daedalus: Journal of the American Academy of Arts and Sciences* 119 (Fall 1990): 83–96.

ACCIDENTS AND DISASTERS

Eric Klinenberg. *Heat Wave: A Social Autopsy of Disaster in Chicago.* Chicago: University of Chicago Press, 2002.
Alwyn Scarth. *Le Catastrophe: The Eruption of Mount Pelee, the Worst Volcanic Disaster of the 20th Century.* New York: Oxford University Press, 2002.

Theodore Steinberg. *Acts of God: The Unnatural History of "Natural" Disasters.* New York: Oxford University Press, 2000.

Graham A. Tobin, and Burrell E. Montz. *Natural Hazards: Explanation and Integration.* New York: Guilford Press, 1997.

David Von Drehle. *Triangle: The Fire That Changed America.* New York: Atlantic Monthly, 2003.

VIOLENCE AND WARFARE

Philip Bobbitt. *The Shield of Achilles: War, Peace, and the Course of History.* New York: Knopf, 2002.

📖 Zlata Filipovic, "Zlata's Diary: A Child's Life in Sarajevo," pp. 175–178.

📖 James Garbarino, "Challenges We Face in Understanding Children and War: A Personal Essay," pp. 169–174.

Dave Grossman. *On Killing: The Psychological Cost of Learning to Kill in War and Society.* Boston: Little, Brown, 1995.

📖 Ice T, "The Killing Fields," pp. 178–181.

Walter Laqueur, ed. *The Holocaust Encyclopedia.* New Haven, Conn.: Yale University Press, 2001.

📖 Daniel Leviton, "Horrendous Death: Improving the Quality of Global Health," pp. 165–168.

📖 Jack Lule, "News Strategies and the Death of Huey Newton," pp. 33–40.

Eric H. Monkkonen. *Murder in New York City.* Berkeley: University of California Press, 2001.

Colin Murray Parkes. "Genocide in Rwanda: Personal Reflections," *Mortality* 1, no. 1 (1996): 95–110.

📖 Nancy Scheper-Hughes, "Death Without Weeping: The Violence of Everyday Life in Brazil," pp. 41–58.

Jonathan Shay. *Odysseus in America: Combat Trauma and the Trials of Homecoming.* New York: Scribner, 2003.

Herbert S. Strean and Lucy Freeman. *Our Wish to Kill: The Murder in All Our Hearts.* New York: St. Martin's Press, 1991.

Fred Turner. *Echoes of Combat: The Vietnam War in American Memory.* New York: Anchor-Doubleday, 1996.

Franklin E. Zimring and Gordon Hawkins. *Crime Is Not the Problem: Lethal Violence in America.* New York: Oxford University Press, 1997.

CAPITAL PUNISHMENT

Roman Espejo, ed. *Does Capital Punishment Deter Crime?* Farmington Hills, Mich.: Greenhaven, 2003.

Richard J. Evans. *Rituals of Retribution: Capital Punishment in Germany, 1600–1987.* New York: Oxford University Press, 1996.

TERRORISM

Bruce D. Berkowitz. *The New Face of War: How War Will Be Fought in the 21st Century.* New York: Free Press, 2003.

Cindy C. Combs and Martin Slann. *Encyclopedia of Terrorism*. New York: Facts on File, 2002.

Christopher Hewitt. *Understanding Terrorism in America: From the Klan to Al-Qaeda*. London: Routledge, 2003.

William Langewiesche. *American Ground: Unbuilding the World Trade Center*. New York: North Point Press, 2002.

Walter Laqueur. *The New Terrorism: Fanaticism and the Arms of Mass Destruction*. New York: Oxford University Press, 1999.

Tom Pyszcynski, Sheldon Solomon, and Jeff Greenberg. *In the Wake of 9/11: The Psychology of Terror*. Washington, D.C.: American Psychological Association, 2003.

AIDS and Emerging Diseases

📖 Harold Brodkey, "To My Readers," pp. 295–300.

Kenneth J. Doka. *AIDS, Fear, and Society: Challenging the Dreaded Disease*. Washington, D.C.: Taylor & Francis, 1997.

Madeline Drexler. *Secret Agents: The Menace of Emerging Infections*. New York: Penguin, 2003.

Laurie Garrett. *The Coming Plague: Newly Emerging Diseases in a World Out of Balance*. New York: Farrar, Straus and Giroux, 1994.

Gina Kolata. *Flu*. New York: Farrar, Straus & Giroux, 1999.

📖 Charles E. Rosenberg, "What Is an Epidemic? AIDS in Historical Perspective," pp. 29–32.

Jonathan B. Tucker. *Scourge: The Once and Future Threat of Smallpox*. New York: Atlantic Monthly, 2001.

Organizations and Internet Resources

AIDS Hotline: <www.cdc.gov>. Centers for Disease Control and Prevention, Division of STD/HIV Prevention, 1600 Clifton Road, NE, Mail stop E-2-7, Atlanta, GA 30333. (800) 342-AIDS. Information, support, and resources for emerging diseases, including AIDS.

American Ex-Prisoners of War: <www.axpow.com>. National Headquarters, #40, 3201 East Pioneer Parkway, Arlington, TX 76010. (817) 649-3398. Fax: (817) 649-0109. National organization for individuals who were prisoners of war.

Children with AIDS Project: <www.aidskids.org>. Information and education about children with AIDS, along with a variety of services for children affected by AIDS, including foster or adoptive care.

Illinois Coalition Against the Death Penalty: <www.icadp.org>. Suite 2300, 180 North Michigan Avenue, Chicago, IL 60601. (312) 849-2279. Fax: (312) 201-9760. Promotes abolition of the death penalty.

National Association of People with AIDS: <www.napwa.org>. 1413 K Street NW, Washington, DC 20005. (202) 898-0414. Fax: (202) 898-0435. Provides support for people diagnosed with AIDS, AIDS-related complex, or HIV. Advocates community awareness of AIDS and promotes participation of local organizations in AIDS-related health care and social services.

National Center for Victims of Crime: <www.nvc.org>. Suite 480, 2000 M Street NW, Washington, D.C. 20036. (202) 467-8700. Fax: (202) 467-8701. Outreach and resources for victims of crime, including teens and 9-11 survivors.

National Native American AIDS Prevention Center: <www.nnaapc.org>. Suite 1020, 436 Fourteenth Street, Oakland, CA 94612. (510) 444-2051. Fax: (510) 444-1593. E-mail: <info@nnapc.org>. AIDS research, prevention, care, public policy, and resources.

Parents of Murdered Children, Inc. (POMC): <www.pomc.com>. National POMC, Suite B-41, 100 East Eighth Street, Cincinnati, OH 45202. (513) 721-5683 or (888) 818-POMC. Fax: (513) 345-4489. National support group for families and friends of individuals who died by violence with local chapters in some areas.

Wings of Light: <www.wingsoflight.org>. Suite 1-448, 16845 North 29th Avenue, Phoenix, AZ 85023. (602) 516-1115. Support network for survivors, family members, and rescue personnel involved in aircraft accidents.

❧ Additional resources are available online at mhhe.com ❧

Major Points in This Chapter

- Life unavoidably involves risk, but personal choices and social conditions can increase our exposure to potentially lethal risks.
- Accidents involve events over which individuals have varying degrees of control; thus, the choices we make can affect the probabilities of accidents. Considering such factors as carelessness, lack of awareness, and neglect can lead to a better understanding of how and why accidents occur.
- Disasters are defined as life-threatening events that affect a large number of people within a relatively brief period of time, bringing sudden and great misfortune. The risk of death from disasters can be minimized when precautionary measures are taken to lessen their impact.
- Interpersonal violence is recognized as a public health problem. Violence can affect our well-being even though we ourselves have not been directly victimized.
- Community standards of morality and justice play major roles in determining how an act of killing is assessed by a society and its judicial system. The killer's motivation and intent, along with the relationship between killer and victim, are among the factors considered in assessing whether a homicide is lawful or unlawful and, if unlawful, whether it is murder.
- Capital punishment has a twofold purpose; namely, to punish the offender and deter potential offenders. However, many people believe it is inconsistent for a society to try to prevent murder by itself engaging in killing.
- Avoiding the use of derogatory labels, eliminating conditions that underlie dehumanizing perceptions of oneself and others, and promoting communication between potential adversaries are among ways of lessening the potential for violence.
- War abrogates conventional social sanctions against killing by substituting a different set of conventions and rules concerning moral conduct.

- Modern warfare is characterized by technological alienation and psychic numbing; the traditional distinction between combatants and noncombatants has become increasingly blurred, if not erased.
- Terrorism seeks to cause political, social, and economic disruption through planned as well as indiscriminate acts of murder.
- AIDS is viewed by some experts as the harbinger of an unknown number of emerging deadly diseases that will increasingly threaten the health of human beings worldwide.

Observations and Reflections

Because of the wide range of topics included in this chapter, you may wish to focus on one of the topics mentioned. Take this opportunity to explore your interest in greater depth. One way to do additional research is to consult the list of organizations and Internet resources in this chapter. There you will find contact information for such organizations as Parents of Murdered Children (POMC) and AIDS education and support organizations, as well as other organizations of interest. All have websites that can be visited for further information.

Identify a topic that you would like to explore further. Use this page and the next to describe the results of your additional research.

⟫➡ *Movies and War*

Directions: *Watch a movie that depicts war, such as* Platoon, Full Metal Jacket, Hamburger Hill, Born on the Fourth of July, Gone with the Wind, Saving Private Ryan, *or* Schindler's List. *After viewing the film, answer the following questions:*

1. How accurately do you believe the film depicted reality?_____

   _____

2. What did the film tell the viewer about war? _____

   _____

   _____

3. How were the dead treated? _____

   _____

   _____

4. Was grief depicted? _____

   _____

   _____

5. Were funerals or other mourning rituals shown? _____

   _____

   _____

   _____

6. Were the deceased ever mentioned again?_____

   _____

   _____

   _____

7. What does the film communicate about the long-term effects of war? _____

_____

_____

_____

8. What suggestions could you make for improving the filmmaker's depiction of

war? _____

_____

_____

_____

_____

_____

_____

_____

_____

9. Could you serve in combat and kill an enemy? Why or why not? _____

_____

_____

_____

_____

_____

_____

_____

_____

_____

_____

_____

⇒ *Violence and Your Environment*

Directions: *Imagine that you visit a store within walking distance of your home. As you start to open the door, you notice the sign below posted on the glass at eye level. Read it carefully, paying attention to your reactions. Remember, this is in your neighborhood.*

1. Use the space below and on the following page to describe your thoughts and reactions to this sign being posted in your neighborhood.

_____

_____

_____

_____

_____

_____

_____

_____

_____

_____

2. Now imagine that this poster is on the door of a store that is NOT in your neighborhood. What are your reactions? Do you think twice about going into the store?

_____

_____

_____

_____

_____

_____

_____

_____

_____

_____

_____

_____

_____

_____

_____

_____

_____

_____

_____

_____

⇒ *Violent Death and Children's Attitudes*

Directions: *Here is a child's list of the ways people die. Count the number of violent deaths. Compare it to the number of natural deaths.*

```
1. Heart Attack
2. Smoke/Cancer
3. Drugs
4. Choke on food
5. Shot to death
6. Car Accident
7. Stabbed
8. Stroke
9. Killed by a bomb
10. Fire in house
11. Cut your head off
12. Drinking too much
13. Drown
```

Note the incidence of sudden death owing to accidents. What proportion of the list are they?

_____

_____

List the kinds of deaths that are violent to you.

_____

_____

_____

_____

_____

_____

_____

_____

_____

_____

_____

Review the statistics for your community. How many people were murdered last year? Did any of these involve decapitation?

_____

_____

_____

_____

_____

_____

_____

_____

_____

_____

_____

_____

_____

_____

_____

Beyond Death / After Life

Chapter Summary

Chapter 14 explores the major philosophical, religious, and parapsychological views concerning immortality. The notion that earthly existence continues on in some form following death is one of the oldest concepts held by human beings, as attested to by discoveries made in the earliest known graves. In traditional societies, death usually represents a change of status for the deceased, some kind of transition from the land of the living to the land of the dead.

In the West, our views about immortality have been influenced by the Judaic, Hellenistic, and Christian traditions, as well as by secular ideas of the modern era. At the risk of oversimplifying, a capsule statement of the conventional Western view is that human beings live a single life, that the individual soul survives the death of the body, and that conduct during earthly life determines the ultimate fate of the soul. For the most part, the emphasis on survival of the individual soul is a later development, having been preceded by an emphasis on some type of corporate survival involving the continued existence of the community as a whole. Even so, the emphasis on one's conduct in the present life as a determinant of some future state is ancient. The concept of immortality in the Islamic tradition shares many features with the other Abrahamic traditions, Judaism and Christianity. Although neither the Bible nor the Qur'an provides a systematic treatment of death, the subject is not ignored. Rather, the emphasis is on living righteously and on moral accountability.

Whereas Western thought is noted for its tendency to make distinctions, point up contrasts, and establish differences, Eastern philosophies and religions typically seek to discover the unity that lies behind apparent opposites. Distinctions are subsumed within a holistic "both/and" perspective. The Eastern view is that life and death are complementary aspects of an essentially undivided reality. This viewpoint informs both Hinduism and Buddhism, and it is reflected throughout the holy books of the East, although individual sects exhibit a diversity of opinion with respect to how these insights should be applied in daily life. The doctrine of reincarnation, for example, can be understood as referring to physical transmigration (the passing of the soul from one body to another at death) as well as to continuous transmigration (the insubstantial and ineffable process of psychophysical events that constitute moment-to-moment experience). Either way, the aim is to know the unconditioned state beyond both birth and death.

For many people, death has been divorced from its mythic and religious connotations. The underpinnings for traditional beliefs no longer carry the same weight in a culture that emphasizes scientific method and empirical verification. The present milieu is one in which secular alternatives to religion are pervasive. It is not unusual for a person to hold several competing worldviews at the same time, combining a vague religious faith (perhaps carried over from childhood) with a more secular faith in scientific modes of knowledge and humanitarian ideals of conduct. Despite the option of unbelief, most people still affirm belief in God and, to a somewhat lesser degree, belief in more or less conventional notions of heaven and hell. It may be that, for persons steeped in the materialist culture of the modern West, religious beliefs about the afterlife represent a comforting backdrop to more concrete forms of immortality found in the biological continuity represented by one's children or the social continuity represented by creative work or heroic deeds.

Stories of travel to another realm beyond the earthly existence can be found in virtually all cultures. Near-death experiences (NDEs) represent a modern variation of such otherworld journeys. These accounts by persons who have reportedly glimpsed the afterworld, or the path that leads to it following death, have been interpreted variously. Some believe these journeys are proof of personality survival after death. Others view them as nothing more than a psychological or neurophysiological response to the stress of life-threatening danger. An individual's own model of reality is likely to favor one or the other of these differing interpretations. Each requires a form of faith. In the fragmented religious situation that characterizes modern society, the accounts that derive from near-death experiences (and experiences resulting from the ingestion of LSD and other psychedelic substances) remind us of the universal human need to make meaning of life and death.

Whether we view death as a wall or as a door, our beliefs about the nature of the cosmos and our place in it exert a powerful influence on how we choose to live and on how we care for and relate to persons who are dying or bereaved.

Objectives

- To compare and contrast the views of immortality in the Judaic, Hellenistic, Christian, Islamic, and secular traditions.
- To compare and contrast Eastern religious views of life after death.
- To describe the main features of near-death experiences.
- To analyze the alternative interpretations of near-death experiences.
- To summarize death-related experiences associated with dreams and the use of psychedelic substances.
- To demonstrate how beliefs about what follows death influence a person's understanding of death and how they evidence themselves in choices regarding care of the dying as well as in daily life.

Key Terms and Concepts

afterlife	death dreams
bardo	eschatologies
cosmic dualism	*hades*

heaven

hell

immortality

Judgment Day

kaddish

karma

moksha

near-death experience (NDE)

nirvana

otherworld journey

panoramic life review

paradise

psychedelic experience

purgatory

rebirth

reincarnation

resurrection

samsara

secularization

She'ol

soul

spiritual dimension of dying

symbolic immortality

transmigration

yahrzeit

Questions for Guided Study and Review

1. How does the question of life after death relate to the meaning of life?
2. What are some key features of traditional concepts about life after death, such as those associated with Hawaiian beliefs?
3. How is the idea of "judgment" related to beliefs about the afterlife?
4. How did Jewish beliefs about death and resurrection change over time?
5. What is the Hebrew concept of *She'ol,* and how was this concept refined?
6. How do the customary mourning rituals of Judaism relate to reaffirmation of life?
7. What are the main views of death and immortality associated with Hellenistic (Greek) traditions?
8. In ancient Greece, how did heroism relate to immortality?
9. What is the relationship among Hebrew, Hellenistic, and Christian concepts of the soul?
10. Contrast the idea of resurrection of the body with the concept of an immortal soul.
11. What are the characteristics of afterlife beliefs in the Islamic tradition?
12. What role do Munkar and Nakir play in visiting the grave?
13. How does the *Book of Deeds* relate to Islamic concepts of the Last Judgment and a person's eternal state?
14. What are the key features of a traditional Islamic funeral, and why are they important?
15. How do Eastern and Western thought differ regarding life and death?
16. How are *samsara* and *karma* related?
17. With respect to the afterlife, what is the view of self and selfhood in Hinduism and Buddhism?
18. What is the Zen Buddhist understanding of *transmigration?*
19. How is *nirvana* related to birth and death?
20. In Tibetan Buddhism, what is the meaning of the term *bardo?*
21. Why is the period immediately following death of special importance to Buddhists?
22. What is the effect of secularization on traditional beliefs about the meaning of death?
23. How do *positivism* and *humanitarism* relate to the secularization of death?
24. How does the concept of personal immortality persist in secular, or nonreligious, responses to death?

25. What are near-death experiences (NDEs)?
26. How do NDEs relate to other forms of *otherworldly journeys?*
27. What are the core elements of the NDE?
28. What is *panoramic life review?*
29. What are the three main theories for interpreting or explaining near-death experiences?
30. In the typical near-death experience, what are the three stages distinguished by Russell Noyes and Roy Kletti?
31. What cautions should be kept in mind regarding NDEs?
32. How do "death dreams" relate to near-death experiences?
33. In pioneering studies of the therapeutic effects of LSD (lysergic acid diethylamide) with patients suffering intense pain, what were the results?
34. How does the "wall and door" metaphor help to summarize various beliefs after the afterlife?

Practice Test Questions

MULTIPLE CHOICE

1. Which of the following statements is most in keeping with traditional Hawaiian beliefs about the afterlife?
   a. "The afterlife is non-existent."
   b. "There is a place in heaven for everyone."
   c. "We cannot change the fate chosen by the Gods."
   d. "Wrongdoers will suffer eternal punishment."

2. Of the following statements, the ancient Hebrew writers would most likely have said
   a. "We have a right to an afterlife."
   b. "Because there is no afterlife, we must make the most of this life."
   c. "If there is life after death, it is God's gift."
   d. "Eternal damnation is inevitable."

3. According to Islamic tradition, funerals should be
   a. occasions for a community-wide celebration.
   b. elaborate.
   c. simple.
   d. occasions for intense grief.

4. Which of the following are the three stages of NDEs according to Russell Noyes and Roy Kletti?
   1. life review
   2. panoramic journey
   3. transcendence
   4. resistance

   a. 1 and 2
   b. 1 and 3
   c. 1, 2, and 4
   d. 1, 3, and 4

5. In terms of the "wall/door" metaphor discussed in the text, Christians would most likely view death as
    a. a wall.
    b. a door.
    c. both a wall and a door.
    d. neither a wall nor a door.

TRUE/FALSE

_____   1. Exploring your beliefs about immortality will always result in an easier acceptance of death.

_____   2. The Bible provides a systematic theology of death and the afterlife.

_____   3. The idea of the resurrection of the body is NOT found in Judaic thought.

_____   4. Humanism is a secular concept.

_____   5. Death dreams can include themes associated with the growth of vegetation.

MATCHING

Match each of the following terms on the left with the appropriate description on the right.

_____   1. minyan   a. period of mourning after a person has been buried

_____   2. kaddish   b. requires a minimum number of individuals

_____   3. shivah   c. anniversary of a death

_____   4. yahrzeit   d. prayer for the dead

❧ Answers to practice questions can be found in Part IV ❧

Related Readings

📖 Indicates selection from *The Path Ahead: Readings in Death and Dying,* ed. Lynne Ann DeSpelder and Albert Lee Strickland (Mountain View, Calif.: Mayfield, 1995).

GENERAL STUDIES

📖 Thomas Attig, "Coping with Mortality: An Essay on Self-Mourning," pp. 337–341.

Thomas Attig. "Respecting the Spirituality of the Dying and the Bereaved," in *Dying, Death, and Bereavement: A Challenge for Living,* 2nd ed., ed. Inge Corless, Barbara B. Germino, and Mary A. Pittman, 61–75. New York: Springer, 2003.

International Work Group on Death, Dying and Bereavement. "Assumptions and Principles of Spiritual Care," *Death Studies* 14, no. 1 (1990): 75–81.

📖 Robert Kastenbaum, "Reconstructing Death in Postmodern Society," pp. 7–18.

CULTURAL AND RELIGIOUS PERSPECTIVES

Carl B. Becker. *Breaking the Circle: Death and the Afterlife in Buddhism.* Carbondale: Southern Illinois University Press, 1993.

Caroline Walker Bynum. *The Resurrection of the Body in Western Christianity, 200–1336.* New York: Columbia University Press, 1995.

John J. Collins and Michael Fishbane. *Death, Ecstasy, and Otherworldly Journeys.* Albany: State University of New York Press, 1996.

Neil Gillman. *The Death of Death: Resurrection and Immortality in Jewish Thought.* Woodstock, Vt.: Jewish Lights, 1997.

Stephen Greenblatt. *Hamlet in Purgatory.* Princeton, N.J.: Princeton University Press, 2001.

Kenneth Kramer. *The Sacred Art of Dying: How World Religions Understand Death.* Mahwah, N.J.: Paulist Press, 1988.

Hiroshi Obayashi, ed. *Death and Afterlife: Perspectives of World Religions.* New York: Praeger, 1991.

Jack Riemer, ed. *Wrestling with an Angel: Jewish Insights on Death and Mourning.* New York: Schocken, 1995.

Margaret Stutley. *Shamanism: A Concise Introduction.* New York: Routledge, 2002.

Carol Zaleski. "In Defense of Immortality," *First Things* (August-September 2000): 36–42.

NEAR-DEATH EXPERIENCES

Paul Badham. "Religious and Near-Death Experience in Relation to Belief in a Future Life," *Mortality* 2, no. 1 (1997): 7–21.

Bruce Greyson. "Near-Death Experiences," in *Varieties of Anomalous Experience: Examining the Scientific Evidence,* eds. Etzel Cardeña, Steven Jay Lynn, and Stanley Krippner, pp. 315–352. Washington, D.C.: American Psychological Association, 2000).

Kenneth Ring and Evelyn Elsaesser. *Lessons from the Light: What We Can Learn from the New-Death Experience.* New York: Plenum, 1998.

Carol Zaleski. *Otherworld Journeys: Accounts of Near-Death Experience in Medieval and Modern Times.* New York: Oxford University Press, 1987.

SYMBOLIC IMMORTALITY AND CONTINUING BONDS

📖 Dennis Klass, "Solace and Immortality: Bereaved Parents' Continuing Bond with Their Children," pp. 246–259.

📖 Nancy Scheper-Hughes, "Death Without Weeping: The Violence of Everyday Life in Brazil," pp. 41–58.

📖 Phyllis R. Silverman, Steven Nickman, and J. William Worden, "Detachment Revisited: The Child's Reconstruction of a Dead Parent," pp. 260–270.

Organizations and Internet Resources

Center for Aging, Religion, and Spirituality: <www.aging-religion-spirituality.com>. 2481 Como Avenue, Saint Paul, MN 55108. (651) 641-3581. Fax: (651) 641-3425. Educational programming, research, and publications that identify and explore the interface between spirituality and psychosocial variables of aging.

Center for Spirituality and Healing: <www.csh.umn.edu>. 420 Delaware Street, S.E., Mayo Memorial Building, 5th floor, MMC #505, Minneapolis, MN 55455. (612) 624-9459.

Fax: (612) 626-5280. Innovative programs designed to integrate complementary, cultural, and spiritual care into medicine.

Faith in Action: <www.fiavolunteers.org>. Wake Forest University School of Medicine, Medical Center Boulevard, Winston-Salem, NC 27157. (877) 324-8411 or (336) 716-0101. Fax: (336) 716-3346. An interfaith volunteer caregiving program of the Robert Wood Johnson Foundation.

First Spiritual Temple: <www.fst.org>. The Ayer Institute, 16 Monmouth Street, Brookline, MA, 02446. (617) 566-7639. A nondenominational Christian Spiritualist Church founded in 1883 and dedicated to the study, advancement, and practice of healing, spirit communication, and related areas.

The George Washington Institute for Spirituality and Health: <www.gwish.org>. Suite 510, 2131 K Street, NW, Washington, D.C. 20037. (202) 496-6409. Fax: (202) 496-6413. Educational and clinical issues related to spirituality and health.

Intermountain West Foundation for Spirituality and Healing in Medicine: <www.SHIMFoundation.org>. 684 East Vine Street, #3, Murray, UT 84107. (801) 641-3030. Dedicated to promoting spirituality and healing in medicine through research and education.

International Association for Near-Death Studies: <www.iands.org>. P.O. Box 502, East Windsor Hill, CT 06028. (860) 882-1211. Fax: (860) 882-1212. Information and support related to near-death experiences.

Union for Reform Judaism: <www.uahc.org>. The UAHC Department of Jewish Family Concerns, 633 Third Avenue, New York, NY 10017. (212) 650-4294. Fax: (212) 650-4239. Information and resources from the perspective of the Reform Jewish community.

❧ Additional resources are available online at mhhe.com ❧

Major Points in This Chapter

- The belief that human personality continues in some form after death is among the oldest concepts held by human beings. In traditional societies, death is usually viewed as a change of status, a transition from the land of the living to the land of the dead.
- Traditional Hawaiian beliefs about death and the afterlife emphasize the clan and punishment for wrongdoing.
- Western views of immortality have been influenced by Judaic, Hellenistic, and Christian traditions as well as by secular ideas of the modern era.
- Hebrew tradition views the human person as an undivided psychophysical entity; it is not as if the soul inhabits a body, but rather that the body has life.
- Plato refined the Hellenistic concept of the soul and advanced a number of "proofs" that the soul is eternal and is released from the body at death.
- Christian beliefs about the afterlife emphasize the resurrection of the body and the destiny of the individual soul.
- Islamic teachings embody a vision of the afterlife that is both spiritual and physical; Allah (God) determines the span of each life, and each person's deeds, good or

evil, determine whether the nature of the after-death existence will be eternal bliss or everlasting torment.

- A distinguishing feature of Hinduism is belief in the transmigration of the soul; at death, the soul passes from one body or "being" into an incarnation in another form, animal or human.
- Buddhism emphasizes the impermanence of the self, and the after-death state is conceived of as involving successive reincarnations toward the ultimate goal of nirvana, literally implying extinction, as when the flame of a candle, deprived of fuel, goes out.
- Otherworld journeys, stories of travel to other realms beyond the earthly, are found in virtually all cultures.
- Near-death experiences (NDEs) are accounts by people who have seemingly returned from the edge of death. These accounts are interpreted variously, with some people taking them as an indication that the human personality survives death while others believe that the phenomena associated with NDEs reflect a psychological or a neurophysiological reaction to the stress of a life-threatening experience.
- Suggestive hints about the afterlife are also associated with "death dreams" and experiences related to the ingestion of psychedelic, or mind-altering, substances.
- The spiritual component of care for dying patients should be acknowledged by caregivers so that the appropriate resources can be made available to individuals who desire them.

Observations and Reflections

This chapter explores different beliefs about whether there is life after death and, if so, what form it may take. Which beliefs discussed in the text are similar to those you hold? What do you notice about beliefs that bring you comfort or resolution in coping with or thinking about death?

You may discover differences between what you actually believe and what you would like to believe. Such differences may be important information for you. Beliefs can provide a basis for appropriate change and may reflect the recognition that what served us well at one point in our lives does not necessarily serve us equally well later on.

Use the space below to record your notes and responses to the topics covered in this chapter.

➠ *Beliefs and How They Serve*

Directions: *People generally hold beliefs about death and afterlife that serve a purpose. Here is a chance to examine your beliefs and the purpose they serve. Pay attention to distinctions between what you* actually *believe and what you would* like *to believe. Answer the following questions.*

1. In the space below, write in detail what you believe happens at and shortly after the moment of death.

_____

_____

_____

_____

_____

_____

_____

_____

_____

_____

_____

_____

_____

_____

_____

_____

_____

2. As you think about the purpose of your beliefs, use this space to answer the question: How does this belief serve or comfort you?

_____

_____

_____

_____

_____

_____

_____

_____

_____

_____

_____

_____

_____

_____

_____

_____

_____

_____

_____

_____

⌨ 🖥 *Near-Death Experiences*

Directions: *Begin your Internet search with the information provided by the International Association for Near-Death Studies located at <http:www.iands.org>. From there, locate five websites that have interesting information about NDEs. List each site's address, include a summary of the content, and rate it from 1 (very useful) to 5 (useless).*

1. URL _____ Rating_____

_____

_____

_____

_____

_____

_____

_____

_____

2. URL _____ Rating_____

_____

_____

_____

_____

_____

_____

_____

_____

_____

3. URL _____ Rating_____

_____

_____

_____

_____

_____

_____

_____

4. URL _____ Rating_____

_____

_____

_____

_____

_____

_____

_____

_____

5. URL _____ Rating_____

_____

_____

_____

_____

_____

_____

_____

_____

⟿ 🖥 *Internet Beliefnet*

Directions: *One of the most interesting sites on the Internet for information about religious traditions and spiritual support is Beliefnet [http://beliefnet.com]. Access this site and select religious issues or traditions. Explore the issues by topic or by religion and summarize the information found on the website. Also rate the usefulness of the information from 1 (extremely useful) to 5 (useless). Include the URL of the pages you visit.*

1. URL _____ Rating_____

_____

_____

_____

_____

_____

_____

_____

_____

2. URL _____ Rating_____

_____

_____

_____

_____

_____

_____

_____

_____

_____

3. URL _____ Rating_____

_____

_____

_____

_____

_____

_____

4. URL _____ Rating_____

_____

_____

_____

_____

_____

_____

_____

_____

5. URL _____ Rating_____

_____

_____

_____

_____

_____

_____

_____

_____

The Path Ahead:
Personal and Social Choices

Chapter Summary

Chapter 15 brings our survey of death and dying to a close with opportunities for reflection on the topics discussed throughout the text. Acknowledging the impact of death in our lives can awaken us to just how precious life is and lead us into a greater appreciation of relationships. One of the benefits gained through an exploration of death and dying lies in the new choices such study offers. Death is taken out of the closet and scrutinized from a variety of perspectives. The close examination of death often brings insights that help to dissipate or resolve feelings of guilt or blame related to grief over a loved one's death. New and more comforting perspectives may shed light on experiences that were previously unsettling.

Many people discover that their study of death and dying has application not only to personal or professional concerns but also to issues facing society at large. Questions concerning such issues as the allocation of scarce health care resources, care for dying patients and the elderly, and the use of life-sustaining medical technologies require an informed public, individuals who can participate knowledgeably in the shaping of public policy. Confronting the meaning of death in social as well as personal contexts may alter our political consciousness and offer a deeper dimension of reality to issues involving public safety, disarmament, environmental pollution, and violent crime.

Death education is a young discipline, one in which curricula and standards for measuring outcome are still being defined. The tag line of virtually every journal article, regardless of discipline, states: "More research is needed." This is perhaps especially so in the field of thanatology. Students who undertake further work in the discipline will find innumerable opportunities to make significant contributions. Because thanatology deals with both scientific and humanitarian concerns, the qualities of objectivity and caring are both necessary. Needed, too, is a dedication to maintaining communication among theorists, researchers, and practitioners.

The field of thanatology—and, by extension, death education and the death awareness movement—has already made important contributions to the quality of our communal life with respect to humanizing medical relationships, advancing appropriate care for the dying, and calling attention to the essential human values that sustain us through experiences of loss and grief. The compassionate acts of service that have been encouraged and promoted thus far are founded on a recognition of the identity and worth of each human being.

As we look to the future, and as the field of death education continues to mature, new questions and issues will demand our attention. Will care of the dying become big business? Or will dying be brought back into the personal realm of the individuals and families who are closest to a particular death? Individuals who have become sensitive to issues of terminal care as a result of studying death and dying will be equipped to make meaningful choices and to share information with others as they move toward the goal of ensuring compassionate care. The pace of social change is such that most people devote little time to the rituals of celebration and gathering together that were so central to traditional communities. If we believe that funerals are a time-honored means for facilitating the expression of grief and coping with loss, how can the essential features of such ritual be maintained or altered in such a way that the therapeutic importance of the ritual remains intact? Again, individuals who have gained some understanding of the meaning of funeral ritual and the process of grief will be in a position to make personally meaningful choices as well as to share their insights with others.

Death is an intensely human experience. In beginning to make room for loss and change in our lives, we may find it useful to balance our fears with openness, our anxieties with trust. But in gaining more familiarity with death, we ought to be wary about becoming overly casual about it—or it might turn out that we have confronted only our image of death, not death itself. In facing death, perhaps we should let go of our desire for a "good" death and attend rather to the possibility of an appropriate death. In the context of such a death, the social and emotional needs of the dying person are met to the fullest extent possible, and suffering is kept to a minimum. There is no place for dehumanizing or demeaning procedures. An appropriate death is the death that someone would choose for himself or herself—if there were a choice.

Objectives

- To identify and evaluate the social and personal consequences of studying death and dying.
- To assess the current state of death education and to suggest concerns that should be addressed.
- To analyze speculation about attitudes and practices related to death in the future and to assess the potential effects of these changes on individuals and society.
- To identify and appraise for oneself the qualities associated with an appropriate death.

Key Terms and Concepts

appropriate death
death anxiety
death awareness movement
"death without regrets"

death education
death in the future
ethical will
horrendous death

Questions for Guided Study and Review

1. What is the lesson learned in the story of the "mortal king"?
2. What are some benefits of studying death and dying?
3. What are some of the challenges and areas of concern facing death education?
4. What do studies of death anxiety tell us?
5. What are some of the problems and difficulties with research into death anxiety?
6. What are some of the significant contributions of death education and the death-awareness movement on our collective well-being?
7. How have spiritual values been important in the evolution of palliative and hospice care?
8. How might death education help to alleviate instances of "horrendous death"?
9. Projecting from current trends in modern societies, what are some possible future concerns related to death and dying?
10. What is the personal value of exploring issues related to dying and death?
11. How can we "humanize" death and dying?
12. What are the characteristics of a "good" death?
13. What is an "appropriate" death?
14. How was the death of Charles Lindbergh an example of an appropriate death?
15. What have you learned through taking this course?

Practice Test Questions

MULTIPLE CHOICE

1. According to Robert Fulton, mourning is
   a. the most important function in overcoming death.
   b. not always necessary.
   c. a dynamic process.
   d. the least important part of the death process.

2. Herman Feifel asserts that the death-awareness movement has
   a. helped humanize medical relationships and health care.
   b. little effect in broadening our grasp of the phenomenology of illness.
   c. little to say about the vitality of human responses to loss.
   d. made few contributions to well-being, but there is reason for optimism.

3. In the context of humanizing death and dying, what can help balance fears and anxieties about death?
   1. casualness
   2. openness
   3. control
   4. trust

   a. 1 and 2
   b. 1, 2, and 3
   c. 1 and 3
   d. 2 and 4

4. In ancient Greece, to die young was considered
    a. exceptional luck.
    b. tragic.
    c. quite normal.
    d. unusual.

5. In the context of an appropriate death, the dying person's
    a. self-identity is diminished.
    b. suffering is controlled.
    c. wishes are controlled.
    d. choices are limited.

TRUE/FALSE

_____ 1. Depending on one's personal and cultural resources, death may be devalued, denied, and eluded.

_____ 2. Hospices and suicide prevention programs are examples of a movement to confront issues surrounding death.

_____ 3. Cultural attitudes about death are reflected in a society's programs for the aged and its care of the dying.

_____ 4. According to Dan Leviton and William Wendt, death education should address human-caused large-scale deaths.

_____ 5. The concept of a good death is essentially the same in all cultures.

MATCHING

Match each of the following quotes related to a particular concept on the right with the appropriate person on the left.

_____ 1. Robert Kastenbaum

_____ 2. Avery Weisman

_____ 3. Herman Feifel

_____ 4. Alfred Killilea

a. *appropriate death:* "a death someone might choose for himself had he a choice"

b. *death anxiety:* "thanatology's assembly line"

c. *death awareness:* "deepens appreciation of life"

d. *death awareness movement:* "integrate existing knowledge concerning death and grief into communal and public institutions"

❧ Answers to practice questions can be found in Part IV ❧

Related Readings

📖 Indicates selection from *The Path Ahead: Readings in Death and Dying,* ed. Lynne Ann DeSpelder and Albert Lee Strickland (Mountain View, Calif.: Mayfield, 1995).

DEATH EDUCATION

Clifton D. Bryant, ed. *Handbook of Death & Dying.* Thousand Oaks, Calif.: Sage, 2003

Charles A. Corr and Kenneth J. Doka. "Master Concepts in the Field of Death, Dying, and Bereavement: Coping Versus Adaptive Strategies," *Omega: Journal of Death and Dying* 43, no. 3 (2001): 183–199.

Patrick Vernon Dean, "Is Death Education a Nasty Little Secret? A Call to Break the Alleged Silence," pp. 323–326.

Glennys Howarth and Oliver Leaman, eds. *Encyclopedia of Death and Dying.* New York: Routledge, 2001.

Robert Kastenbaum, ed. *Macmillan Encyclopedia of Death and Dying.* New York: Gale, 2002.

Robert Kastenbaum and Beatrice Kastenbaum, eds. *Encyclopedia of Death.* Phoenix: Oryx Press, 1989.

Carla J. Sofka. "Social Support 'Internetworks,' Caskets for Sale, and More: Thanatology and the Information Superhighway," *Death Studies* 21, no. 6 (1997): 553–574.

Maura Spiegel and Richard Tristman, eds. *The Grim Reader: Writings on Death, Dying, and Living On.* New York: Anchor-Doubleday, 1997.

Robert G. Stevenson, ed. *Curing Death Ignorance: Teaching Children About Death in Schools.* Philadelphia: Charles Press, 1994.

Tony Walter. *The Revival of Death.* London: Routledge, 1994.

Hannelore Wass, "Visions in Death Education," pp. 327–334.

LIVING WITH AWARENESS OF MORTALITY

Thomas Attig, "Coping with Mortality: An Essay on Self-Mourning," pp. 337–341.

Sandra L. Bertman, "Bearing the Unbearable: From Loss, the Gain," pp. 348–354.

Allan B. Chinen, "The Mortal King," pp. 335–336.

Herman Feifel, "Psychology and Death: Meaningful Rediscovery," pp. 19–28.

F. Gonzalez-Crussi. *The Day of the Dead and Other Mortal Reflections.* New York: Harcourt, Brace, 1993.

International Work Group on Death, Dying, and Bereavement. "Existential Questions and Their Moral Implications," *Omega: Journal of Death and Dying* 43, no. 1 (2001): 1–6.

Robert Kastenbaum, "Reconstructing Death in Postmodern Society," pp. 7–18.

Alfred G. Killilea, "The Politics of Being Mortal," pp. 342–347.

Daniel Leviton, "Horrendous Death: Improving the Quality of Global Health," pp. 165–168.

Robert A. Neimeyer, ed. *Death Anxiety Handbook: Research, Instrumentation, and Application.* Washington, D.C.: Taylor & Francis, 1993.

Organizations and Internet Resources

The Death Clock: <www.deathclock.com>. A friendly reminder from the Internet that life is slipping away. Enter your personal information and see how long you have to live statistically.

Death Today: <http://death.monstrous.com/death_today.htm>. Michael Kearl's review of the sociology of death, including discussion of changes in practices and beliefs.

Find A Grave: <www.findagrave.com>. An Internet database containing about five million grave records, including photographs of graves and cemeteries.

Goodbye Magazine: <www.goodbyemag.com>. An online and print journal of contemporary obituaries.

International Network on Personal Meaning: <www.meaning.ca>. c/o Trinity Western University, Graduate Counselling Psychology Department, 7600 Glover Road, Langley, B.C. V2Y 1Y1 Canada. (604) 513-2034. Fax: (604) 513-2010. Network for education, research, and news concerning the quest for meaning, including coping with death anxiety.

Morbidity and Mortality Weekly Report: <www.cdc.gov/mmwr/>. The CDC's weekly publication with links to reports related to illness and death.

The Tombstone Traveller's Guide: <www.tombstonetravel.com>. What will the American cemetery look like in the future?

‿ Additional resources are available online at mhhe.com ‿

Major Points in This Chapter

- Death may be viewed as a threat or as a catalyst toward greater awareness and creativity in life.
- Death is inseparable from the whole of human experience; the study of death touches on the past, present, and future.
- The study of death takes into account the actions of individuals as well as the customs of entire societies; it leads naturally to the arena of political decisions and ultimately brings us to choices of an emphatically personal nature.
- Coming to terms with personal mortality can be understood as a process of mourning—a lifelong experience in coping with uncertainty, impermanence, and vulnerability, all qualities inherent in being mortal.
- Thanatological studies create movement—individually and as a society—toward knowledge and actions that allow us to deal with death intelligently and with compassion.
- Research on death anxiety and its related concepts of fear, threat, and concern with the prospect of one's own death should be applied to practical issues that human beings experience in their encounters with dying, death, and bereavement.
- The interrelated disciplines of death education, counseling, and care of the dying continue to evolve; one of the most pressing needs involves a deeper recognition of the diversity of experiences present in modern, pluralistic societies.
- The conceptualizing of death in the future raises intriguing questions relating to technology, ethics, law, and the whole range of customs and practices that have been part of the way humans traditionally have dealt with death. For example, given an ever growing population and increasing demand for land, will ground burials continue to be a reasonable option for future generations?
- Achieving an appropriate death (defined as the death a person would choose for himself or herself should such a choice be possible) requires that we first rid ourselves of the notion that death is never appropriate.

Observations and Reflections

Do you envision the future as one wherein technology dominates our decisions about death, dying, and bereavement? Or are you confident about the evolution of a more humane approach to dealing with death?

Use the space below and on the next page to record your thoughts and reflections about dying, death, and bereavement in the present and in the future.

⇒ *Death in the Future*

Directions: *Imagine yourself as an anthropologist arriving on Earth from another planet in the year 2050. Your job is to look at the behaviors related to death, dying, and bereavement. Be imaginative in your responses to the following:*

1. What do you envision? Recall each of the chapters in *The Last Dance* and write about the changes you imagine will come.

    _____

    _____

    _____

    _____

    _____

    _____

2. What kinds of life-threatening illnesses prevail? Is AIDS still a threat? _____

    _____

    _____

    _____

    _____

    _____

    _____

3. How are the dying treated? _____

    _____

    _____

    _____

    _____

    _____

4. How is death defined? _____

_____

_____

_____

_____

_____

5. Does the imagined future include "neomorts," bodies in suspended animation from which parts are taken when needed? _____

_____

_____

_____

_____

_____

6. What kinds of death rituals are observed? _____

_____

_____

_____

_____

_____

7. What beliefs would be present in such a future society? _____

_____

_____

_____

_____

_____

⇒ 🖳 *Death Predictions*

Directions: *Will medical scientists develop techniques to accurately predict the time of a person's death? Access the sites listed below. Note the similarities and differences between the predictions of your death date. Describe your reactions to the information contained on each site.*

1. <www.deathclock.com>

_____

_____

_____

_____

_____

_____

_____

_____

_____

_____

2. <www.msnbc.com/modules/quizzes/lifex.asp>

_____

_____

_____

_____

_____

_____

_____

_____

_____

_____

3. <www.dinkytown.net/java/LifeTime.html>

_____

_____

_____

_____

_____

_____

_____

4. <www.am-i-fat.com/Life_Expectancy.html>

_____

_____

_____

_____

_____

_____

_____

5. <http://home.worldonline.dk/eskemj/>

_____

_____

_____

_____

_____

_____

_____

⫸ *Influence of the Pioneers*

Directions: *Review your readings about the beginnings of death education. Below is a recent photograph of Elisabeth Kübler-Ross. Remembering what you know about her contributions, write several paragraphs summarizing what you believe to be her impact.*

© 2000 PATRICK DEAN

Now, imagine that you are in a conversation with Dr. Kübler-Ross at this time in her life. She is ailing from a series of strokes that have left her immobile. You ask, "How are you?" In the next section, construct the response you imagine she would have based on the stages of her model of coping with illness.

1. Stage one response: _____

_____

_____

_____

_____

2. Stage two response: _____

_____

_____

_____

_____

_____

3. Stage three response: _____

_____

_____

_____

_____

_____

_____

4. Stage four response: _____

_____

_____

_____

_____

_____

_____

5. Stage five response: _____

_____

_____

_____

_____

_____

_____

⟫➡ *Ethical Will*

Directions: *An ethical will is intended to communicate and describe to your survivors your values, beliefs, blessings, life's lessons, and other inspirational advice. Use the space below to place your thoughts for an ethical will.*

What I'd most like my family and friends to understand about my life, what was important to me, and what I learned are described below. The last thing I'd like to say is this:

_____

_____

_____

_____

_____

_____

_____

_____

_____

_____

_____

_____

_____

_____

_____

_____

_____

_____

262 ∼ Chapter 15

Journey Through The Last Dance, 7th ed.
Activities and Resources

⟫➡ *Create Your Own Activities*

Directions: *The activities in this book are designed to give you added experiences with the material in* The Last Dance. *Here is an opportunity for you to give us some ideas for activities to include in the next edition of this book. Some of these activities might use the Internet. Following the format for the activities you've completed in this book, include a title, directions and content.*

⭢ *Create Your Own Activities*

Directions: *The activities in this book are designed to give you added experiences with the material in* The Last Dance. *Here is an opportunity for you to give us some ideas for activities to include in the next edition of this book. Some of these activities might use the Internet. Following the format for the activities you've completed in this book, include a title, directions and content.*

⟩⟩➡ *Postscript and Farewell*

We hope you have enjoyed using this companion to *The Last Dance: Encountering Death and Dying*. We would like to have your suggestions and submissions for the next edition. If you have developed activities that might be included, please send them to us.

It will also be helpful for us to know which parts of this book were most beneficial in your course of study.

Please consider using the following response form. When you fill it out, you can send it to Pacific Publishing Services, Post Office Box 1150, Capitola-by-the-Sea, California 95010-1150.

We appreciate all of your comments.

1. Which parts of *Journey Through The Last Dance* did you use?

	Always	Usually	Some of the time	1–2 times	Never
Chapter Summary					
Objectives					
Key Terms and Concepts					
Questions for Guided Study and Review					
Practice Test Questions					
Related Readings					
Organizations and Internet Resources					
Major Points in This Chapter					
Observations and Reflections					
Learning Activities					

2. What particular parts of *Journey Through The Last Dance* were most helpful?

_____

_____

_____

_____

_____

3. What comments can you make about improvements?

_____

_____

_____

_____

_____

4. What other activities or materials would you like to see included?

_____

_____

_____

_____

_____

5. Did you share the activities with classmates or with others? If so, what kind of re-sponses did you get?

_____

_____

_____

_____

_____

Thanks for your help! We appreciate hearing from you.

Reading a Journal Article

Academic journals are among the most reliable sources for information about death studies. The articles in such journals are scholarly and well-researched. Furthermore, the articles are generally reviewed by academic peers to ensure their scholarliness and accuracy. They should nevertheless be read critically. In evaluating studies, sample size and composition is important.

If a journal or article is unavailable at your school's library, most libraries are now able to take advantage of services that make it possible to fax or send articles from elsewhere. You may wish to check with your librarian early in the semester to see if this service is available to you. Many opportunities also exist to gather information through the Internet. Many journals have websites that contain the table of contents from the journals, while others have abstracts or complete articles available. Check with your librarian and academic computing personnel to see which resources you can access.

The Structure of Scholarly Articles

Scholarly articles generally have six sections: Abstract, Introduction, Methods, Results, Discussion, and References. These sections may be briefly described as follows:

Abstract. Summarizes the article. It briefly gives you the hypothesis, theories, methodology, results, and interpretation of the findings.

Introduction. Discusses the topic, reviews previous research, and states the study's hypothesis and predictions.

Methods. Describes how the research was conducted. It is usually broken up into three subsections: (1) Subjects, describing the people studied; (2) Materials, describing materials used in the study; and (3) Procedure, describing how the study was done.

Results. Gives the results of the research. It provides the statistics and quantitative results.

Discussion. Refers to ideas, hypotheses, and studies examined in the Introduction; it also suggests future research or argues for or against a theory.

References. Provides a bibliography of the article's sources.

Useful Reading Tips

1. *Read the abstract first.* The abstract gives you a general idea of what to expect.

---

2. *Scan the article.* This will give you a feel for what is being covered.

3. *Skip around.* You don't have to read the article in any particular order. Reading the Introduction and Discussion sections first may make it easier to understand the article.

4. *Read the article at least twice.* Don't think that something is wrong with you if you don't understand everything after the first reading. Scholarly articles can be difficult to comprehend.

5. *Read the Methods and Results sections for general information.* Usually all you need to know from these sections is how the research was conducted and what its results were. You usually don't need to know every detail.

6. *Think critically.* Just because an article is scholarly doesn't mean it is without errors or biases. Its research, for example, may not support its conclusions.

Evaluating the Article

In evaluating a journal article, keep in mind the following considerations about research samples and methodological limitations.

Sampling Issues. The choice of a sample is critical. To be useful, a sample should be representative, meaning that this small group represents a larger group in terms of age, sex, ethnicity, social class, orientation, and so on. Samples that are not representative of the larger group are known as biased samples. Many samples in death studies research are limited because they rely on volunteers and because ethnic groups may be underrepresented.

Clinical Research. A major limitation of clinical research is its focus on unhealthy behavior. Ask yourself how a condition was defined as healthy or unhealthy, whether inferences gathered from the behavior of patients can be applied to others, and whether the individuals in the study are representative of the group.

Survey Research. Limitations of survey research include people inaccurately reporting their behavior; interviewers allowing preconceptions to influence the way they frame their questions, thereby biasing their interpretations; the discomfort some respondents feel about revealing information; the interviewer's gender, which may influence respondents' comfort level; and the reluctance of some ethnic groups to reveal information.

Observational Research. Limitations of observational research include volunteer bias, whether awareness of being observed affects behaviors, whether participant observation affects objectivity, and ethical responsibilities regarding informing those being studied.

Differences in sampling and methodological techniques help explain why scientific studies of the same phenomenon may arrive at different conclusions. Sometimes conclusions differ because of errors concerning different assumptions about death studies.

Journals

If we were to choose only seven journals with which to stay current with the field, they would be the ones listed below in alphabetical order. They should be part of your library's basic journal collection. (If not, see if they will acquire the missing titles.)

Death Studies

Illness, Crisis, and Loss

Journal of Loss and Trauma (formerly *Journal of Personal and Interpersonal Loss*)

Journal of Palliative Care

Mortality

Omega: Journal of Death and Dying

Suicide and Life-Threatening Behavior

Other useful journals are listed below. Although most of them are not solely devoted to death studies, they all frequently publish relevant articles.

AIDS Care: Psychological and Socio-Medical Aspects of AIDS/HIV

AIDS Patient Care and Standards

American Journal of Nursing

American Journal of Orthopsychiatry

American Journal of Psychiatry

American Journal of Public Health

American Psychologist

American Sociological Review

Archives of Suicide Research

Australian Journal of Psychology

Australian Psychologist

British Journal of Guidance and Counseling

Cambridge Quarterly of Healthcare Ethics

Cancer Nursing

Cancer Practice

Counselling Psychology Quarterly

European Journal of Psychotherapy, Counselling and Health

Gerontologist

Hastings Center Report

Health Communication

JAMA: Journal of the American Medical Association

Journal for the Scientific Study of Religion

Journal of Advanced Nursing

Journal of Applied Social Psychology

Journal of Clinical Ethics

Journal of Consulting and Clinical Psychology

Journal of Gerontological Social Work

Journal of Law Medicine & Ethics

Journal of Medical Ethics

Journal of Medicine and Philosophy

Journal of Personality

Journal of Personality and Social Psychology

Journal of Psychosocial Oncology

Journal of the American Academy of Child and Adolescent Psychiatry.

Journal of the American Geriatrics Society

Journal of Traumatic Stress

Kennedy Institute of Ethics Journal

Lancet

Medical Care

Milbank Quarterly

New England Journal of Medicine

Nursing Clinics of North America

Psycho-Oncology

Psychodynamic Practice

Social Science and Medicine

Social Work

Sociology of Religion

Theoretical Medicine and Bioethics

Adapted by permission from Bobbi Mitzenmacher and Barbara Werner Sayad, *Study Guide to Accompany Human Sexuality*, 3rd ed., Strong, DeVault & Sayad. Copyright © 1999 Mayfield Publishing Company, Mountain View, Calif.

Writing a Research Paper

There are nine basic steps to writing a research paper. The following information will help guide you through the decisions you will need to make and the tasks you will need to accomplish in writing a research paper. Note that actually writing the paper doesn't occur until step eight.

Step One. Start with an idea that interests you. Begin with a subject, idea, or question that you find interesting. Because you may be spending considerable time working on it, make sure it's not boring. This initial idea may evolve into something entirely different, but you need to find a starting point.

Step Two. Make sure your idea is specific. Once you've found an idea that interests you, do some background reading and researching to get a feel for the topic. See what research has been done. Talk with your instructor or teaching assistant to make sure that your topic is specific and that there are available resources.

Step Three. Create a bibliography. Once you know your idea is workable, create a bibliography on your topic. Use general bibliographies of scholarly articles, such as Sociological Abstracts or Psychological Abstracts, or do a search on computer bibliographic databases, such as PsycLit and Sociofile. Your reference librarian can assist you.

Step Four. Read relevant articles and books. Read other works on your topic to find whether your idea has already been researched, other research changes what you want to do, and you can incorporate earlier research into your paper.

Step Five. Decide on your methodology. Decide which methodology you will use: survey, observational, or clinical methods.

Step Six. Write an outline. Writing an outline will help you organize your ideas and clarify the steps you will need to do in your research. Remember, however, that writing a research paper is an evolving process. You will probably change your outline as you go along.

Step Seven. Conduct your research. At this point you need to conduct your actual research. This involves constructing the materials for the survey or experiment; planning how to conduct the survey, interviews, or observation; and collecting the data.

Step Eight. Write your paper. Use your outline to write a first draft. If you use the American Psychological Association (APA) style, your paper will be divided into six parts. See the discussion on the structure of scholarly articles in the previous resource section, "Reading a Journal Article."

Step Nine. Rewrite. Rewriting is the key to good writing. After you've written your paper, put it aside for a few days, then come back to it fresh and reread it, pencil in hand. (If you've input the paper on a computer, read the hard copy.)

An excellent technique for refining your paper is to read it aloud. Reading it aloud will help you "hear" awkward sentences, bad grammar, and incomplete sentences. It will also help you "see" typos and misspellings.

Show your paper to a friend and ask for his or her reactions: Is the paper well organized? Is it complete? Does it read smoothly?

Finally, retype your paper. Be sure that you have corrected all typographical and spelling errors. A carefully typed or printed paper reflects the care you put into your project.

Adapted by permission from Bobbi Mitzenmacher and Barbara Werner Sayad, *Study Guide to Accompany Human Sexuality,* 3rd ed., Strong, DeVault & Sayad. Copyright © 1999 Mayfield Publishing Company, Mountain View, Calif.

Guidelines and Suggestions for Research Projects

A research project involves selecting a topic, designing a small-scale study around that topic, collecting data, and presenting your findings. Although research projects are similar in some ways to writing a library research paper, they involve a particular set of requirements that must be considered if the outcome is to be successful. In this assignment, you are asked to plan, complete, and report on your research by creating a poster presentation of your findings.

Poster Format

At conferences and other group situations, poster sessions allow authors (also known as presenters) and attendees to engage in extended one-on-one discussions about the author's research. Posters detailing research findings, new ideas, innovations, and advances in a field of study can be shared with many individuals at the same time. Several posters are usually displayed simultaneously in a large room, giving attendees an opportunity to browse the various poster displays and talk with the authors, who typically also have handouts available that summarize their research methods and results.

All research projects of this kind are presented in a "poster" format. The poster is generally about four by six feet, and is displayed in a way that viewers can understand both the project and the results in a clear, interesting manner.

Research Assignment

This activity contains specific guidelines for the preparation of a project poster. (For this assignment, you will also hand in a text-only copy with your poster; the text-only copy is typed in a regular-size font [10 point or 12 point] and should be between 8–10 pages long, including references.)

You may work alone, in pairs, or in a group of not more than three members. If you work with others, the workload for each member must be equivalent to the workload of a single person's project. Students working in pairs or in groups must submit a brief individual report, summarizing their own contribution to the project. Be sure to exchange phone numbers and e-mail addresses because you will need to be in contact with your group members. Find a compatible out-of-class meeting time.

References

One goal of this assignment is to acquaint you with the scholarly literature. Your study should include at least four references from the literature on death and dying, not including your text. Students working in groups will need to include one additional reference for each group member, resulting in *at least* six citations for a three-person group.

To begin, locate one reference related to your research project. This reference does not necessarily have to exactly match what you plan on doing with your project, but it should pertain to the topic in some way. Type a summary of your reference. You will use the summary to guide your work on the project outline and to determine how the references can be incorporated into the final project presentation.

References should be from journals, books, or articles from an edited collection of readings in the professional literature. You can review the Related Readings in this book for ideas. To locate an overview of your chosen topic, look in one of the secondary source encyclopedias in the field of thanatology.[1] These encyclopedias contain succinct and useful articles on various topics in thanatology. Check your library's holdings, both in the reference section and on the general shelves.

Secondary references are useful for background information. Examples of such references include assigned readings from your text or other books, magazine articles, dissertation abstracts, dictionaries, and encyclopedias. Such references should *not* be used as primary references for your poster. "Pop psych" books, popular magazines, and newspaper articles are unacceptable as primary references, although they may be helpful in providing background or guidance as you begin investigating your topic.

In addition to the sources listed in this book by chapter under the heading Related Readings, check journals in the field, such as *Omega, Mortality,* and *Death Studies,* as well as articles from scholarly journals in related disciplines. You can review pages 269–270 in this book for listings of journals that are likely to be of interest. Check your library's journal holdings, both in print and online.

In accessing information available on the Internet, use the guidelines for evaluating Internet sites provided on pages 5–8 of the Introduction to this book. Take care in selecting your reference sources. You might want to ask your professor for advice about information you find online, particularly regarding the reliability and validity of theory, research, or practices described. All of the sources used in developing your poster presentation are placed in the reference section of the poster in the format shown in the fifth edition of the *Publication Manual* of the American Psychological Association.[2]

Designing a Research Project

Once you have selected a topic to investigate and have completed the write-up of one of your references, you will need to think about the overall design of your project. This assignment is intended to be a small-scale study. You do not have to find hundreds of participants, but you must find a sufficient number of participants or data sources to allow you to see some trends.

THE OUTLINE

An outline allows you to organize your thoughts in a hierarchical or logical sequence. You can refer to reference books that describe how to prepare an outline for a research project or paper.[3] Choose one of three types of outlines:

1. The *keyword outline* in which each outline level is restricted to keywords.

2. The *topic outline* in which phrases and clauses are used at each level of description.

3. The *sentence outline* in which each level of description is a full sentence.

The outline view of your word-processing program can be used to help make sure that you have addressed all of the key points of your idea. You will turn in your outline to your professor before you begin to collect data or make observations.

THE IDEA

The goals and objectives for your project are developed by working with your idea. This process also involves tying your initial background research into your overall study plan. Here is a fictitious example of a small-scale study to give you an idea of how to proceed.

In this example, two researchers were interested in using children's drawings to examine how children think about death as well as what they say causes death. The hypothesis was that children who live in violent environments would attribute cause of death to more violent acts in comparison to those who live in less violent circumstances. The researchers were also interested in finding out if the leading cause of death stated by most of the children in each sample correlated with official statistics on the leading cause of death in the child's community. This project required at least two sample populations in which adults would be willing to have their children participate in the study. (Several noteworthy results came about just from seeking permission to conduct the pilot study.) Instead of using interview questions, a survey, or direct observation, the researchers decided to use a script with each sample. They also decided on a method for obtaining drawings and entering into a dialogue with the children to verify the cause of death depicted in the drawings.

In your own project, remember that it is important to be respectful of your participants. Explain that you are collecting data for a class project, but wait until *after* you have collected the data to describe the purpose of your project (unless, as in our fictional case, adult permission is needed to survey the children). Assure your participants that they have the right to withdraw from your project at any time. Develop a systematic way of coding your observations or results. In our fictional example, the researchers used the drawings and causes of death reported by each child in the study.

THE RESEARCH METHODS

After obtaining permission to conduct research with four age-matched samples, the researchers in our example developed a method of collecting information. Here is the introduction they used with the children:

"Hi, my name is _____. I'm working on a project that only children like you can help me with. I am here today to see what you all know about the ways people die. Please use the paper and crayons on your table to draw a picture of the ways people die. It can be anything you think. Please start your drawings or write your thoughts on a piece of paper now. We'll talk about what you have drawn and what you are thinking after you finish. We will have time to talk about your ideas and feelings."

The research section of your study is where your professor may choose to review your interview questions, surveys, or narrative before you use them with participants. After you have your professor's response, you can begin collecting information. Remember that this project does *not* work well as a last-minute activity.

In our fictitious research project, after obtaining the latest official statistics on causes of death from county and city sources, these statistics were compared with the leading causes of death stated by each sample population of the children who participated in the study.

THE RESULTS

In the results section of your poster presentation, you will discuss your findings. What did you discover? Did the results prove or disprove your hypothesis? What insights did you arrive at concerning the topic? How do the results you obtained compare with the information from your references? What surprises occurred? Where did you discover possible flaws in your plan? What suggestions could you offer for further research or observations on this topic? Be sure to compare and contrast your findings with your search of the literature (your references), as well as what you have learned in class.

In our fictional example, the samples showed a correlation between the number of violent deaths in the environment and the number of children depicting such events in their drawings. The researchers noted that there was a possibility that the content of the drawings might have been influenced by having the children in groups, with some children possibly copying a neighbor's idea. One of the most interesting findings about this study was the difficulty in getting adults to allow children to participate. A contact in Greece reported that, even with her status as a university professor in child development, none of the schools in her area would allow the children to participate. Comments like "Why would we want them to think about *death?*" and "That's something that would *not* be good for our children" revealed that discussing death was taboo in some social environments.

THE REFERENCES

Follow APA style for all references.

Preparing Your Poster Presentation

A well-constructed poster is self-explanatory and addresses the questions a reader is likely to have about your project. Successful posters achieve both coverage of the topic and clarity of presentation. In order to effectively communicate the nature of your work, your poster should be succinct, clearly presented, well written, and checked for spelling and grammatical errors.

COVERAGE AND CLARITY

Posters must be easy to read. In preparing text for your poster, aim for clarity of communication. Your goal is to educate your readers about what you have learned through studying an interesting topic. The APA guidelines for posters include the following points about coverage and clarity:

> Have you provided all the obvious information? Will a casual observer walk away understanding your major findings after a quick perusal of your material? Will a more careful reader learn enough to ask informed questions? Ask yourself, What would I need to know if I were viewing this material for the first time? Then state the information clearly.[4]

To achieve clarity, check whether the sequencing of the material and visual aids follows your idea and the steps you took to reach your conclusions. The APA guidelines offer useful advice:

> Indicate the ordering of your material with numbers, letters or arrows, when necessary. Is the content being communicated clearly? Keep it simple. Place your major points in the poster and save the non-essential but interesting sidelights for informal discussion. Be selective. Your final conclusions or summary should leave observers focused on a concise statement of your most important findings.[5]

FORMATTING A POSTER

Conference posters have a standard layout that is composed of four columns that read from top to bottom and left to right. This arrangement allows several people to read the poster at the same time without bumping into one another.

Posters are visual. Think about color and design. Use graphs and tables to display ideas and results. Add drawings, cartoons, photos, or other visuals to arouse interest and sharpen clarity. Posters should not be dry and boring, but neither should they be flamboyant. Avoid gaudy colors and patterned backgrounds. You can use color effectively by restricting yourself to harmonious three-color schemes while avoiding the kind of excess that will give your poster the look of an elementary school project. The APA guidelines advise:

> Choose two to three colors and keep them consistent throughout the poster. Use strong primary colors (for example, red, blue, and yellow). They provide the best contrast and create the most professional impression. Keep lots of empty (white) space on your poster to enhance the effect of colored sections.[6]

Use a large type font. Many experienced poster presenters recommend a sans serif font for the text (for example, Arial or Helvetica). You may want to use 20-point type for text and 48-point type for the title.[7] Posters should be prepared in upper and lower case; do not use all capital letters. For your method and results sections, you can use "bullets" to summarize your procedures and findings.

Preparing Graphics

You can use graphs, illustrations, photographs, videos, tape recordings, computer displays, and other supplementary materials to enhance your work and make it clearer to your readers.[8] A professional poster presentation is *not* decorated just to make it "pretty." Each visual element relates to the study. Hand drawings and handwriting are sloppy and amateurish. The computer program Microsoft PowerPoint may give you ideas for planning and preparing your graphics.

Placing Information on Your Poster

Mount the pages of your poster on construction paper or matte board that is large enough to provide a 1" to 2" border. You can also use large sheets of poster board. Do not overlap the pages or have pages hanging over the edge of the mounting material. All the information should be contained within the borders of the construction paper or poster board.

You may want to attach your poster to a free-standing tripod. (A tri-folding cardboard device for presentations is available at office supply stores.) If you decide to present your poster this way, make sure that the board is light and portable. In placing the information on your poster, be sure to check the following:

1. Type font and size are consistent both in the headings and in the text.

2. Material has been placed in the correct sequence.

3. Only information that is absolutely necessary appears.

What Does a Finished Poster Look Like?

Elements of a Poster

A poster presentation includes a set of standard components that resemble the sections of a research article, as described in the APA's *Publication Manual*.

Layout

Here we'll look at an example that includes the major areas of a poster presentation. The design of a poster presentation usually includes four columns. The abstract, introduction, and research questions are usually in the first column, followed by a column devoted to research methods, then one to the results, and the last to your conclusions, references and, if appropriate, acknowledgements (see Figure 1.1). Each of these elements is discussed with detailed illustrations in the following sections.

The title of a presentation and its authors occupies a long box—sometimes called a banner—at the top of a poster. Authors' names and each person's affiliation is placed in this section. The large font san serif type allows attendees to easily see who prepared the poster.

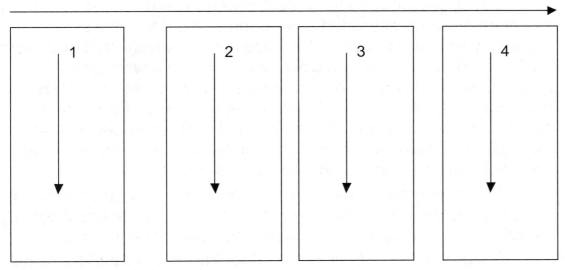

Figure 1.1 *Overview of a four-column poster layout*

Ways People Die: Environmental Influences on Children's Views of Death

Puddley P. Purrpott, Ph.D., and A. Jamal Garcia, M.A.

University of Hawaii, Honolulu

Figure 1.2 *Title, author(s)and their affiliation(s)*

Begin with your banner. (see figure 1.2) Then, in the first column, place your abstract, followed by the rest of your information in four columns that read from top to bottom and left to right, ending with your references in the lower right hand corner of the last column.

Abstract

The abstract is a brief summary of your work. It is the first item in the left-hand column of your poster. The abstract includes your research questions or hypotheses, method(s) used to collect data, synopsis of the main results and the conclusions drawn from the results. Write the abstract after all the other pieces of your research are complete. Like the title, the abstract should be self-explanatory and self-contained (see Figure 1.3).

Abstract

When questioned about the "ways people die," children living in violent or death-saturated environments tend to answer quite differently from those whose lives are comparatively sheltered from such experiences. Children's drawings provide a window for examining the impact and consequences of environmental exposure to chronic acts of violence. James Garabino says, "Few issues challenge our moral, intellectual, and political resources as does the topic of children and community violence, war, violent crime, and other forms of armed conflict." (Garabino, 1993).

This pilot project studied the responses of young children in matched samples from the inner city of South Central Los Angeles; Detroit, Michigan; Santa Cruz, California; and Bonn, Germany.

Children ages 7–9 were asked to draw a picture of the ways people die. When children in a lower-middle class, urban school in Germany were asked about the ways people die, the influence of environment was apparent: Violent deaths were described as being caused by "weapons" and "sharp knives." Conspicuously absent was any use of the word *gun.* Handguns are illegal in Germany and carried only by the police.

Comparisons were made between population statistics regarding causes of death and those cited by the children in each sample. In violent environments, violent death was drawn by a majority of the sample. In samples where the death rate from violent events was low, children were much more likely to draw natural deaths or deaths from accidents. The population living near the Pacific Ocean depicted an unusually high number of deaths from falling off the local cliffs into the ocean and drowning. However, this cause of death was very low in the statistics collected, leading researchers to wonder if children in safer environments related more to *parental warnings* about the dangers of death than actual deaths.

Figure 1.3 *Abstract section of a poster*

Introduction

You'll want to provide an introduction to your topic. In this section of your poster, give a brief description of the topic you are investigating, at least one reference citation that supports your study, and a description of your goal(s) in conducting the study (see Figure 1.4). Consider including the answers to these basic questions:

1. What previous research led to your study?

2. What does your research add to the knowledge base?

3. Why is your study important or interesting?

4. What is the major objective of your study?

5. Who does your study impact?

Introduction

An important aspect of this study is to address questions regarding the cultural and therapeutic relevance of art therapy for inner-city children and youth experiencing trauma, violence, and loss.

Besides possessing a more mature conceptual orientation toward death, children who experience firsthand the reality of death because of war or pervasive violence or in connection with other forms of catastrophe often exhibit a fatalistic attitude toward death that contrasts with children whose experiences of death occur in more benign circumstances (Schonfeld and Smilansky, 1989).

In comparing these four populations it is clear that the environment (social, physical, religious, and psychological) has an impact on children's concepts of the ways people die.

[Individuals interested in collaborating on this research project through the provision of additional cross-national samples are encouraged to contact the authors.]

Figure 1.4 *Introduction section of a poster*

Research Questions

Research questions or hypotheses are derived from your basic topic idea. In developing research questions, think about the various aspects of the particular topic you have selected and your goals for the study. Do you want to explore the limits of an idea? Are you trying to extend a theory or add to what others have said about it? Do you want to generate a similar theory? Or perhaps you want to challenge a theory or the evidence used in developing it. An example of how research questions are presented is shown in Figure 1.5.

Research Questions

1. Will children in violence-saturated environments report more violent ways of dying?

2. How does a child's perception of the ways people die correlate to official statistics on the cause of death in that child's environment?

3. What other environmental factors contribute to a child's understanding of the ways people die?

Figure 1.5 *Research Questions section of a poster*

As you look over the project suggestions beginning on page 286, identify a topic that interests you. Perhaps you already have selected a topic from your research of the literature during your selection of a reference (see page 274). Whether you are starting from a reference, a suggested project, or an idea of your own, be mindful of the questions you are interested in answering through your study. State your research question(s) clearly in short sentences. As you continue to develop your idea, review and revise these questions as necessary.

Clearly stated research questions or hypotheses will help you conduct your study in the most efficient manner. For example, let's say you are going to use an instrument that has already been deemed reliable and valid, such as a death anxiety scale. Imagine that you are curious about whether death education lessens death anxiety. You will want to compare your classmates' death anxiety scores before and after the majority of your class time has passed. Here your research question will be very basic: Is students' death anxiety decreased after taking a course in death education?

Methods

In the methods section, you describe the source(s) of your data and how you went about collecting it. Choose the most important information about who, what, when, and where the study was conducted. This is where you give readers a picture of how you did your study (see Figure 1.6).

Method

PARTICIPANTS

Four sample populations of children averaging 25 in each group, ages 7–9, selected from communities in South Central Los Angeles; Detroit, Michigan; Santa Cruz, California; and Bonn, Germany

PROCEDURE

Each potential adult participant was approached by the interviewer and asked, "I am collecting data for a class project. Would you be willing to allow your children to participate in a study of children's views about the ways people die? Subjects will draw or write their responses to the question: 'What are the ways people die?' Death and dying will be discussed with the group, and individual drawings will be reviewed with each child and collected for analysis."

DIRECTIONS

"Hi, my name is _____. I'm working on a project that only children like you can help me with. I am here today to see what you all know about the ways people die. Please use the paper and crayons on your table to draw a picture of the ways people die. It can be anything you think. Please start your drawings or write your thoughts on a piece of paper now. We'll talk about what you have drawn and what you are thinking after you finish. We will have time to talk about your ideas and feelings."

Figure 1.6 *Methods section of a research poster*

Results

In the results section, describe your discoveries. Here you provide a summary of the most interesting findings. The order in which results are reported is important. The most interesting or relevant results are presented first. Less interesting or less relevant results are reported later. First report a general conclusion or interpretation and then follow it with descriptive information that supports this general statement.[9] The results section can be enhanced with tables, figures, photographs, or other illustrations to help demonstrate your results (see Figure 1.7).

Results

1. Children living in violent environments depicted causes of death relating to murder, expecially detailing "drive-by" shootings in the South Central, Los Angeles population complete with accurate gang colors and dead bystanders, including babies.

2. Children living in high-crime neighborhoods were more likely to accurately portray the leading causes of death, especially handgun-related shootings.

3. Children with religious backgrounds living in a benign environment attributed the cause of death to "God's will" (in more than half the drawings from the Santa Cruz, California sample).

Death Data by Sample

	Total Population	Total # Deaths	Homicide	Suicide	Accidental	Natural	Gun Related
South Central Los Angeles California	3,537,000	10,344	1,788	970	n/a	4,364	1,374 [1]
Bonn, Germany	293,072	2,988	20 [2]	35	44	2,924	2
Eastside Inner City Detroit Michigan	992,000	11,397	565	102	316	10,364	8 [3]
Santa Cruz [4] California	325,000	1,646	9	27	39	1,562	9 [5]

[1] designated "hand gun"   [2] 8 murder; 12 violent = 20   [3] designated "firearms"
[4] county population figures   [5] 1 homicide, 8 suicide

Source: Purrpott, P.P. & A. J. Garcia, Ways People Die

Figure 1.7 *Results section of a research poster*

Conclusions

Identify the most important aspects of your research, including both general and specific conclusions. Incorporate information about what you discovered as well as results that did *not* show up in your study. (see Figure 1.8).

Conclusions

1. Children living in violence-saturated environments depicted more violent ways of dying, including murder and suicide than deaths from natural causes or accidents.

2. In environments where children were exposed to violent death either directly or via adults or the media, the rate of violent death reported by the children correlates to increased death rates from these causes.

3. Religious beliefs influenced the children's depiction of the ways people die in the population attending Catholic school.

4. Dangers to child safety as emphasized by adults in the environment showed up in the children's drawings in less violent environments depicting the physical environment (falling from the cliffs into the ocean and drowning and burning to death in a house fire) and adult warnings concerning loss of life.

Figure 1.8 *Conclusions section of a poster*

References

List sources most important to your study, usually in a smaller type font than the rest of your poster text (see Figure 1.9).

References

Garbarino, J. (1993). Challenges we face in understanding children and war: A personal essay. *Child Abuse & Neglect,* 17(6), 787-793; reprinted in L. A. DeSpelder & A. L. Strickland (Eds.), (1995), *The path ahead: Readings in death and dying* (169-174). New York: McGraw-Hill.

Garbarino, J. (1992). *Children in danger: Coping with the consequences of community violence.* San Francisco: Jossey-Bass.

Schonfeld, D. J., & Smilansky, S. (1989). A cross-cultural comparison of Israeli and American children's death concepts. *Death Studies,* 13, 593-604.

U.S. Census Bureau. (2001). Murder Victims by age, sex and race. In *Statistical abstract of the United States* (186). Washington, DC: U.S. Government Printing Office.

Figure 1.9 *References section of a poster*

Project Evaluation Criteria

Poster projects are graded based on the following criteria:

1. The quality of your initial outline and reference summaries.

2. Whether the project is complete and conforms to the guidelines, including timely submission of your reference summary and outline.

3. How you designed the observation or research.

4. The quality of your observations or research.

5. Your interpretation and discussion of the findings.

6. Professional appearance. This includes careful editing, elimination of grammar and other writing mechanics errors, and the use of formal language.

7. Your choice of scholarly references written up in APA style.

8. If you worked with others, you will be evaluated on your individual contribution as well as on your ability to work collaboratively with the group.

Project Suggestions

1. Themes of death and dying are abundant in art, literature, and music. Choose works in one of the these fine arts and analyze their death-related content according to their main themes. One way to do this is by choosing a particular historical era (for example, World War II or the Victorian Age) and then comparing the art of that time with the prevalent social issues. You might ask the questions: What insights about dying, death, and bereavement are communicated in the art of that era? How have death-related themes in art reflected and influenced attitudes toward death and dying?

2. The lyrics of popular music contain death-related content. Analyze and compare the death-related themes that are present in the music of the present youth generation and those of earlier generations. What changes have occurred? Alternatively, you might analyze and compare death-related themes across several different genres of popular music. What do these themes in popular music communicate about young people's experiences with and conceptions of death? You might also interview or survey adolescents about their attitudes toward such lyrics.

3. A study can be designed around assessing death anxiety for a group of participants. Such a study can be based on death anxiety scales that are available in the published literature. For example, it would be interesting to find out if students who take a death education course are more or less death anxious or death phobic than those who do not take such a course. It would also be of interest to determine whether death anxiety scores change as a result of death education. Does taking a course about death increase or decrease anxiety? You might also focus on studying death anxiety as it relates to age, gender, religion, college major, past experiences, and so on. Other possibilities include investigating how death anxiety relates to occupation (for example, medical personnel or teachers) or to afterlife beliefs. Published literature can be found on these topics to guide the development of your research project.

4. Obituaries can be good sources of information about attitudes toward death and toward the dead. A content analysis of obituaries may reveal regional differences, gender differences, age differences, and cohort differences. You might compare your findings with previous studies of obituaries and death notices. Or you might compare recently published obituaries with those published in the past to identify and describe changes in attitudes towards death and dying. In searching for obituaries, both library and Internet resources are useful.

5. Cemeteries are another source of information about attitudes toward death and toward the dead. You might compare cemeteries across regions, ages of the deceased, religion, gender, or other variables that you identify as being relevant. Observe as many different representations of death as you can, both individual symbols (for example grave ornaments and headstones) and the symbolism of the place itself as revealed in its setting and architectural styles. Notice examples of different styles of epitaphs. What themes do you find? What information is typically given about the deceased? The materials used to construct headstones or monuments, as well as their placement within the cemetery, can also be an area of study. Or you might interview individuals who create or manufacture monuments and grave markers to obtain their insights about the significance of such memorialization. The published literature on the history of the American cemetery can be used to support your points.

6. Research children's books about death, dying, and bereavement by using your local libraries and bookstores. Read the books and compile a bibliography of children's literature in which the primary subject is death. Then expand the bibliography by annotating or describing each source. Include details such as the date and place of publication, point of view from which the story is told, religious or cultural settings, developmental level of the presentation, conceptualization of death, portrayal of grief and mourning, and any illustrations or artwork. Use the literature on development of the mature concept of death to create a list of relevant criteria, then evaluate each book for its appropriateness and sensitivity with respect to the developmental evolution of the death concept. In your evaluation, consider using a scale of 1–10, with one being the lowest rating and 10 the highest. You might also obtain responses to some or all of the books from children and their parents.

7. Similarly, you might want to review books on death and dying that are written for adolescents. You could compare these books to those written for younger children and determine in what ways they differ. The books you gather could be evaluated for their appropriateness based on what you have learned about adolescents' concepts about death and their experiences with bereavement. Based on your knowledge, how would you improve upon these books?

8. Another culture's death-related rituals and customs can be the object of in-depth analysis. In addition to accessing published research or descriptions relating to death as viewed through the eyes of another culture, you might want to interview one or more individuals from the culture you have chosen to study. Alternatively, you could interview someone who is familiar with that culture. People on campus and in your community can be helpful to you in conducting this kind of cross-cultural study. Most colleges and universities have a number of international students who might be willing to be interviewed and talk about their cultural practices.

9. Portrayals of dying, death, and bereavement in the news or entertainment media could be the subject of study and scholarly analysis. This project can take a num-

ber of directions. If television is chosen as the medium to be studied, you might focus on either news programs or on television shows in which death and dying are commonly depicted (for example, police or medical dramas). If you select film as the medium to be studied, you could examine a range of movies in which a person's death forms the main focus of the storyline. You might choose to study and report on differences in how foreign and domestic films depict stories involving death and dying. Whether you decide to study television or films, you will probably need to conduct a careful content analysis that includes discussion of how death and dying are portrayed by that medium. This kind of study must go beyond mere description to include detailed analysis of death-related content with specific information about typology, images, language, symbolism, and any other variables that you have selected to study.

10. Humor in its various forms represents one way that people cope with death. A study can be designed to examine how humor is used to encounter, deflect, or otherwise deal with death. For example, you might compile a collection of jokes or cartoons and analyze them regarding how they address or portray themes or current issues that involve dying or death. You could recruit and survey a group of individuals who are willing to rate (perhaps on a scale of 1 to 5) the jokes or cartoons you've collected on the basis of various factors and qualities to answer the question, "What do people find funny about death?" Your analysis could include differences by gender, age, and religious affiliation or background, along with other variables.

11. The Internet and World Wide Web represent an evolving aspect of the "death system" that can be examined and studied. What death-related topics can be found on the Internet? Is it possible to see patterns in themes or issues reflecting contemporary approaches to dying, death, and bereavement? You could compile a list of what you think are the best web sites and include a detailed description of what they offer, their links, and an evaluation of how useful each one is. In your evaluation, consider the target population(s), the background and motivation of the individual(s) who created the sites, and the value of the information presented.

12. The rise of *virtual cemeteries* and *memorial sites* on the Internet is another topic that can be studied and presented in a poster session. How do these innovations compare to traditional cemeteries and memorialization? Investigate sites devoted to memorializing individuals who died in a particular manner or sites devoted to grieving specific types of bereavement, such as the deaths of children, parents, friends, or pets. How do the memorials and postings for pets differ from those created for humans? Do postings differ by gender? Are more males or females memorialized on a particular site? There are many approaches and research questions that could be used to guide this kind of study.

13. Many businesses and corporations have felt the need to reevaluate their company policies on worker absences owing to bereavement. The impact of grief in the workplace (for example, with the death of a colleague) on morale and productivity is also a matter of concern to employers and managers. Studies in this topic area could begin by identifying local companies and interviewing personnel managers about their policies regarding bereavement leave for employees. Another approach could involve interviewing the employees themselves to determine their experiences and attitudes about grief in the workplace.

14. A study can be designed to investigate some particular aspect of individuals' attitudes toward death, such as attitudes toward physician-assisted suicide. It could

be interesting to compare the range of attitudes expressed on the basis of such factors as gender, occupation (or college major), religiosity, or death anxiety.

15. Sympathy and condolence cards are a source of information about attitudes and beliefs relative to loss and grief. A study of this topic might investigate issues such as the frequency with which euphemisms or metaphors are used in expressing condolences. Different types of stores (for example, stationery shops, drugstores, supermarkets) may offer a different selection of cards for sale. By collecting and analyzing a range of sympathy and condolence cards, you could create a poster presentation that describes specifically how your results reflect this diversity, perhaps comparing secular cards to religious cards.

We have listed these suggestions both for your use and to help jumpstart your imagination in choosing a topic of interest. Feel free to create and design your project in a manner that reflects your own special interests in studying death and dying.

Adapted from Research Project Guidelines developed by Illene Noppe, Ph.D., University of Wisconsin, Green Bay. Used by permission.

Notes

1. Glennys Howarth and Oliver Leaman, eds., *The Encyclopedia of Death and Dying* (New York: Routledge, 2001); Robert Kastenbaum, ed., *MacMillan Encyclopedia of Death and Dying,* 2 vols. (New York: Thompson-Gale, 2003); and Robert Kastenbaum and Beatrice Kastenbaum, *Encyclopedia of Death* (Phoenix, Ariz.: Oryx Press, 1989).

2. *Publication Manual of the American Psychological Association,* 5th ed. (Washington, D.C.: American Psychological Association, 2001).

3. Robert J. Sternberg, *The Psychologist's Companion: A Guide to Scientific Writing for Students and Researchers,* 2nd ed. (New York: Cambridge University Press, 1988) pp. 21–26.

4. *APA Poster Instructions* (Washington, D.C.: American Psychological Association, 2003).

5. Ibid.

6. Adelheid A. M. Nicol and Penny M. Pexman, *Displaying Your Findings: A Practical Guide for Creating Figures, Posters, and Presentations* (Washington, D.C.: American Psychological Association, 2003).

7. Ibid.

8. Edward R. Tufte has written three excellent resources for gaining an understanding of how to present visual information: *Envisioning Information* (1990); *Visual Explanations: Images and Qualities, Evidence and Narrative* (1997); and *The Visual Display of Quantitative Information,* 2nd ed. (2001). All are published by Graphics Press, Cheshire, Conn.

9. Sternberg, *The Psychologist's Companion,* p. 51.

Answers to Practice Test Questions

Chapter 1 Attitudes Toward Death: A Climate of Change

MULTIPLE CHOICE

1. b   (page 5)
2. c   (page 15)
3. a   (page 32)
4. b   (page 32)
5. a   (page 36)

TRUE/FALSE

1. False   (page 20)
2. True   (page 23)
3. True   (page 28)
4. False   (page 34)
5. True   (page 35)

MATCHING

1. c
2. a
3. d
4. b

(page 34)

Chapter 2 Learning About Death: The Influence of Sociocultural Forces

MULTIPLE CHOICE

1. d   (page 42)
2. c   (page 45)
3. a   (page 53)
4. d   (pages 64, 66)
5. b   (page 81)

TRUE/FALSE

1. True   (page 42)
2. False   (page 54)
3. False   (page 61)
4. True   (page 66)
5. True   (page 82)

MATCHING

1. b
2. a
3. d
4. c

(pages 55, 58, 60)

Chapter 3 Perspectives on Death: Cross-Cultural and Historical

MULTIPLE CHOICE

1. b   (page 90)
2. c   (page 92)
3. a   (page 95)
4. b   (page 113)
5. d   (page 120)

TRUE/FALSE

1. True   (page 87)
2. True   (page 94)
3. False   (page 101)
4. False   (page 111)
5. True   (pages 113, 121)

MATCHING

1. d

2. a
3. b
4. c

(pages 89–90, 91, 99, 103)

Chapter 4 Health Care Systems: Patients, Staff, and Institutions

MULTIPLE CHOICE

1. a   (page 125)
2. b   (page 129)
3. c   (page 132)
4. a   (page 141)
5. a   (page 144)

TRUE/FALSE

1. False   (page 125)
2. True   (page 133)
3. True   (page 137)
4. False   (page 140)
5. True   (page 148)

MATCHING

1. b
2. c
3. d
4. a

(page 143)

Chapter 5 Death Systems: Matters of Public Policy

MULTIPLE CHOICE

1. c   (page 156)
2. c   (pages 157–158)
3. d   (page 165)
4. d   (page 177)
5. b   (page 176)

TRUE/FALSE

1. True   (page 163)
2. False   (page 169)
3. True   (page 170)
4. False   (page 176)
5. True   (page 180)

MATCHING

1. d
2. c
3. a
4. b

(page 156)

Chapter 6 Facing Death: Living with Life-Threatening Illness

MULTIPLE CHOICE

1. b   (page 186)
2. a   (page 188)
3. c   (page 195)
4. a   (page 195)
5. b   (page 202)

TRUE/FALSE

1. True   (page 185)
2. False   (page 189)
3. True   (page 197)
4. True   (page 209)
5. False   (pages 214–215)

MATCHING

1. c
2. d
3. a
4. b

(pages 190, 192, 193)

292   ～   Answers

Journey Through The Last Dance, 7th ed.
Activities and Resources

Chapter 7 End-of-Life Issues and Decisions

MULTIPLE CHOICE

1. d   (page 221)
2. c   (page 224)
3. d   (page 235)
4. a   (page 227)
5. a   (page 246)

TRUE/FALSE

1. True   (page 220)
2. False   (page 226)
3. True   (page 238)
4. True   (page 259)
5. True   (page 264)

MATCHING

1. c
2. a
3. b
4. d

(pages 225, 246, 253, 263)

Chapter 8 Survivors: Understanding the Experience of Loss

MULTIPLE CHOICE

1. a   (page 268)
2. a   (page 270)
3. a   (page 283)
4. b   (page 284)
5. c   (pages 277, 279)

TRUE/FALSE

1. False   (page 270)
2. True   (page 275)
3. True   (page 286)
4. False   (page 292)
5. False   (page 305)

MATCHING

1. c
2. a
3. d
4. b

(pages 268, 277, 279, 298)

Chapter 9 Last Rites: Funerals and Body Disposition

MULTIPLE CHOICE

1. a   (page 309)
2. b   (page 310)
3. a   (page 320)
4. c   (page 323)
5. d   (page 339)

TRUE/FALSE

1. True   (page 315)
2. True   (page 321)
3. False   (page 323)
4. True   (page 332)
5. True   (page 336)

MATCHING

1. b
2. d
3. a
4. c

(page 311)

Chapter 10 Death in the Lives of Children and Adolescents

MULTIPLE CHOICE

1. c   (page 348)
2. d   (page 353)
3. d   (page 359)
4. a   (page 362)
5. b   (page 372)

TRUE/FALSE

1. True   (page 348)
2. True   (page 351)
3. False   (page 353)
4. False   (page 367)
5. False   (page 373)

MATCHING

1. b
2. c
3. d
4. a

(pages 347, 359, 360, 364)

Chapter 11 Death in the Lives of Adults

MULTIPLE CHOICE

1. b   (page 381)
2. c   (page 383)
3. b   (page 390)
4. a   (page 395)
5. d   (page 404)

TRUE/FALSE

1. True   (page 385)
2. False   (page 389)
3. False   (page 396)
4. True   (page 401)
5. True   (page 402)

MATCHING

1. c
2. d
3. a
4. b

(page 385)

Chapter 12 Suicide

MULTIPLE CHOICE

1. c   (page 411)
2. a   (page 414)
3. b   (page 415)
4. b   (page 423)
5. d   (page 429)

TRUE/FALSE

1. True   (page 409)
2. True   (page 415)
3. False   (pages 427–428)
4. True   (page 440)
5. True   (page 443)

MATCHING

1. c
2. d
3. a
4. b

(pages 415, 417, 418)

Chapter 13 Risks of Death in the Modern World

MULTIPLE CHOICE

1. a   (page 453)
2. c   (page 459)
3. a   (page 465)
4. b   (page 477)
5. b   (page 492)

TRUE/FALSE

1. True   (page 450)
2. False   (pages 461–462)
3. True   (page 465)
4. True   (page 477)
5. False   (page 487)

294 ～ Answers

Journey Through The Last Dance, 7th ed.
Activities and Resources

MATCHING

1. d
2. b
3. a
4. c

(pages 466, 467, 476, 482)

Chapter 14 Beyond Death / After Life

MULTIPLE CHOICE

1. d   (page 496)
2. c   (page 500)
3. c   (page 506)
4. d   (page 521)
5. c   (pages 526–527)

TRUE/FALSE

1. False   (page 496)
2. False   (page 498)
3. False   (page 499)
4. True   (page 514)
5. True   (page 524)

MATCHING

1. b
2. d
3. a
4. c

(page 500)

Chapter 15 The Path Ahead: Personal and Social Choices

MULTIPLE CHOICE

1. c   (page 534)
2. a   (page 540)
3. d   (page 548)
4. a   (page 548)
5. b   (page 549)

TRUE/FALSE

1. False   (page 529)
2. True   (page 532)
3. True   (page 534)
4. True   (page 540)
5. False   (page 548)

MATCHING

1. b
2. a
3. d
4. c

(pages 538, 539, 546, 549)

Glossary

Abrahamic traditions. The three major religions that trace their origin to the Hebrew patriarch Abraham: Judaism, Christianity, and Islam.

accident-prone. Being involved in a greater than average number of accidents or having personality traits that predispose to accidents.

accommodation. A process whereby a new group adapts to the values or customs of a dominant social group by making adjustments that allow for the existing group's interests.

acquired immunodeficiency syndrome (AIDS). A life-threatening disease of the human immune system that diminishes the body's natural defenses against infection.

active dying. The end phase of a terminal illness when death is expected to occur within hours or a few days and involving a set of physical signs or symptoms usually associated with the period just before death occurs.

active euthanasia. The intentional act of ending the life of a patient who is suffering from an incurable and painful disease.

acute care. The use of aggressive medical techniques to diagnose illness or injury, relieve symptoms, provide treatment, and sustain life.

acute grief. The intense expression of the reaction to significant loss.

acute pain. A biological signal of the potential for or extent of injury that can serve as a protective mechanism, prompting the sufferer to remove or withdraw from the source of pain.

acute suicidal crisis. A period of brief duration during which an individual is at the peak of self-destructive potential.

adjunctive therapy. A therapy used to counteract the side effects of the primary treatment or relieve other symptoms.

adoption loss. Loss associated with giving up a child for adoption.

advance directive. A legal form or statement made by an individual to express his or her preferences about life-sustaining treatment in the event he or she becomes unable to make such decisions or communicate them in the future.

Aesculapian authority. The traditional "godlike" place of honor given to physicians in society and referring to Aesculapius, the first physician according to Greek legend. The components of such authority include (1) *sapiential authority,* based on the physician's special knowledge or expertise; (2) *moral authority,* based on the rightness and goodness of the enterprise of medicine and doing what is expected of a good physician; and (3) *charismatic authority,* which derives from the original unity of medicine and religion and the involvement of the physician in matters of life and death.

aftercare. Counseling or other bereavement support services provided by a funeral home to bereaved individuals and families.

afterlife. Occurring after death of the physical body; an existence after death.

allowing to die. Withholding or withdrawing life-sustaining treatment.

altruistic suicide. In Durkheim's model, a category of suicide associated with an excessive degree of social connectedness, resulting in the values of the social group predominating over the individual's valuing of his or her own life; also known as *institutional suicide.*

amplification effect. A process whereby the actions of terrorists are broadcast through the mass media to a larger audience than such acts would have in the location where they occur.

ancestor worship. A term sometimes used to describe customs that can be more accurately described as reverence for the dead and a sense of communion between the living and the dead.

anomie. A sense of confusion, alienation, and uncertainty, due to social instability resulting from a breakdown of standards and values. In Durkheim's model, such instability and lack of social regulation creates conditions for anomic suicides.

anticipatory grief. A reaction to the awareness of an impending loss; also known as *forewarning.*

appropriate death. A death that is relatively pain free and in which suffering is minimized and the social and emotional needs of the dying person are met to the fullest extent possible; in short, as Avery Weisman says, "a death that someone might choose for himself or herself—if he or she had a choice." See also **peaceful death**.

ars moriendi. (1) Art of dying. (2) The notion that there is a "right" way to die that applies to everyone.

artificial nutrition and hydration. The use of medical technologies, such as feeding tubes and intravenous lines, to provide nourishment and liquids to patients who are unable to take nourishment or liquids by mouth.

assimilation. A process whereby the values or customs of a new group are incorporated by a dominant social group so that the values of the new group fit into the existing social network.

attachment theory. The belief that psychological maturing is dependent on a succession of attachments. When a person recognizes that an object (someone loved) to which he or she is attached no longer exists, grief arises, along with a defensive psychological demand to withdraw libido (energy) from the object.

autonomy. An individual's right to be self-governing, to exercise self-direction and moral independence.

autopsy. A medical examination of a body after death to determine cause of death or investigate the nature of changes caused by disease.

bardo. In Tibetan Buddhism, an intermediate or transitional state between death and rebirth.

beneficence. Doing good or conferring benefits that enhance personal or social well-being.

beneficiary. The person designated to receive money, property, or other distributions from the settlement of an estate or named to receive other benefits.

bequest. A gift or distribution of money, property, or other possessions.

bereavement burnout. A state associated with the experience of multiple losses in which a bereaved individual is overwhelmed by loss such that he or she becomes emotionally numb and disoriented, obstructing or impairing the normal expression of grief.

bereavement. The objective event of loss.

bibliotherapy. The use of books (especially literature and poetry) as an aid to coping with loss or other experiences.

biological markers. In suicidology, biochemical substances such as serotonin and other neurotransmitters whose levels in the brain appear to be correlated with suicidal behavior.

biopsy. The surgical removal of a small amount of tissue for diagnostic purposes.

Black Death. The mass deaths caused by plague, which came to Europe via a Black Sea port in 1347.

brain death. Irreversible cessation of all functions of the entire brain, including the brain stem.

broken heart phenomenon. The idea that severe or unresolved mental stress related to grief can disrupt the normal rhythm of the heart and cause irregularities and even cardiac arrest.

burial. A form of body disposition that encompasses a range of practices, including a grave dug in the soil as well as entombment in a mausoleum or burial at sea; may involve disposal of the whole body or just the bones or cremated remains.

burnout. A reaction to stress in which a caregiver goes beyond the state of exhaustion and depression to "past caring."

butsudan. In Japanese culture, a family altar containing memorial tablets honoring deceased ancestors and a focal point for ongoing relationships between the living and dead members of a household.

cancer. A condition in which there is a proliferation of cells capable of invading normal tissues, which unchecked (malignant) can be lethal.

cardiopulmonary resuscitation (CPR). A medical procedure intended to restore normal breathing and heartbeat after cardiac arrest.

caregiver stress. A category of stress related to frequent exposure to suffering and multiple losses, as well as to nonreciprocal giving, excessive demands, feelings of inadequacy at inability to provide cure, and institutional constraints.

casket. A rectangular container for the disposition of a corpse.

cause of death. Condition or circumstance that results in death.

cellular death. The death of cells and tissues of the body, which occurs as a progressive breakdown of metabolic processes, resulting in irreversible deterioration of the affected systems and organs of the body.

cemetery. A burial ground or place for burial.

certification of death. A process involving the official registration of death and providing legal proof of death by certifying the pertinent data and facts regarding the deceased and the mode and place of death.

ch'ing ming. In Chinese culture, an annual festival celebrating the return of deceased ancestors and during which family members visit graves and burn paper replicas of money and other necessities as a way of showing respect and care for ancestors.

charnel house. An arcade or gallery, usually associated with a church or cathedral, where the bones of the dead were kept after being removed from common graves.

chemotherapy. The treatment of disease using chemicals (drugs).

chronic illness. An illness of long duration or frequent recurrence.

chronic pain. As contrasted with acute pain, chronic pain usually lasts longer than three to six months.

chronic suicide. A term coined by Karl Menninger that refers to individuals who harm themselves by means of drugs, alcohol, smoking, reckless living, and other self-destructive behaviors.

clinical death. Determined on the basis of either the cessation of heartbeat and breathing or the criteria for establishing brain death.

closed awareness. An awareness context in which a person with a terminal prognosis is not aware of his or her impending death and, although others may know, there is no communication about this prospect.

cluster suicides. The phenomenon of a number of suicides occurring within the same locale, closely related in time, and involving similar methods.

CMO (comfort measures only). A message to medical staff that a patient does not want attempts made to revive him or her in the event of cardiac or respiratory failure.

codicil. An amendment or change to a will.

coffin. A container for the disposition of a corpse that, in contrast to a casket, is hexagonal and has shaped shoulders.

cognitive transformations. In Piagetian theory, the manner in which an individual's mode of understanding the world changes in sequential stages from infancy to adulthood, especially with respect to organizing and reasoning about ideas and experiences.

collective destiny. A view emphasizing death as the collective fate of humankind, that "we all shall die," in contrast to an emphasis on the destiny of the individual.

columbarium. A structure with a series of vaults or niches for urns that usually contain human remains.

coma. A state of profound unconsciousness (may be reversible).

committal. A ceremony held at the grave or crematorium focusing on disposition of the deceased's remains.

complementary therapy. A therapy used along with primary or conventional therapies to help alleviate symptoms and restore healthful functioning.

complicated mourning. A manifestation of grief that affects the bereaved's ability to adapt to life without the deceased.

conversion of the warrior. The process by which the social conventions and norms regarding homicide in ordinary interpersonal circumstances is altered so that killing in warfare is deemed acceptable and even heroic.

coping potency. The capacity to maintain a sense of self-worth, set goals and strive to meet them, sustain hope for the future, and exercise choice with an awareness of one's power to interactively engage with the environment; also known as *resiliency*.

coping strategies. As contrasted with defense mechanisms, coping strategies involve conscious, purposeful efforts intentionally directed toward solving a problem or establishing control over a stressful situation. They include emotion-focused coping to regulate the level of distress, problem-focused coping to deal with the problem itself, and meaning-based coping to maintain a sense of positive well-being.

coroner. An individual, usually an elected official, whose job it is to conduct investigations into the cause and circumstances of suspicious or sudden deaths.

cremation. The process of reducing a dead body to ashes by burning or intense heat.

crisis suicide. A pattern of suicidal behavior associated with sudden, traumatic change in a person's life.

cry for help. The idea that much suicidal behavior involves a drastic action whose goal is not death, but rather to force some change or solve some problem.

cryogenic suspension. The practice of subjecting a corpse or body part (typically a head) to extremely cold temperature with the aim of "suspending" biological activity until some time in the future when a cure for the disease that caused the death has been developed and life can be restored.

crypt. Historically, an underground burial vault or chamber, often situated beneath the floor of a church or cathedral; more recently, a chamber or vault in a mausoleum.

cultural competency. An understanding that involves awareness of oneself and others as cultural beings so that ethnocentrism and stereotyping are avoided and culture is recognized as diverse and as involving multiple identities that are not defined simply by ethnicity.

cultural lag. A situation whereby a society falls behind in dealing with new social problems that result from technological advances and rapid social changes.

culture. Everything in human society that is socially rather than biologically transmitted; the ways of thinking, feeling, and acting—that is, the lifeways—of a given group of people.

cybermourners. Mourners who participate in funeral services by watching live video of a funeral via the Internet.

danger-of-death narratives. Stories or accounts of close calls with death.

danse macabre. The "Dance of Death," a cultural and artistic phenomenon influenced by mass deaths caused by plague in the fourteenth century and conveying through drama, poetry, music, and the visual arts ideas about the inevitability and universality of death, that it comes to everyone and when least expected.

death anxiety. Fearful or apprehensive uneasiness of mind about the threat of personal annihilation or ultimate prospect of one's own death.

death certificate. A document that constitutes official registration and legal proof of death by certifying the facts of a death and recording pertinent data about the deceased.

death dreams. Imagery and symbols of death that occur during the dream state.

death education. Formal or informal instruction about dying, grief, and related topics.

death knells. The ringing of a bell, usually in a distinctive pattern, to provide public notice that a death has occurred and, in some instances, to drive away evil spirits or convince a spirit not to remain with a dead body.

death notice. A standardized report giving brief details about a person's life and published, usually in small type in a single column, in a newspaper after his or her death. See also **obituary.**

death notification. The process of announcing that a death has occurred. See also **death notice; obituary**.

death songs. An acknowledgment of one's preparation for death, often composed spontaneously and expressing a resolve to meet death with equanimity and to accept it with one's whole being as the final act of earthly existence.

death system. All the elements of a society—people, places, times, objects, and symbols—that have an impact on how people deal with dying and death and through which an individual's relationship to mortality is mediated by society.

death talk. Language about death, especially the use of metaphors, euphemisms, and slang.

Death with Dignity Act (Oregon). A ballot initiative passed by Oregon voters in 1994 and reaffirmed in 1997 that allows physicians under certain conditions to prescribe lethal medication to terminally ill patients. See also **physician-assisted suicide**.

deathbed promises. A form of unfinished business in which a dying person elicits some promise from his or her survivors to perform some action after the person dies.

deathbed scene. The customary scene surrounding the bed of a dying person as influenced by cultural attitudes and practices.

defense mechanisms. As contrasted with coping strategies, defense mechanisms occur unintentionally and without conscious effort or awareness; they function to change a person's internal psychological states, not the external reality. Such mechanisms may be adaptive in dealing with a stressful situation in the short term, but can hinder mobilization of resources and the taking of appropriate action over the longer term.

definition of death. The conceptual understanding of what constitutes death, which seeks to answer the question "What is so essentially significant about life that its loss is termed *death?*"

demographics. The size, shape, distribution, and other statistical information about a population.

depersonalization. An aspect of the scientific method applied in medicine which results in focusing more on the disease than on the patient.

determination of death. The process of using a set of criteria, tests, and procedures to assess whether an individual is living or dead according to an accepted definition of death.

developmental push. A phenomenon associated with the death of a parent whereby a bereaved person assumes a more mature self-image or attitude because he or she no longer thinks of himself or herself as a "child."

diagnosis-related groups (DRGs). A program of reimbursement for medical care that makes use of a predetermined schedule of fees for various services provided to patients.

Dies Irae. Literally, "Day of Wrath"; a musical symbol of death; a spoken, chanted, or sung segment of the mass for the dead. See also **dirge.**

direct cremation. A method of body disposition in which the corpse is immediately taken for cremation without formal viewing of the remains or any visitation or ceremony with the body present.

directive mourning therapy. Rituals or other actions designed to help bereaved persons take symbolic leave of the deceased or move from a maladaptive to an adaptive style of grieving.

dirge. A solemn and mournful song or hymn expressing grief; often accompanying funeral or memorial rites. See also **Dies Irae.**

disaster. A catastrophic, life-threatening event that affects many people within a brief period of time, bringing sudden and great misfortune, destruction, and loss.

disenfranchised grief. Grief experienced in connection with a loss that is not socially supported or acknowledged.

distancing strategies. A method of coping with a difficult experience or situation by limiting the number of people with whom one has contact through the reduction of opportunities for potentially stressful interactions.

DNR (do not resuscitate). A message to medical staff that a patient does not want attempts made to revive him or her in event of cardiac or respiratory failure.

donor card. A document used to specify the intent to donate organs or body parts after the donor's death.

double effect. The doctrine that a harmful effect of treatment, even if it results in death, is permissible if the harm is not intended and occurs as a side effect of a beneficial action.

double suicide. A type of suicide pact that generally occurs among older couples who are heavily dependent on each other, isolated from other sources of social support, and in which one or both partners are ill.

dual-process model of grief. A framework for understanding grief as consisting of both loss-oriented and restoration-oriented coping behaviors, which are expressed by the bereaved in varying degrees at different times.

durable power of attorney for health care. See **health care proxy.**

dying trajectory. The duration and progression of a disease or injury toward death. Two contrasting patterns are (1) the lingering trajectory, when life fades away slowly from a disease and (2) the expected quick trajectory such as occurs in emergencies that result in sudden death.

effigy. An image or representation of a person, reflecting the belief that the bereaved maintain bonds with the deceased by perpetuating their memory.

egoistic suicide. In Durkheim's model, a category of suicide associated with an inadequate sense of social connectedness, causing individuals to feel alienated from others and overly dependent on their own resources.

el Día de los Muertos. The Mexican celebration of the Day of the Dead, which is held each year in late October and early November at the same time as the Catholic feast days of All Souls' Day and All Saints' Day.

elder care. Comprehensive care for chronically ill older adults, which can range from limited assistance with independent living to supervised, institutional care in a variety of settings.

elegy. A song or poem expressing sorrow in a pensive or reflective manner and commemorating a person's life and death.

embalming. A process of treating a corpse with chemicals or other substances to temporarily retard decay or deterioration.

emerging adulthood. A period of human development associated with the late teens through the mid-twenties when people in modern societies may no longer view themselves as adolescents but may not see themselves entirely as adults.

emerging diseases. Infectious diseases that emerge suddenly as potential epidemic threats to health and well-being.

entombment. To place in a tomb or grave. See also **burial; crypt.**

epidemiologic transition. An historical shift in disease patterns causing a redistribution of deaths from the young to the old.

equivocal death. A death that occurs in circumstances that are unclear or questionable as to the mode of death and the deceased's intent. See also **psychological autopsy.**

eschatology. Ideas or beliefs about the ultimate state of human beings after death, the end of the world, or the ultimate destiny of mankind.

estate. The money, property, and other possessions belonging to an individual.

ethical will. A document written as a nonmaterial bequest or gift to pass on to relatives and future generations one's personal values, life's lessons, beliefs, blessings, and inspirational advice.

ethics. The discipline dealing with what is good and bad and with moral duty and obligation.

ethnocentrism. The fallacy of making judgments about others solely in terms of one's own cultural assumptions and biases.

---

ethnomedicine. Methods of holistic medical treatment based on indigenous or folk beliefs.

euphemisms. Substitution of indirect or vague words or phrases for ones considered harsh or blunt.

executor. A person named in a will to see that the provisions of the will are carried out properly.

existential dread. Anxiety or fear related to the ultimate prospect of one's own death.

extraordinary measures. Medical interventions intended to sustain life temporarily until a patient's own restorative powers allow the resumption of normal biological functioning.

fantasy reasoning. The use of unrealistic examples or arguments to explain what causes death and what it means in biological and empirical terms.

fatalistic suicide. In Durkheim's model, a category of suicide associated with excessive social restraint and absence of choice, causing individuals to feel there is nowhere to turn and nothing good that can be achieved.

fêng-shui. An art of divination concerned with the proper positioning of elements in harmonious relation to one another.

filial piety. A translation of the Chinese *hsiao,* which emphasizes interdependence between the living and their ancestors whereby the living perform necessary ancestral rites and the dead dispense blessings to their descendants.

five stages. A model of emotional and psychological response to life-threatening illness devised by Elisabeth Kübler-Ross and consisting of denial, anger, bargaining, depression, and acceptance.

forensic pathology. The application of medical knowledge to questions of law.

FTC Funeral Rule. The Trade Regulation Rule on Funeral Industry Practices, implemented by the U.S. Federal Trade Commission in 1984, requires that funeral service providers give detailed information about prices and legal requirements to people who are purchasing funeral services. See also **itemized pricing**.

funeral director. A person engaged in the business of professionally managing or arranging funerals and related services, typically including preparing the dead for burial or other disposition; also known as *mortician* or *undertaker.*

funeral home. A business establishment with facilities for preparing the dead for burial or cremation as well as for viewing of the body and other funeral ceremonies.

funeral. An organized, purposeful, time-limited, group-centered response to death (William Lamers). A rite of passage for both the deceased and his or her survivors, usually with the body present in a place of honor; typically includes music, prayers, readings from scripture or other poetry or prose, a eulogy honoring the deceased, and sometimes a sermon on the role of death in human life.

futile treatment. A medical intervention that is ineffective or serves no useful purpose, especially one capable of postponing death but offering no reasonable hope of improvement.

gallows humor. Humor that makes use of incongruity or inconsistency to transgress or extend the boundaries of social norms concerning death with the aim of defusing anxiety or putting fearful possibilities in a manageable perspective; also known as *black humor.*

genocide. The deliberate and systematic destruction of a racial, religious, political, cultural, or ethnic group.

geographical mobility. Demographic pattern whereby large segments of a population move frequently.

gerontology. The study of older people and the processes of aging.

grave goods. Items that a bereaved person or group believes to be significant in some way to the deceased that are buried or cremated with a corpse; also known as *funerary artifacts.*

grave liner. See **vault**.

grave marker. An inscribed tablet, usually made of bronze or stone, that serves to identify or commemorate the person buried in a grave. See also **monument**.

grief work. Based on attachment theory, the idea that bereaved individuals must actively confront a loss and work to detach previously invested (ego) energy from the deceased (object) so it can be reinvested in new relationships.

grief. The reaction to loss, encompassing thoughts and feelings, as well as physical, behavioral, and spiritual responses.

Hades. The underground realm of the dead in Greek mythology; usually depicted as a shadowy place inhabited by bloodless phantoms. See also **She'ol**.

haiku obit. A term used to describe the brief vignettes that highlighted the life stories and interests of individuals killed in the terrorist attack on the World Trade Center in September, 2001 and printed in a series entitled "Portraits of Grief" as a unique form of tribute, witness, and solace.

haka. In Japanese culture, a family gravesite where ashes of deceased family members are interred.

Harvard criteria for brain death. Standards published in 1968 by a Harvard Medical School Ad Hoc Committee to Examine the Definition of Brain Death. The criteria include: (1) lack of receptivity and response to external stimuli, (2) absence of spontaneous muscular movement and spontaneous breathing, (3) absence of observable reflexes, including brain and spinal reflexes, and (4) absence of brain activity, as signified by a flat electroencephalogram (EEG).

health care proxy. A form of advance directive whereby an individual appoints another person, known as a proxy, as a representative to make decisions about medical treatment if the individual becomes unable to do so.

heaven. In Abrahamic religious traditions, the dwelling place of the blessed dead; a spiritual state of everlasting communion with God.

hell. See **Hades; She'ol**.

hibakusha. A Japanese word meaning "explosion-affected"; originally used to describe survivors of the atomic bombings of Hiroshima and Nagasaki; more broadly, refers to pervasive anxiety about the threat of annihilation.

higher-brain theory. The idea that irreversible loss of the capacity for consciousness, rather than simply loss of the capacity for biological functioning, should be used in defining and determining death.

Hippocratic Oath. A guide for the conduct of physicians that traces its origin to the ancient Greek physician Hippocrates.

home care. Medically supervised or supportive care provided in a person's home.

homicide. The killing of one human being by another. See also **manslaughter; murder**.

hopelessness. A key aspect of depression, especially as it occurs in suicidal thoughts and behavior.

horrendous death. A term coined by Daniel Leviton and William Wendt to describe deaths that originate in human activity and affect large numbers of people; examples include terrorism, assassination, and genocide.

hospice care. A program of health care oriented toward the needs of dying patients and their families in which the emphasis is placed on comforting the patient rather than curing a disease.

hospital. A medical institution designed to provide short-term intensive care of patients.

iconics. Objects that communicate meaningful symbolic information, such as distinctive clothing worn by medical staff.

immediate burial. A method of body disposition in which the corpse is taken immediately for burial without formal viewing of the remains or any visitation or ceremony with the body present.

immortality. Survival after physical death; the quality or state of unending existence or lasting fame.

induced abortion. The termination of a pregnancy brought about with the aid of mechanical means or drugs; also termed artificial or therapeutic abortion.

infertility. A condition in which the capacity to produce offspring is diminished or absent, resulting in lack of success in achieving pregnancy.

informed consent. The duty of physicians to disclose information about treatment to patients and to obtain their consent before proceeding with treatment.

inner representation. A set of memories and other mental or emotional images that allow a bereaved person to maintain a sense of continuing interaction with a deceased loved one.

institutional denial. Socially institutionalized avoidance of death-related thoughts and emotions.

institutional neurosis. In routinized and bureaucratic environments, the increasing dependence of residents on staff for even mundane needs and the erosion of their unique personality traits.

intervention. In suicidology, short-term care and treatment of persons who are actively experiencing a suicidal crisis.

interventional cascade. The use of multiple sophisticated medical technologies to sustain life and delay death.

intestate succession. The distribution of an estate according to guidelines established in state law when a person has not made a will.

intuitive vs. instrumental grieving. The idea that, in coping with loss, people may express grief both emotionally (intuitive grieving) and physically (instrumental grieving).

invisible death. A phrase used to describe attitudes toward death in the modern era in which most aspects of dying and death are less public and less part of common experience than in earlier times.

irreversibility. A component of the mature concept of death that recognizes biological death as final and not reversible.

itemized pricing. As a requirement of the FTC Funeral Rule, funeral businesses must provide itemized information on a general price list to allow customers to compare prices or choose only those elements of a funeral that they wish to purchase.

Judgment Day. An event involving final judgment of one's moral actions by God at the end of the world.

justice. Right and proper action; fairness; finding balance among competing interests.

kaddish. A Jewish prayer, after a death, recited by mourners in the daily ritual of the synagogue and at public gatherings. The kaddish praises God and is an affirmation of life.

kanikau. A traditional Hawaiian poetic lament, carefully composed or spontaneously created, commemorating a person's death.

karma. In Hinduism, the moral law of cause and effect that determines the nature of a person's future existence.

karoshi. Literally, "overwork-death"; a Japanese word meaning "sudden death from overwork" and referring to the buildup of biologically devastating fatigue resulting from job-related stress.

lament. A musical expression of ritual leave-taking; an emotionally moving expression of loss and longing.

lethality. In suicidology, the progressive nature of suicide intention whereby vague thoughts or fantasies of suicide are followed by concrete actions or steps toward carrying out the suicidal act.

life expectancy. The number of years a newborn child is expected to live based on statistical averages.

life insurance. An element of estate planning that provides for payment of funds to a designated beneficiary or beneficiaries upon the insured's death.

life review. A review of the course of one's life, including past relationships and significant events, resulting in the possibility of discussing existential concerns and completing unfinished business.

life-extending technologies. Medical techniques and associated devices employed to sustain functioning of the biological organism.

life-threatening illness. An illness that potentially may cause the patient's death.

linking objects. Objects that symbolize in some way the relationship between the bereaved and the deceased.

little deaths. Ordinary losses that occur in the course of changes and transitions in life.

living dead. In African traditions, the ongoing community of deceased ancestors who are recalled in the minds of the living.

---

living will. A form of advance directive that enables individuals to provide instructions about the kind of medical care they wish to receive if they become incapacitated or otherwise unable to participate in treatment decisions.

local identity. A shared appreciation of the geography, people, and culture associated with a particular place and the values commonly held by its residents.

loss. An instance or event of being deprived of something valued.

loss-oriented coping. An aspect of the dual-process model of grief that involves behaviors such as yearning for the deceased, looking at old photographs, and crying.

magical thinking. (1) The notion that one's angry thoughts or feelings can cause harm or even death to others. (2) The notion that one is responsible for bringing an illness on oneself even though there is no evidence for making this assumption.

maintaining bonds. The activity of sustaining interactions with a deceased loved one through memories and other forms of both inner and environmental representation of the deceased.

managed care. Efforts to control where, when, and from whom medical services can be obtained by standardizing policies and procedures to reduce costs.

managed death. The attempt to control or seek mastery of the threat of death or the circumstances of dying by application of medical technology and by personal and social choices.

manslaughter. The unlawful, but unplanned killing of a human being without malice.

mass suicide. A special form of cluster suicide in which a large number of individuals die by suicide at the same time and place.

mature concept of death. An understanding of death that includes recognition of the observable facts about death—universality (all living things eventually die), irreversibility (death is final), nonfunctionality (it involves cessation of all physiological functioning), and causality (there are biological reasons for the occurrence of death)—as well as an understanding of personal mortality; that is, one's own eventual death.

maturity. According to Eriksonian developmental theory, the eighth and final stage of the human life cycle.

mausoleum. An aboveground structure of concrete, marble, or other stone in which one or more bodies are entombed in vaults or chambers. See also **crypt.**

mean world syndrome. A situation in which the symbolic use of death contributes to a "discourse of fear" leading to a heightened sense of danger and irrational dread of dying.

medical examiner. A qualified medical doctor, generally with advanced training and certification in forensic pathology, usually appointed to conduct investigations into the cause and circumstances of suspicious or sudden deaths.

Medicare Hospice Benefit. A legal provision enacted by the U.S. Congress in 1982 whereby qualifying for hospice care requires a doctor's certification that a patient's life expectancy is six months or less if the illness runs its normal course.

memento mori. A phrase meaning "Remember, you must die!" which emphasizes individual responsibility for the destiny of one's soul.

memorial service. A ceremony held in memory of a person who has died, typically without the body present. See also **funeral.**

memorial society. A cooperative, usually nonprofit, organization that offers body disposition services to members at reduced cost by arranging such services on the basis of volume purchasing.

memorialization. (A) An act of remembrance or commemoration; specifically, an act performed with the aim of honoring and remembering the dead. (B) The practice of preserving the identity of a person buried in a particular place by recording his or her name on a grave marker.

mental first aid. Providing comfort and support to a person undergoing a painful experience or a difficult medical procedure.

metastasis. The spread of multiple sites of cancer additional to the primary or original site.

middle knowledge. An aspect of coping with life-threatening illness that involves fluctuation between acceptance and denial as patients and those close to them seek a balance between acknowledging the reality of the patient's condition and sustaining hope for recovery.

middlescence. A term used to describe the sometimes turbulent years of middle adulthood.

miscarriage. The death of a fetus occurring prior to the twentieth week of pregnancy; also termed spontaneous abortion.

mizuko. Literally, "water children"; a Japanese term used for children conceived but never born due to abortion.

mode of death. As contrasted with *cause* of death, four modes of death—natural, accidental, homicidal, suicidal—are commonly recognized on death certificates. Investigation of intentions and subconscious factors may be required to assign a particular death to one of these four categories.

moksha. In Hinduism, liberation from one's fate and the cycles of history. See also **karma.**

monument. A memorial structure, usually of stone, bronze, or other metal, erected in remembrance of a person.

mortality rates. A statistical measure used to compare the frequency of deaths occurring due to different causes or among different populations.

mortician. See **funeral director.**

mortuary. See **funeral home.**

mourning restraints. Among the LoDagaa of Africa, items made of leather, fabric, or string that are worn by mourners and used to indicate degree of relationship between the bereaved and the deceased and to moderate the bereaved's behavior during the period of intense grief.

mourning. The process by which a bereaved person integrates a loss into his or her ongoing life, as influenced by social and cultural norms for expressing grief.

murder. The unlawful killing of a person with deliberate intent (malice aforethought).

mutual pretense. An awareness context in which individuals know that a patient's condition or prognosis is likely to be terminal, but everyone, including the patient, avoids direct communication about this prognosis and instead acts to sustain the illusion that the patient is getting well; also known as *conspiracy of silence.*

name avoidance. The practice of refraining from using the name of deceased persons to avoid disturbing the living.

National Organ Transplant Act. Enacted by the U.S. Congress in 1984, this Act instituted a central office to help match donated organs with potential recipients.

near-death experience (NDE). A psychological event with mystical and transcendental elements, typically occurring to individuals close to death or in situations of intense physical or emotional danger.

necromancy. From the Greek, meaning "corpse-prophecy," a way of contacting the dead through shamanistic rites and bringing back messages to benefit the living.

neonatal death. The death of an infant occurring during the first four weeks following birth.

neonatal intensive care. Sophisticated medical care for seriously ill newborns.

niche. A recess in a wall into which an urn is placed. See also **columbarium.**

nirvana. Literally, "extinction"; a transcendent state beyond birth and death reached after ignorance and desire have been extinguished and all karma, the cause of rebirth, has been dissolved.

noncorporeal continuity. The notion, usually related to spiritual or religious beliefs, that the human personality or soul survives in some form after the death of the physical body.

nonempirical ideas about death. Ideas about death that are not observable and not subject to confirmation as factual.

nonfunctionality. An understanding of death as involving the cessation of all physiological functioning or signs of life.

nursing home. A medical facility designed to provide long-term residential and supportive care for patients whose illness does not require acute, intensive care.

obituary. An account of a person's life and death printed in a format similar to other feature stories. See also **death notice.**

object of hope. A focus of hopefulness that changes over time during the course of a terminal illness, from the early hope that symptoms do not mean anything serious, to hope for a cure, to hope for more time, to hope for a pain-free and peaceful death.

o-bon. A Japanese midsummer festival that marks the return of ancestral spirits to their families.

open awareness. An awareness context in which the prospect of an individual's dying from terminal illness is acknowledged and discussed openly.

organ transplantation. The transfer of living organs, tissues, or cells from a donor to a recipient with the intention of maintaining the functional integrity of the transplanted tissue in the recipient.

origin-of-death myths. Stories told in traditional cultures about how death became part of human experience, usually because of transgression of divine or natural law or because of failure to carry out some crucial action that would have ensured immortality.

otherworld journey. A parapsychological or spiritual phenomenon associated with travel to a world beyond death or beyond present reality.

otherworld. In Celtic culture, the realm of the dead where the life of the soul continues in a world apart from that in which mortals dwell. According to Arthurian legend, the name of the paradise to which King Arthur was carried after his death was known as Avalon.

pain management. The treatment of pain by attending to its severity, location, quality, duration, course, and meaning to the patient, among other factors. Effective treatment generally occurs in a stepwise approach that begins with simple non-opiod pain medications and, if necessary, progressively moves to more powerful drugs.

palliative care. The active total care of patients whose disease is not responsive to curative treatment; emphasizes healing of the person and relief of distressing symptoms rather than curing of a disease.

panoramic life review. An element of the near-death experience that consists of vivid and almost instantaneous visions of a person's whole life, or selected highlights of it, which may include visions of events in the person's future life.

paradise. A place or state of bliss or delight. See also **heaven.**

parental messages. Direct or indirect communications from parents to children about what death is and how to behave appropriately toward it.

passive euthanasia. See **allowing to die.**

paternalism. The assumption of parentlike authority by medical practitioners, potentially infringing on a patient's freedom to make medical decisions even though such authority is exercised with benevolent intent.

pathological grief. A manifestation of grief that is unhealthy, excessive, or markedly abnormal.

Patient Self-Determination Act. Legislation enacted by the U.S. Congress in 1990 that requires providers of services under Medicare and Medicaid to inform patients of their rights to appoint a health care proxy and to document their wishes for treatment by using advance directives.

peaceful death. The aim of an approach to end-of-life care in which successful management of pain and other distressing symptoms, along with provision of emotional and spiritual support, allows a patient to live as fully as possible until the end of life.

perceived similarity. (1) The idea that the more similar to the deceased a survivor believes he or she is, the greater the grief reaction is likely to be. (2) In social support, the idea that people who have experienced similar losses can be more empathetic and understanding in sharing their experiences.

persistent vegetative state (PVS). A state wherein brain stem functions are intact and involuntary bodily functions such as spontaneous breathing are sustained, but there is severe mental impairment and no cognitive awareness of self or environment due to lack of higher brain functions.

personal mortality. The understanding that not only do all living things die eventually, but that "I will die."

physician-assisted suicide (PAS). A situation in which a physician, at the patient's request, intentionally helps a patient hasten his or her death by providing lethal drugs or other interventions with the understanding that the patient plans to use them to end his or her life.

placebo. A substance lacking active pharmacologic properties given as medicine for its suggestive effect or for mental relief of the patient rather than its actual effect on a disease.

postmodernism. Characterized by a reappraisal of taken-for-granted beliefs and an exploration of and openness to ideas and customs from all historical periods and cultures.

postmortem. Occurring after death.

postneonatal death. The death of an infant occurring after the first four weeks and up to eleven months following birth.

posttraumatic stress disorder (PTSD). A psychological reaction to a highly stressful event (as in wartime combat or disaster); symptoms may include depression, anxiety, flashbacks, recurrent nightmares, and avoidance of reminders of the stressful event; also known as *delayed grief syndrome* and *posttraumatic grief disorder*.

postvention. (1) In suicidology, assistance given to all survivors of suicide, including those who attempt suicide as well as families, friends, and associates of those who die by suicide. (2) In the aftermath of disasters, aid given to all those affected.

primary caregiver. An individual who is available on a more or less full-time basis to provide home care for a patient. This may be the patient's spouse, partner, parent, other relative, or someone hired by a family or funded by a public agency to carry out such duties.

probate. The legal process by which an estate is settled and property distributed.

procession. A journey of mourners to convey the corpse from the site of the funeral to the place of burial or cremation.

prognosis. The expected course and duration of a disease.

protothanatic behavior. Behavior, such as the child's game of "peekaboo," that involves preparation for concepts about life and death that eventually emerge in later interactions with the environment.

proximics. The study of how spatial and temporal factors affect individuals in social and interpersonal situations and how differences in the use of space and time relate to environmental and cultural factors.

psych-ache. A word coined by Edwin Shneidman that refers to unbearable mental pain caused by frustration of a person's most important needs.

psychedelic experience of death. A transcen-tal experience associated with drugs with mind-altering effects such as LSD (lysergic acid diethylamide) that evoke profound encounters with critical aspects of human existence and an examination of the spiritual or religious meaning of life, as well as reevaluation of previously held attitudes about death.

psychic maneuvers. Personal, social, and cultural factors that tend to facilitate violence and homicidal acts.

psychic numbing. A self-protective psychological response to horrific death that causes individuals to become temporarily insensitive and unfeeling.

psychological autopsy. An investigative technique used by behavioral scientists in cases of equivocal death that involves gathering information about the deceased and circumstances of death to determine the probable mode of death.

psychosocial development. In Eriksonian theory, a model of human development that focuses on significant turning points, or crises, that require a response from the individual in the context of his or her relationships with the environment and with other individuals.

public vs. private loss. A distinction between the public and private aspects of a loss-event whereby the private sorrow of the bereaved may either conflict with or be comforted by the dimensions of the loss as a public event.

purgatory. In Christian theology, an intermediate state after death for purification to eliminate obstacles to enjoyment of eternal union with God.

quality-adjusted life years (QALYs). A concept associated with health care rationing that aims for a balance or trade-off between the length of life and quality of life whereby a person might equate the prospect of living fewer years in perfect health with the prospect of living more years in less-than-perfect health.

rational suicide. A type of suicide associated with the desire to gain release from burdensome suffering as, for example, in severely debilitating or terminal illness. See also **physician-assisted suicide**.

rationing. In health care, the allocation of scarce medical resources among competing individuals or groups; occurs when not all care expected to be beneficial is provided to all patients, usually because of cost; also known as *lifeboat ethics*.

rebirth. Spiritual regeneration; the idea that the soul or spirit is reborn in another body or form following death of the physical body.

recuerdo. A form of remembrance intended to memorialize the dead and comfort the living that is usually presented as a written narrative or ballad that tells the story of a person's life in an epic, lyrical, and heroic manner.

reframing. A process of reconceptualizing the behavior of another person in a way that explains the behavior in positive rather than negative terms.

reincarnation. In Asian religions, the idea that the soul, or some essential spiritual element of life, takes rebirth in new bodies or forms of life.

religiosity. The relative importance of religion in a person's life as displayed through emotional ties and commitment to the religion, participation in its ceremonies, the degree to which it is integrated in the person's life, and knowledge about the religion and its traditions, beliefs, and practices.

remission. Temporary relief or disappearance of evident active disease, occurring either spontaneously or as the result of therapy.

replaceability. In the context of socialization about how to cope with loss, the notion that grief can be minimized by quickly replacing, for example, a pet who has died with another pet without allowing the griever time to acknowledge the loss.

resocialization. The restructuring of basic attitudes, values, or identities that occurs when adults assume new roles that require a reevaluation of their existing values and modes of behavior.

respite care. Temporary care that allows family members or other caregivers a break in caring for a patient.

restoration-oriented coping. An aspect of the dual-process model of grief that involves behaviors, such as mastering tasks that had been taken care of by the deceased, reorganizing one's life, and developing a new sense of identity.

resurrection. In Christianity, the belief that Jesus rose from the dead in physical form and that all of the human dead will rise again to life before the final judgment.

revictimization. A situation in which media coverage or publicity about a horrific death evokes a "second trauma" for the bereaved in addition to the initial trauma of the loss itself.

right to die. The argument that individuals have a right to decide for themselves when suffering outweighs the benefit of continued life and can therefore refuse further medical treatment intended to sustain life and even take steps to actively hasten their death.

rigor mortis. Temporary rigidity of muscles that occurs following death.

rites of passage. Rituals that enact themes of separation, transition, and reincorporation in marking significant changes of status for individuals and their community.

rituals of dying. Customs and behaviors that have cultural meaning during the terminal phase of life.

samhain. In Celtic culture, a festival marking the end of one year and beginning of the next, during which supernatural communication with the gods and the dead takes place; a precursor of Halloween.

samsara. In Hinduism, the journey or passage of beings through a series of incarnational experiences. See also **karma**.

secondary morbidity. Physical, mental, emotional, social, or other difficulties that may be experienced by individuals closely involved in long-term care of a terminally ill person.

secularization. The process in modern societies whereby religious ideas and practices lose influence because of scientific and other nonreligious knowledge.

selective memory. A way to cope with difficult experiences by reconstructing memories in such a way that painful memories are "forgotten."

senescence. The biological process of aging or state of being old.

separation distress. A form of anxiety experienced by an infant or a young child caused by separation from a significant person or familiar surroundings; more generally, yearning, longing, or searching behaviors associated with loss or bereavement.

seppuku. Literally, "ritual disembowelment"; a type of culturally accepted suicide associated with samurai warriors in feudal Japan who sacrificed their lives to maintain the honor or reputation of their lords, also known as *hara-kiri*. See also **altruistic suicide**.

shaman. A visionary who projects his or her consciousness to the supernatural realm and acts as intermediary between the worlds of the living and the dead.

She'ol. In Hebrew tradition, the underworld of the dead, a shadowy realm of ghostly, disembodied souls. See also **Hades**.

sites of memory. Focal points for public grief and mourning, as well as memorialization.

skilled nursing facility. A health care institution designed to provide a comprehensive level of non-acute care, including medical and nursing services as well as dietary supervision.

slippery slope. The argument that one should not permit acts that, even if moral in themselves, would pave the way for later acts that would be immoral.

social construction of reality. The notion that every society constructs or shapes its own version of how the world works, as well as its truths or meanings, including the meaning and place of death in people's lives.

social death. A pattern of avoidance stemming from the confrontation with mortality represented by life-threatening illness that leads people to abandon seriously ill patients and treat them as non-persons.

social learning theory. The idea that individuals learn how to behave as members of a society through a process of conditioning that involves reinforcement of social norms by means of rewards and punishments.

social norms. Rules and guidelines that prescribe what a given society considers to be appropriate behavior (normal) in particular situations.

social structure. Aspects of a society's institutional structure that influence social life by helping make it orderly and predictable.

social thanatology. See **urban desertification**.

socialization. The process of learning and internalizing the beliefs, values, rules, and norms of a society.

society. A group of people who share a common culture, a common territory, and a common identity, and who interact in socially structured relationships.

soul. The essence of an individual's life or self; the spiritual principle in human beings.

spiritual care of the dying. See **total care**.

spontaneous abortion. See **miscarriage**.

sterility. Inability to produce offspring due either to inability to conceive (female) or to induce conception (male).

stillbirth. The spontaneous death of a fetus occurring between the twentieth week of pregnancy and birth.

subculture. A group that shares a distinctive identity and lifestyle within a larger society. A subculture may share a specific ethnic heritage, or it may be unique because of history, language, place of origin, economic circumstances, or other distinctive qualities.

subintentional death. A death in which an individual plays some partial, covert, subliminal, or unconscious role in hastening his or her own demise.

sudden infant death syndrome (SIDS). A medical syndrome involving the sudden and unexpected death of a child, usually before one year of age, in which postmortem examination fails to show an adequate cause of death.

suffering. Distress endured as a result of disability or because of fear or anxiety about impending and unavoidable loss, including death.

suicide bomber. An individual who willingly sacrifices his or her life in a terrorist attack with the intention of simultaneously harming others.

suicide pacts. An arrangement between two or more individuals who determine to kill themselves at the same time and usually in the same place.

surrogate. In the context of advance directives, a person appointed to make decisions about medical treatment. See also **health care proxy**.

survivor guilt. Feelings of blame or guilt experienced by bereaved persons who question whether they are somehow responsible for a death or question why they survived a particular disaster while others did not survive.

suspected awareness. An awareness context in which a person suspects that his or her prognosis involves death, but this suspicion is not confirmed by those who know the truth.

suttee. A type of suicide occurring among certain castes in India whereby a widow was compelled by prevailing social and religious beliefs to throw herself upon her husband's cremation pyre and immolate herself as an act of devotion.

symbolic healing. Therapies that evoke symbolic meanings that are significant to the patient in achieving their anticipated effects; examples include faith healing, supernatural healing, and folk healing.

symbolic immortality. A nonreligious form of survival or continuity after death related to biological immortality (children), artistic immortality (creative works of art), or communal immortality (heroic or good deeds that benefit the community).

symbolic interactionism. A social theory that emphasizes the freedom of individuals to construct their own reality as well as to potentially reconstruct what has been inherited by actively responding to the social structures and processes in their lives.

symbolic loss. As contrasted with *actual* loss, the meanings a bereaved person associates with his or her bond with the deceased.

tactical socialization. In the context of informal death education, strategies used to change individuals' perceptions and behaviors about some aspect of their social world.

tamed death. A phrase coined by Philippe Ariès to describe an accepting and familiar attitude toward death associated with earlier historical periods.

tasks of mourning. According to J. William Worden's model, the four tasks of mourning include: (1) accepting the reality of the loss, (2) working through the pain of grief, (3) adjusting to a changed environment and (4) emotionally relocating the deceased and moving on with life.

teachable moments. Informal opportunities for learning that arise out of ordinary experiences and occur in an interactive and usually spontaneous process.

technological alienation. A phenomenon associated with advances in the modern weaponry of warfare, which result in bureaucratic calculation and insensitivity to the indiscriminate slaughter of civilians.

technological imperative. The belief or practice that sophisticated medical technologies should always be used to combat disease with relatively little concern about costs or potentially adverse side effects.

terminal illness. An illness defined as having no known cure and likely to result in death.

terminality. A state relating to the final stages of a fatal disease or the patterns and processes associated with the end of life.

terrorism. A synthesis of war and theater in which violence against innocent civilians is perpetrated before an audience with the aim of creating a mood of fear that assists in achieving the terrorists' strategic goals.

testator. A person who makes a will.

thanatology. The interdisciplinary study of death as a significant aspect of human existence and concern.

total care. A personal and comprehensive approach to medical care that attends not only to a patient's physical needs, but also to his or her mental, emotional, and spiritual needs; also known as *whole patient care.*

total pain. Physical, psychological, social, and spiritual components of a person's experience of pain.

transmigration. In Asian religions, the idea that, at death, beings migrate or pass from one body or form of being to another.

trauma/emergency care. Care for accidental injuries and other physically threatening conditions that require immediate medical intervention to sustain life or well-being.

traumatic grief. A form of pathological grief that involves symptoms of separation distress, such as intrusive preoccupation with the deceased, and traumatic distress, a cluster of symptoms that includes feelings of purposelessness and futility about the future and a fragmented sense of trust and security.

triage. A method of responding to emergencies that aims to reduce time between injury and treatment by assigning priorities to patients based on the seriousness of their injuries; lower priority is assigned to patients with only a remote chance of survival and those with minor injuries while higher priority is given to patients whose injuries are serious but survivable.

trigger events. New losses, significant anniversaries, and other reminders that reactivate grief for an earlier loss.

---

undertaker. See **funeral director**.

unfinished business. Aspects of a relationship with the deceased that cause a bereaved person to experience a sense of incompleteness due to unresolved conflicts, ambivalence, or other issues in the relationship, or because future plans made together can no longer be fulfilled. See also **deathbed promises**.

Uniform Anatomical Gift Act. Legislation that sets forth provisions for the donation of the body or specific body parts upon the death of the donor.

Uniform Determination of Death Act. A statute designed to provide uniform laws throughout the United States for determining death by applying criteria for so-called brain death in cases where the irreversible absence of circulatory and respiratory functions is insufficient for making such a determination.

United Network for Organ Sharing (UNOS). Operating under contract with the U.S. government, UNOS maintains lists of people waiting for transplants and tracks the status of donated organs to ensure fairness of distribution and competence of medical centers where transplants are performed.

universality. An understanding of death as all-inclusive, inevitable, and unavoidable; that all living things die.

unorthodox treatment. In contrast to adjunctive and complementary therapies, methods of treatment that the medical establishment considers unproved or harmful.

urban desertification. A term coined by Rodrick and Deborah Wallace to describe the physical and social disruption of inner-city urban areas that tends to intensify pathological behaviors and conditions, thereby promoting the rapid spread of infectious diseases.

Valhalla. Literally "the hall of the slain"; in Celtic and Nordic culture, a place of heavenly honor and glory intended for outstanding heroes chosen to support the god Odin in the final battle.

valkyries. In Celtic and Nordic culture, battle-goddesses who apportion victory or defeat in battle and escort fallen heroes into Valhalla.

vault. A container, usually of metal or concrete, designed to support the earth around and above a casket and into which a casket is placed at burial.

viatical settlement. A process that allows patients with terminal illness to sell their life insurance policies to settlement companies before death and receive payment for a percentage of the policy's face value.

victim-precipitated homicide. A type of suicidal behavior in which an individual deliberately provokes others in ways that lead to their unwitting help in causing his or her own death.

viewing room. A room set aside in a funeral home where the casketed body is viewed by family and friends before a funeral service. See also **visitation**.

vigil. A gathering of relatives and friends to say farewells and show respect for a dying person and to give support to his or her family; also known as a *deathwatch*.

vigilante stories. Stories, such as detective novels, in which a hero strives to avenge evil while becoming corrupted by a self-justifying morality that results in perpetuating violence.

virtual cemeteries. Sites on the Internet that offer space for posting photographs and biographical information about the dead and where visitors have opportunities to sign a guestbook and leave "digital" flowers.

visitation. A modern version of the wake in which time is set aside for viewing of the body before a funeral service, providing opportunities for social support and interaction among the bereaved; also known as *calling hours*.

visualization. A mind-body intervention in which a patient employs imagery or similar creative techniques as a complement to conventional therapy or to help restore well-being; in conjunction with chemotherapy, for example, a patient might imagine the drug working inside his or her body to diminish the cancerous cells.

vital signs. The conventional vital signs, or "signs of life," consist of pulse rate (heartbeat), respiratory rate (breathing), body temperature, and blood pressure. Pain has been increasingly viewed as a "fifth vital sign" that should be monitored on a regular basis.

wake. Traditionally held on the night after death occurs, this practice involves laying out the corpse and keeping a watch or "wake" over it both as a safeguard against premature burial and to pay respects to the deceased. See also **visitation**.

water burial. A method of body disposition that typically involves ceremonially sliding the corpse off the side of a ship ("burial at sea") or, less commonly, placing the corpse inside a boat that is set aflame and then set adrift.

Werther effect. The idea that suicide is contagious or has an imitative effect due to the power of suggestion on susceptible individuals; the name comes from Goethe's *The Sorrows of Young Werther*, which supposedly sparked an epidemic of suicide among young people following its publication in 1774.

whole patient care. See **total care**.

whole-brain theory. In contrast to "higher-brain theory," the idea that irreversible loss of the capacity for bodily integration and biological functioning, as set forth in the Harvard criteria for brain death, should be used in determining death.

widowhood. The fact or state of being a widow or widower as a result of the death of a spouse.

will. A legal instrument expressing a person's intentions and wishes for the disposition of his or her property after death.

wished-for child. The concept or expectation of a "perfect" child that is imagined or dreamed about by parents, but which may be thwarted when a child is born with severe disability.

withholding vs. withdrawing treatment. A competent patient generally has the right to either withhold (not start) or withdraw (stop) an unwanted treatment.

xenotransplantation. The use of animals other than human beings as sources for organ transplants.

yahrzeit. In Jewish tradition, the anniversary of a death.